"The author developed  and approach are presented in an ac̲ ̲ ̲t the author's ideas are new and uniq̲ ̲ ̲ ̲he beautifully describes distinctive fea̲ ̲ ̲ ̲developmental stage. 2. She illustrates ̲ ̲ ̲ ̲are organized around shared ego bou̲. ̲ ̲ ̲e describes why and in what sense non-twins could not easily understand ̲ ̲ ̲icate emotional balance between twins. 4. She demonstrates the key issues to be addressed by mental health professionals who see a twin patient."

—**Koichi Togashi**, PhD, LP, professor, Konan University, Kobe, Japan

"Are you a twin? Have you met a twin? Yes? No? Either way, you need to read *Twin Dilemmas*. It gives the best evidence-based description of issues and applied suggestions for positive communication you can find. The book offers an example of systematic qualitative research based on identity types and transaction patterns. Written with clarity and accuracy, we experience 'the world around the lives of twins' and learn from it. We get to look through the window and see the dilemmas lived by twins—and ourselves! This is a basic reference book for human science research and teaching."

—**Richard L. Lanigan**, PhD, executive director and Fellow, International Communicology Institute, Washington DC, USA; university distinguished scholar, professor of communicology (emeritus), School of Communication, Southern Illinois University; Senior Fulbright Fellow (China 1996, Canada 2007); Fellow of the International Academy for Intercultural Research; Fellow, Polish Academy of Science (Philology)

"Dr. Klein's focus on employing intersubjectivity theory is timely and practical, and her unique expertise will add depth to her discussions."

—**Stu Wolman**, MD, board certified in pediatrics and child and adult psychiatry; private practice; training and supervising analyst, Institute of Contemporary Psychoanalysis, Los Angeles, USA

"It is psychologically hard living as a twin within the non-twin world. Twins facing a wide range of psychological challenges, ranging from depression, loneliness, anxiety, confusion, and disappointment, or those simply seeking greater understanding, will find huge value in Dr. Klein's *Twin Dilemmas*. The culmination of 35 years of professional endeavor, this work continues the amazing expert service she delivers to twins worldwide—that of providing insight into what it means to be a twin."

—**Dr. Stephen Hart**, MA, FRHistS, Department of War Studies, The Royal Military Academy Sandhurst, UK

"A twin's relationship is forever complicated. Barbara's gifted mind combines poignant twin narratives with counseling insights, forming vivid depictions of the certain but changing struggles twins face over a lifetime. Twins/multiples are rising in number, yet this deepest of human connections is still misguided by ill-equipped parents and support specialists, causing paralyzing outcomes. Twins will be grateful beneficiaries of ditching the cultural cuteness obsession for twins and assuming genuine responsibility for each twin's uniqueness."

—**Lynn Kraus Boberg**, BA in psychology and K-8 education; an identical twin

"Non-twins have no clue! The energy and complexity of the twin relationship is very different from usual sibling relationships. This book will be tremendously helpful for parents of twins who seek to nurture and understand their children. Easily accessible and well organized—there are new insights at every page turn."

—**Louise Thomson**, MBChB FRACP, physician; mother of girl-boy twins

Twin Dilemmas

The development of how twins relate to each other and their single partners is explored through life stories and clinical examples in this telling study of twin interconnections. While the quality of a nurturing family life is crucial, Dr. Klein has found there are often issues with separation anxiety, loneliness, competition with each other, and finding friendships outside of twinship. When twin lives are entwined because of inadequate parenting and estrangement, twin loss is possible and traumatic, creating a crippling fear of expansiveness—an inability to be yourself. Therapists and twins seeking an understanding of twin relationships will find this clinically compelling book a valuable resource.

Barbara Klein, PhD, has a doctorate in child development and clinical psychology. She consults nationally and internationally with twins and parents of twins about developing individuality and maturity in twin relationships. She is the author of *Alone in the Mirror: Twins in Therapy* (Routledge, 2012) as well as eight other books.

Twin Dilemmas

Changing Relationships Throughout the Lifespan

Barbara Klein

NEW YORK AND LONDON

First published 2017
by Routledge
711 Third Avenue, New York, NY 10017

and by Routledge
2 Park Square, Milton Park, Abingdon, Oxon, OX14 4RN

Routledge is an imprint of the Taylor & Francis Group, an informa business

© 2017 Taylor & Francis

The right of Barbara Klein to be identified as author of this work has been asserted by her in accordance with sections 77 and 78 of the Copyright, Designs and Patents Act 1988.

All rights reserved. No part of this book may be reprinted or reproduced or utilised in any form or by any electronic, mechanical, or other means, now known or hereafter invented, including photocopying and recording, or in any information storage or retrieval system, without permission in writing from the publishers.

Trademark notice: Product or corporate names may be trademarks or registered trademarks, and are used only for identification and explanation without intent to infringe.

Library of Congress Cataloging in Publication Data
A catalog record for this data has been requested

ISBN: 978-1-138-69356-2 (hbk)
ISBN: 978-1-138-69357-9 (pbk)
ISBN: 978-1-315-53041-3 (ebk)

Typeset in Baskerville
by HWA Text and Data Management, London

Contents

Foreword: Twins in Therapy by Jacqueline M. Martinez — viii
Acknowledgments — x

Introduction: Understanding Twin Interconnections: Harmony, Fighting, and Estrangement — 1

1 What Childhood Memories of Life Experiences and Narratives Reveal About Adult Twin Relationships — 5

2 Parenting Issues with Twins: Strategies to Resolve Conflicts and Uncertainties — 34

3 When Do Separation Issues Begin for Twins? When Do Separation Issues End? — 57

4 Why Twin Fighting Can Lead to Estrangement — 82

5 The Lives of Adult Twins — 108

6 Being a Twin in a Non-Twin World — 128

7 The Healing Process in Psychotherapy for Twins — 151

8 Affirming Relationship Changes for Twins Throughout the Lifespan — 170

Bibliography — 178
Index — 186

Foreword

Twins in Therapy

Jacqueline M. Martinez, PhD

I am a twin. Nothing in my life goes unaffected by this fact. Yet, it wasn't until I was 48 years old that that I began to recognize the full impact of my twinship in my life. I have always known that I can never stop being a twin. "What is it like to be a twin?" I remember being asked this question over and over again starting from the time I was very young. My response was honest, simple, and always the same: "I don't know because I don't know what it's like to not be a twin." I could not have possibly recognized how insightful my answer was when I first spoke it. Only decades later have I come to see the powerful consequences of this simple fact.

 Because I was born a twin, I learned what it's like to be deeply connected to another human being. Twins learn to understand another person as oneself. In my adult life I have been frustrated in my efforts to connect with other people, mostly because my primary measure for connection and understanding came from being a twin. I didn't understand why I couldn't create that twin level of connection with singletons. I didn't recognize the difference between my twin world and the non-twin world that I lived in. It's a double-edged sword because my desire to connect with others has often proven to be an asset. I am a good listener. I work very hard to see the world from other people's perspective. I'm very empathetic. I always try to establish understanding. On the other hand, it is very taxing to spend so much time trying to make such deep connections with people in general. I've been seriously depressed through major portions of my life. I struggled in therapy with therapists who did not recognize the importance of my being a twin in understanding why I was struggling so much. What seems obvious to me now—that my most severe depression emerged shortly after I moved away from my twin—was completely missed, and even dismissed, by therapists. It was only after I began working with Dr. Klein that I began to recognize the reasons why I struggled so much.

 Today my twin and I are "estranged." The tangled web that is our relationship may never be fully worked out. But one thing is clear—we must each work it out for ourselves. Recognizing that we each experience our relationship differently is crucial. For a twin to recognize and embrace their own point of view singularly, without regard to their twin's point of view is an important achievement. It doesn't come naturally. Working with Dr. Klein I learned to see the many, many ways in which my twinness impacts virtually every aspect of my life. Working on my relationship with my twin is a different kind of work than working on how I am a twin in the way I relate to other people. My twin and I have worked in therapy together on our twin relationship, but not enough to be able to move our relationship between the tangled dynamics that define it today. It's better if we each work individually. Will we ever again feel the closeness and trust we felt as children? I don't know. But I do know that as adults we each must come to terms with who we are outside of the twinship.

I have been comforted greatly by connecting with other twins, especially my fellow twins in Dr. Klein's Twin Estrangement Group. I am comforted by recognizing just how much in common I have with each of my fellow group members. The group members have helped me to see all of my twin-tendencies as they continue to hold sway over my life. And yet, we are each so very different. This complex tangled web of each of our twin relationships has some common threads, but our paths of entanglement are unique and include aspects of lives that are very different. I have been amazed at how radically the same and radically different we can all be at the same time. More than anything else, I feel a sense of camaraderie with each of them that is tremendously healing. The feeling of being misunderstood that so often characterized my early adulthood no longer dominates.

Unraveling the tangled web of twin relationship is not an easy task. Therapists who work with twins encounter a very complex terrain of human interrelationships that require tremendous skill, patience, and understanding. I am deeply grateful to Dr. Klein for so many personal reasons. But I am also grateful to her for taking the tremendous time and energy to write this book. Therapists, twins, and non-twins alike will benefit greatly from this work. Therapists especially need to understand the complexity of twin attachment as it plays out over the course of the lifespan. If they don't, then their work with twin clients will be ineffective at best, and deeply harmful at worst.

Acknowledgments

I have had an enormous amount of support and encouragement from my family, twin clients, and Dr. George Zimmar at Routledge. Specifically, first in line for my abundant thanks is my soulmate, editor, and twin replacement, Paul Macirowski, who oversaw every single aspect of the writing and manuscript preparation of *Twin Dilemmas*.

My children, Elizabeth and Jonathan, Richard and Kim, listened patiently to my ideas and progress. Dr. George Zimmar was so thoughtful, kind, sensitive, and brilliant as I marched through the writing of this book.

Dr. Jackie Martinez graciously, and she says, proudly, agreed to write the foreword to this book at a time when she was extremely busy at ASU. Sherry Sweet patiently helped me with the bibliography, acting as if it were a simple task to read my handwriting, which often reflected my state of mind.

Theory and research only made sense with the real lived experiences of the twins in my life. My twin sister is a part of this book and I hope that she can respect my efforts to describe our relationship. The twins who I have worked with over the last 35 years are the backbone of this book and I am grateful to them from the bottom of my heart.

My twin estrangement group agreed to share some of their thoughts and words for this book for the enlightenment of other twins who might not fit the profile of having an ideal relationship. Their support, energy, commitment, and honesty to one another has formed a new twin family, of which I am the humble leader. And, yes, we celebrate Christmas together and exchange Secret Santa gifts. Thank you, in alphabetical order to avoid favoritism, for adding so much flavor and reality to this book:

Vincent Arthurs
Keith Bigelow
Sandy Gillians
Stephen Hart
Dotan Horowitz
Jackie Martinez
Sarah Moukhliss

Introduction

Understanding Twin Interconnections: Harmony, Fighting, and Estrangement

Demystifying the twin relationship has been a lifelong journey for me. Often the path I was on made me confront professional and personal battles that were deeply troubling and often confusing. But as I got to understand the research on twins and twins on a personal and professional level new insights and understanding unfolded which are exciting for twins to understand and for those who are interested in intimate relationships. This book is about what I have learned about twins throughout my long career.

As long as I can remember as a child being a twin was punctuated with the peace and sweetness of compassion and sharing. Unfortunately it was also fraught with problems which my parents and extended family conveniently ignored or arbitrarily blamed on me. Continually my twin sister and I were encouraged to get along and stop fighting. We were told in different ways and at different times that we were the same. We were expected to be able to do everything alike. I think that as children we knew on some level that we were not the same. Unfortunately, we were not able to express our opinions on how and why we're different. Talking back to your parents was not acceptable in the early 1950s. Following parental expectations to be copies of each other was impossible, although we tried.

We played together and made double trouble for our family when ever possible. We walked to school together until we graduated from high school. We dressed alike until seventh grade. We did our schoolwork together. We went to religious school, dance class, piano, and girl scouts together. Our social life brought out our differences. Marjorie had lots of girlfriends who didn't like me. I had boyfriends who didn't like her. More simply stated, friendships separated us, and then separate interests.

In college we studied different courses. She was a diehard English major and I majored in history. We fought a lot about everything and anything as soon as we were away from home. I think we wanted to be our own persons. Valuing different people and ideas was natural for us. After graduating from UC Berkeley, I finally geographically separated from my twin sister. At the age of 21 I was married and living in California while my sister was living with her husband in Sweden. We were happy to be apart and living our own lives, but we missed our deep connection and easy communication style.

Gradually, I became curious about the normality of my twin relationship which was a roller-coaster ride. As I grew into young adulthood I felt like a fish out of water without my sister even though we had a hard time being together. I sought out self-understanding through psychoanalysis and my higher education. I engaged in new friendships. Although my new friendships had roots in my childhood twin identity which was particularly focused on closeness and companionship, my new attachments were not wrought with the serious conflicts of childhood. My young adult relationships were lively, not self-defeating. My children brought me joy and challenges as they were and still are so close to my heart.

In my first long round of psychoanalysis I came to understand that Marjorie and I were told that we were the same, but we were treated differently. I was the bad seed—the twin to be blamed. My sister could do nothing wrong as a child. And it was my job to make sure she felt good about herself by taking responsibility for her mistakes. Both of us suffered from our labeled childhood identities. Understanding and sorting out the mixed messages of our childhood and teenage years took us too many years to overcome as twins and as individuals. Healing and forgiving the mistakes of out past was a persistent theme between us after we left home.

When my children were in elementary school I went back to graduate school. As a doctoral student at USC, sitting in an educational psychology class, I learned that some researchers were proving that identical twins had nearly identical IQs. I had a serious panic attack in class because I had been told that my twin sister was smarter than me for as long as I could remember. Thus, I began my academic quest to understand twin development from the perspective of objective nature versus nurture research and qualitative research which included the existence of the subjective. I did doctoral research on twins which showed that parenting was a strong determinant of twin well-being and mental health (Schave, 1982). I wrote *Identity and Intimacy in Twins* (Schave and Ciriello, 1983) with Janet Ciriello in 1983 for George Zimmar at Praeger Publishers. The most crucial findings which are the basis of my later research work are as follows:

> Identity and the capacity to relate closely to others, intimacy, are the focus of the study. Analysis of the data is based on identity formation in the twin subjects. These data suggested different qualities of individuation and different relationships between the twin pairs. One style of individuation was not present for all of the twinships. There were clear patterns that differentiated types of identity, the degrees of separation-individuation, and the relationship formation among the twins who were interviewed. From these interviews, patterns of twinship emerged naturally. Whereas some twins were able to separate psychologically quite effectively, some twins had great difficulty with psychological separations. The degree to which twins were capable of separation and individual development became the continuum for establishing these patterns of twinship. It became clear that there are dominant patterns of twinship. Indeed, it is possible to group

this adult twin population into six types of twinship experiences: (1) unit identity, (2) interdependent identity, (3) split identity, (4) idealized identity, (5) competitive identity, and (6) sibling attachment identity. While some of the twins fit into more than one type of twinship experience, it was relatively easy to determine the pattern that most clearly characterized each twinship from that of shared identity to individuation. Furthermore, the patterns that began in infancy endured throughout the lives of the twins interviewed.

I also theorized that twins have two distinct identities: as a twin and as an individual. Twin identity creates the deep attachment that consciously or unconsciously twins long to share throughout their lives. Individuality promotes the twin's capacity to cope with the stresses of life and to develop a well-defined expansive sense of self. Both identities are born in early life and evolve with the quality of parenting, luck in life, persistence, and challenges.

Patterns of twinship were looked at more closely in my next book *Not All Twins Are Alike: Psychological Profiles of Twinship* (Klein, 2003). I found that the patterns of twinship were revealed with other twins who I interviewed. I concluded that parents who naturally help their twins to develop individuality are more successful in raising emotionally healthy twins. Therapeutic interventions relieved troublesome issues of being a twin in a non-twin world. Mental health issues from depression to anxiety to eating disorders were also apparent in twins and could be alleviated in various types of psychotherapy.

Alone in the Mirror: Twins in Therapy (Klein, 2012) discussed clinical vignettes of twins in therapy with the intention of understanding and explaining issues that twins had with separation, non-twin relationships, psychotherapy, loneliness, estrangement, and twin loss. Unequivocally twins preferred twin therapists who could understand their intensity with one another and their difficulty relating to non-twins. Another crucial finding was that twins can be influenced by their therapists' conscious and unconscious expectations. Strong attachment to the therapist which is enmeshed can be a serious problem. With twins who are overly close to one another there is an inability to connect with the therapist or with others, someone who is interested in being close as the twin must be the go-to person.

The findings of my three books on twins are juxtaposed with my personal and professional twin experiences over the last 30 years in *Twin Dilemmas*. Because I have written extensively on the intensity and complications of twinship relationships, I receive phone calls and emails from my readers for advice on how to handle twin problems that are troubling and confusing. Because of my own struggles separating, then fighting with my sister, and our estrangement in midlife, helping others is extremely rewarding for me when twins and parents of twins call me for advice. Deep and sometimes profound relief is expressed when twin fighting and estrangement are affirmed as normal and understandable in the context of child, adolescent, and adult development. In my professional and personal experiences with twins, together or alone, I have learned that twins are more able to function effectively in their world of relationships and work when they understand the differences between themselves and their twin and the twin world and the non-twin world.

Twin closeness and harmony provides peace and confidence. Twin fighting which can turn into twin estrangement is very common, painful, and troubling for twins. Fighting too much, alongside too much sharing causes confusion for twins about who is responsible for what in their own twinship and with other people. In general, ego or self boundary confusion is normal, understandable, and predictable with young twins because they don't have a clear sense of what is appropriate to take care of in new relationships or with their twin. But as twins grow up and develop their own sense of self, they need to learn how much to expect from their twin and others who are close. Without sensitivity and acknowledgment of what is possible in interpersonal relationships, twins can become disappointed in their twin or in others. Too much closeness, which is related to fear of being separated and on your own, can emotionally strangle twins who are enmeshed. For example, 40-year-old twins who work together and live together: while they each long for marriage and children, a lack of necessary social skills based on individual experiences prevents them from moving forward. Or there is the example of twins who have too much anger based on disappointment in their co-twin and cannot be in the same room with one another. Extreme anger that is unspoken and unresolved can devastate or cripple self-development. And of course there are the twins who are in between these two extremes: "ordinary twins" who try to get along, but cannot do it consistently like the fairy tales suggest.

While my theories are documented, I know that they are controversial as well because they are so counter to the social mythology about how twins have an ideal relationship. There is an overfocus on twins as subjects in genetic vs environmental research. Ironically, even today after living through the ups and downs of my life as a twin in a non-twin world, my twin sister who has read my books on twins will not totally accept my point of view about how to survive our closeness, dependencies, and anger. Still I believe deeply in my ideas about why being a twin is special and extremely hard. I am hoping that twins who are struggling for whatever reason with each other or their families will find understanding and solace in my presentation. Mental health professionals who understand the difficulties and rewards of a twin's journey to independence will be more effective, and so I am writing this book for therapists who work with twins. Parents and relatives of twins will gain insight into why twins are different and often hard to get along with in a normal non-twin expectable way.

Understanding the twin relationship will help when twins understand why they are fighting or know why they cannot separate from one another; it is possible for them to develop strategies and appropriate expectations for one another and their lives. The joy of closeness and harmony grows when maturity based on adulthood reality is built into the deep and entwined twin relationship. Profoundly accepting that once a twin always a twin is what it is. Twins can't get divorced. The twin relationship, often a mystery and difficult to understand in words, is undoubtedly a source of wonder, contentment, loneliness, anxiety and an enduring part of identity.

1 What Childhood Memories of Life Experiences and Narratives Reveal About Adult Twin Relationships

We did not know that being a twin was unique, so how could we talk about our development as individuals or twins as children?

Amy

Everyone we met as children were fascinated by our relationship. We got so many superficial, cutesy questions about what it was like to be a twin. Who is smarter? Who is better looking? Does your mother have a favorite? We were both annoyed. And sometimes just sick to death about all of the questions.

Nancy

When we are together, we feel like we are alone; even though we have each other.

Daniel

The "We" in "We" is Different: The Psychological Uniqueness of Identity and Separation for Twins

Understanding the twin relationship and how this deep attachment grows and changes throughout the lifespan is a lived but an untold story. The outside observer—the onlooker—may see hints of the difficulty twins have being apart and being together as they age. But the rollercoaster ride of twinship can confuse, tire, and alienate single-born individuals, who tend to idealize the closeness twins share (Klein, 2003). Or in some situations, twins feel ashamed that they don't get along and keep their thoughts and feelings hidden about their anger at one another. Certainly, twins know, whether or not they can talk about their idiosyncratic relationship style, that they have different issues with who they are, and how they interact with others than singletons (Schave and Ciriello, 1983). Explaining how different twinship is from children who are born alone is complicated and a labor-intensive problem. Empathy from outsiders looking in is hard to find because onlookers want to have a twin to complement and mirror them. How can a single person know the complications that they have not experienced? Sharing parents and memories creates unique problems with separation and individuation that need to be described and understood (Klein, 2012). Being a twin in a non-twin world can be frustrating and humiliating for twins who long for the closeness and understanding of their early life (Klein and Martinez, 2016; Lanigan, 2016).

The deep interconnection of psychological identity between twins is real. Unlike single-born infants and toddlers, shared identity is inevitable and normal (Schave, 1982; Tancredy and Fraley, 2006). A twin has an identity as a twin and an identity as an individual. Twins are closer than brothers and sisters because they share an identity based on early life experiences and the reaction of others. Psychoanalytic theorists suggest that twins have issues with intertwined ego boundaries (Burlingham, 1952, 1963; Leonard, 1961; Tabor and Joseph, 1961). Ego boundary confusion is understandable and predictable, although I really think the ego boundary lingo is not accurate for twins because of the primary attachment that they share (Fonagy and Target, 2003). For example, if a pair of twins makes decisions together as young children, is this a sign of abnormal ego boundaries? Even when they are just playing together and sharing? When does sharing become so pathological that egos are merged? When is fighting too much fighting?

"How do I do something new without my twin?" is a difficult issue that is hard to work through as well. Being alone becomes a critical problem as twins grow into adulthood. Unfortunately, it is an easy and often-made mistake for teachers and therapists to glibly say, "This is just an ego boundary problem. If you could just set up realistic rules and follow through on them you would not have problems with your twin."

I have been told this myself far too many times. From my personal and professional experiences, I know it is easier to corral wild horses than to set up ego boundaries for twins. Certainly, parents, twins themselves, and therapists should attempt to acknowledge and hold on to individual differences with the highest regard for empathy, truth, and integrity. Individuality is a necessary part of healthy twins' development. Believing that you can actually dictate individuality in twins is short-sighted, futile, and grandiose. And clearly, some identity that is shared between twins is intractable and life-sustaining.

What Is Mine and What Is Yours? The Meaning of Separateness for Twins

> I baulked in public at being compared to my twin. Inwardly I cringed at my lack of uniqueness. Hiding out in my closet, rejoicing in my privacy, became a secret joy. I felt the luxury of having a bigger closet, accommodating an office of sorts, my private abode. In my solo retreat, I meticulously arranged papers and pens, belonging to me alone.
>
> I yearned to define what was mine. Without separate rooms or friends, I acted out this desire with my dolls. Paula's dolls were perfectly unchanged. Mine were altered. My doll world became my individual creation.

Chopping off my dolls' pretty long blonde hair made them uniquely mine, different from us.

Linda

A sense of separateness is such a personal and subjective experience for each and every twin. Most likely, the emotionally intense dramas of the twin relationship are more accurately portrayed in memoirs, biography, and novels (Baker, 1962; Lamb, 1998; Shawn, 2011). Generalizations about twins reduce the depth of feelings that are shared. This said, I believe that understanding the meaning of being alone and learning to be truly separate individuals is the struggle all twins experience throughout their lifetimes (Klein, 2012; Klein and Martinez, 2016). The real-life experiences of twins reveal the joys and serious hardships that are related to the meaning of being alone and separate and still closely aligned—the reality of being a twin. Touching, intense, and telling twin life stories are completely different from the fantasized popular images of twins as idealized or demonized people.

As I know only too well from my experiences, being a twin has a lot of really good or harmonious times of sharing and caring. Special advantages with emotional and physical closeness that non-twins cannot understand and experience are common everyday happenings. There are downsides as well. The mixture of competition, fighting, criticism, and harmony can be overwhelming for twins and their families. Without a doubt the disadvantages of being born married are intense and complicated. Understanding why it is so hard to disentangle "ego boundaries" is crucial for twins, parents, and their psychotherapists.

Briefly stated, the primary attachment that twins share—their twin identity, which is separate from their individual identity, creates a developmental uniqueness (Fonagy and Target, 2003). Confusion about decision-making is a symptom or sign of this developmental idiosyncrasy. Moods and behaviors can change in an instant for twins, depending on who is making the decision or who is in charge. One twin, or the other twin, or the twins as a pair can have a voice in decision making. Also, twin identity within the pair becomes ingrained in their sense of self and affects decision-making. Who is stronger or more skillful capable of making a decision or being in charge? And which twin will need help trying to solve a problem? Each twin sees life differently. They compare their observations and come up with a decision. In other words, confusing or ambivalent ways of perceiving an event are common. A twin can easily go from the reality of a situation to the role they play in their twinship. The following story illustrates my point.

I remember from my own childhood a fight my twin had with our older brother over french fries. At the time of the crisis, we were 6 and Alan was 13. This french fries fight reveals our deep alliance or identification with each other and the complexity of twin decision-making. French fries were a special treat at our home. I knew that I should leave Margie's french fries portion alone. But Alan stole some fries from her plate when she and I were involved in a conversation. Margie got so upset when she saw that some of her french fries were gone that she picked up the phone and started to call the police.

Immediately I asked her to give me the phone. I calmed her down, and she took on my perspective that mother would order more french fries if there were not enough. The police were left out of the potential escalation of this altercation. Was this a fight over essentially nothing? Or did I lend my reasonable ego sensibility to my sister to avoid chaos and stress?

In our childhood relationship my twin was in charge of anger and reacting and I was responsible for the consequences of events. Consequently, Marge got kicked out of Brownies for being wild and I got an ulcer. As children, at any time we could see one another's point of view and easily change our minds. Getting over our entanglement was very difficult. Decisions were made based on opportunity and consequences, and who was in charge at that moment in time. Suffice to say, as adults we each had literally countless hours of psychoanalytic psychotherapy to learn which problems belonged to me and which ones were my twin's problems.

I share another example of how confusing decision-making and fighting can be for twins. I worked with a family with 6-year-old boy–girl twins. Sandra, their mother, called me to ask if I could help her with Melissa and Nate, who were continually fighting over how to get along with each other. These feisty twins were driving their mother crazy. During the summer, Nate, who was hooked on a video game, would ignore Melissa when she asked him to play with her. Melissa became so upset about being ignored that she told her mother she wanted to kill herself.

After this threat occurred several times Sandy was of course concerned and so was I. I met with mom and her twins. Nate was more reserved than Melissa. Both children were of their own minds. After many play therapy sessions and psychological evaluations I could see that both children had "What belongs to who" and "Whose problem is it" twin issues. When I asked the children if they could try and be more civilized with each other they said NO. In fact, they agreed that Nate could not give up video games and Melissa just wanted her brother to play with her. They wanted what they wanted. In other words, both refused to compromise. I suggested to the mom that more separation would prevent some of the fighting. When Nate heard that he was going to have to stay away from his sister at night he was inconsolable. He began to cry. Melissa comforted him. Nate said that no matter how much he hated his sister they had to sleep together. Melissa agreed.

I was very surprised. I could tell that both twins were serious. Their fighting and unhappiness was temporary. Sharing a bed was a certainty. I have found this need for closeness with other young twins who cannot stop fighting over toys, food, clothing, and attention from parents, friends, teachers, and relatives. Fighting, for twins, is different than fighting is for non-twins. Wanting to be together for life-sustaining comfort is critical especially in young children, where identity can be confused and still be normal (Klein, 2012). The importance of closeness in childhood is discussed on the following pages.

Twins share a primary attachment that is reflected in their earliest memories of being a twin (Schave and Ciriello, 1983). While the twin attachment cannot and will not effectively replace the nurturing that parenting provides, the twin bond is as developmentally significant and irreplaceable as the parent–child bond. Twin attachment forms or creates a distinct twin identity—a sense that there is always another who will complement and comfort you by their presence. In infancy twins may not know that they are separate individuals. If babies could talk they might say, "My leg is your leg or your leg is my leg." As twins grow older, emotional confusion about psychological boundaries that is hard to untangle can develop into enmeshment. What belongs to me and what belongs to you can become a serious issue. Whose problem is it anyway? is a theme of twin fighting. Belonging, responsibility, and identification are significant aspects of twin identity development and individuality. What separateness means to twins is very different than what single children experience when they are not with their families.

Patterns of Twinship

The variety of issues that twins deal with are related to the pattern of twinship that develops in infancy and early childhood. In my earlier research I observed six patterns of twinship, which I labeled unit identity, interdependent identity, split identity, idealized identity, competitive identity, and sibling attachment identity. In later research I observed interdependent identity, split identity, and competitive identity.

Clearly, not all twins are alike. Patterns of twinship are based on the quality of parenting which determines the depth of attachment that twins share. In other words, there are different parenting styles that affect the qualities of individuation and differences between the twin pairs (Baumrind, 1995). One style of separation and individuation is not seen in all twinships. How the parents view the twin relationship is crucial (Schave, 1982). Are the twins a burden and ignored? Are the twins tolerated because of the special attention they receive from onlookers? Or are twins seen as a gift and treated as individuals? The more attention each child receives for his or her individuality and the deeper the attachment between parent and child, the more likely twins will be able to separate successfully from one another.

Fortunately and out of necessity for long-term psychological health, each child becomes aware of their relationship with their parents and primary caregivers. At birth, awareness and attachment to the parents or primary caregiver is the basis of their individual sense of self (Stern, 1985). When caregivers have a distinct psychological and physical sense of each twin's special needs for attention, whether or not they are identical or fraternal twins, unique selfhood is energized. When caregivers see their twins as a unit or halves of a whole, twins turn to each other for the nurturing that parenting should be providing. Disinterested or indifferent parenting promotes an interdependent twin attachment that is very difficult to disentangle. For example, when the co-twin gives comfort because their parents are not available, deeply rooted interdependence is established and entangled with individual identity. Fears of expansiveness are entrenched and shared, making separation very traumatic.

In this observational and clinical research three patterns of twinship were apparent. In order of difficulty separating from one another they are the following:

1. Interdependent-identity twins report that their co-twin is more important than their parent because of limited, negligent, hostile, or indifferent parenting styles. Parents are burdened or disappointed by their children. Twins turn to each other for support and love which intensifies their attachment and makes separation very difficult.
2. Split-identity twins are accepted as twins but not as individuals in their own right. Parents like the attention that twins bring to a family. Individual differences between split-identity twin children are based on how the mother and father perceive their children rather than on real observable distinctions. Split-identity twins are opposites at times and a valued pair at other times. Mixed messages about who they are in relation to one another creates a great deal of ambivalence and shame about their twin. Often split-identity twins see their twin as the bad part of themselves or a horrendous burden. Separation and estrangement is common as they grow in adulthood.
3. Individual-identity twins are seen as distinct from one another based on real observational differences. While parents may feel overworked, they do not feel overwhelmed by their children. Attempts are made to separate these toddlers and young children so that separation is possible in adolescence. Over-reliance and shame are not prominent in this pattern of twinship. However, in spite of parental efforts to develop a strong core sense of self, individual-identity twins do seek out psychotherapy to deal with fitting into the non-twin world.

Early Memories Reveal the Direction of Separation Experiences

Early memories of the twin relationship reveal the pattern of twinship that is the foundation of personality development. Early memories predict the ability of twins to separate from one another as these memories are windows or mirrors to how parents react to raising twins (Klein, 2003; Schave and Cirello, 1983). Understanding the type of attachment shared helps therapist and twins be realistic about how much separation is possible and how much work it will take to overcome estrangement. Clearly, goals for twins in therapy will vary based on their ability to change and adapt in the world without their sister or brother. The world around the lives of twins—the social and financial milieu—affects their development as well. The following examples show twins who have an established attachment in different life circumstances.

When Two Are One: Interdependent-Identity

"Interdependent-identity" twins use one another for companionship, support, and reassurance. Parental attention to individuality is left dormant as they grow up. Far too often, uniqueness and individuality is crippled if twins are left to rely on one another for a great deal of their childhood. A fear of expansiveness is common for interdependent-identity twins, who prefer to be copies of one another by sharing values and decision-making. Taking themselves out of the twin equation and seeing themselves as truly psychologically separate is extremely hard for over-identified twins. Or interdependent-identity twins may assign roles to one another. One is outgoing while the other is shy and keeps a look out for trouble. These roles become fixed. Too much time together—forced interconnections—reduce the development of individual life skill abilities drastically. Although resentment and anger at interdependence is obvious, what is missing in each twin's life skill abilities is very difficult to overcome. Being apart is truly traumatically challenging in so many ways for interdependent-identity twins. While it is possible to work with interdependent-identity twins in psychotherapy, outcomes will vary. The psychotherapeutic process is very slow because the therapist will be seriously challenged to replace the closeness of the twin no matter how skillful that clinician may be. In other words, interdependent-identity twins have difficulty trusting the insight of their therapist, especially in areas of achieving independence from each other.

There are of course different types of attachments that twins who are too interconnected share. Here are some examples of twin life experiences that indicate how primary the twin attachment can be. These particular life experiences reflect the importance of early memories that grow into characteristics of personality and lifelong relationships. Life circumstances contribute to separation and individuation process as well. Death for any reason mobilizes independence.

Vince and Victor

> Vince: I remember when we were just five years old holding on to Victor during a terrible thunder and lightning storm that rocked our house at its foundation. I felt safe because I was with my twin brother.

Unfortunately, there was way too much comfort and safety just being together. Separation for these twins was truly challenging. Vince elaborates:

> Who was shaking our house? Why did my mother appear as a ghost when the light flashed? Thunder and lighting. The crashing of the thunder shook the house. Or was I so afraid I was shaking? The illumination of the house turning known surroundings and people into ghost images like the flash of a camera bulb.
> In a double bed with my twin. Safe, secure, reaching out, comfort. Finding my twin next to me. Safety. No more shaking. Just safety and comfort even though the storm continues on. Strength in union and closeness. Sleep, happiness, and peace when two become one.

Vince and Victor were raised in a small, poor, and rural community. Their mother told them that their biological father abandoned them at birth. Later Vince learned that his mother did this in order to receive a hefty amount of child support for her twins when they were infants. Their young mother was angry and abusive. When their stepfather came home their mother told their stepfather to punish them. They were physically abused for their slight behavior indiscretions. Their younger stepbrother was favored and not punished. While other relatives provided love and care, these adorable twins were left to rely on one another as surrogate parents for each other. Working together they warded off the pain of abuse as well as the emptiness of parental indifference.

Vince verbally portrays their early life in this story of reparation.

> There was a huge granite rock that lived in our backyard. We called our rock "the good ship lollypop." Helen, Susan, Ruth, and little Michael lived up the road from us in a tent camp for indigent families. They often came down to our place to play. We climbed on the huge rock and sometimes pretended we were on a cruise ship like the *Love Boat*. Victor, who was six minutes older than me, and Helen, who was also the oldest, were the captains. The rest of us were cooks or stewards or whatever was needed to run the ship. For hours we would pretend that there were huge waves threatening our very existence or movie stars were coming aboard to entertain us. Our play was about what we wanted our lives to be, not what they were. Victor and I were living in a world of hell, abuse, and poverty. Helen and her gang from the tent camp often had to go hungry because there was no money for food. Playing made us feel like we were going to be ok. We ended each meeting singing, "We all live in a yellow submarine."

Their play was a courageous attempt to overcome and repair the pain of their childhood. In their years of schooling Victor and Vince were too important to each other providing comfort and reassurance. When their mother put their hands over the red-hot burner on her stove because they were playing campfire outside, they turned to each other for solace. Twinship seemed to reduce all of their physical and emotional pain as children. Or said differently, being together shoved their bad feelings underground. In school they also received a great deal of attention for being twins, which was life enhancing.

Separating from one another as high school graduates was possible but difficult. They went their own ways in their early twenties. Both twins had already adopted a gay lifestyle, and disappointed their mother by openly coming out of the closet at a time when people were horrified by homosexuality. After searching for a professional identity Vince became a nurse and Victor a nursing assistant. In their late twenties and early thirties they performed as drag queens. They were popular and sought out entertainers. As adults, they lived together and apart. Victor often impersonated Vince to gain a better sense of himself.

The after-effects of separation and the traumatic abuse they experienced as children were both overwhelming and torturous. As Victor and Vince grew into their thirties and early forties life became harder and harder to bear. Vince cared for his brother in a mature and positive way. His caring was not enough. Victor, after many years of a mental illness, committed suicide at age 44. Vince attempted suicide unsuccessfully after he lost his brother. He spent six years of his life trying to make sense of his brother's loss. Recovery from twin loss was extremely hard won and still is an ongoing battle. Vince wrote a book called *Naked Angels* (Arthurs, 2014) that narrates his reaction to losing his brother and the beginning of his recovery.

There are several crucial lessons in this memoir. Child abuse can create deep scars that cripple children well into adulthood emotionally. Twins are vulnerable to abuse because they are hard to raise. Twins need their parents' nurturing. Counting on one another for parental love is not in any way enough to develop an individual sense of themselves. Trying to overcome physical and emotional abuse through the inter-twin connection leads to unfixable problems.

Madeline and Vicki

> Vicki: I do not remember thinking otherwise—thinking of myself as an individual. I remember being in twin strollers and our mom took us out on errands or walks. People would stop and comment about us being twins.

Madeline and Vicki, fraternal twins, were born in Japan while their father was in the air force. Their mother was Dutch and their father was Caucasian from the Midwest. The family spoke both English and Japanese with their older brother and the twins. Financial resources were limited and the family moved with dad's work in the military almost every year. Madeline and Vicki relied on one another for friendship. Making new friendships after moving every year was very difficult. Throughout early childhood Madeline and Vicki were always kept busy together. Both share that they never felt that they were poor because they had one another to play with. Vicki shares her memories of early childhood:

> When we were between two and three we were living in Tucson, Arizona. Madeline and I made mud pies to decorate the outside of our house. When mom found our creative works she immediately removed them. She did not yell at us. She never got angry. We knew that we were both going to have to stop making mud pies.

Madeline and Vicki were treated as one unit by both parents. Interestingly, Madeline and Vicki remember that they were not parented differently than their brother, who was two years older. They describe their older brother as a genius and a loner. As children they were disciplined as a unit—as one person. In other words they were told as a twin pair what to do and not to do. Individual discipline was directed by dad as they got older. Vicki remembers that she was in charge of helping Madeline feel better about herself and follow the house rules. Vicki was the comforting twin. She shares:

> As children we would walk with mother to do all the household errands and we would get a small surprise before we headed home. We were poor so Madeline was always disappointed in our surprise. I always tried to find something special to comfort and help her feel important.

Madeline shares:

> As children, we were dressed alike until sixth grade. We shared a bedroom until the end of high school. We were given the same toys and the same projects and given equal simultaneous attention. We did everything together and we were never apart except during school.

The family finally settled down in Moreno Valley, California, before Madeline and Vicki started kindergarten. Vicki shares:

> In kindergarten the teachers picked up how close we were to one another and that we had our own special way of communicating with each other. We were separated in school from kindergarten onward. We started to develop different ways of reacting to others. I was the quiet, serious child. Madeline was more rebellious and outgoing. Making new friends was easier for Madeline as she was more of a show off. She made more friends than I did. No matter what had happened between us, we were always close and took care of the other if necessary. We felt that we were a part of one another.

Separation at school helped these twins establish a unique sense of who they were when they were not together. Their mother began to notice that there was a great deal of anger between them. Separating was easier for Madeline who felt that being a twin was abnormal. Vicki kept to herself more and she was the more serious problem-solving twin. Shy in comparison to Madeline, Vicki was more careful and a perfectionist. Observable competition that was not talked about at home began between these school-age children. Madeline liked getting her way and found Vicki to be too strict and mean. Vicki was heartbroken that her sister was so different from her. They blamed one another and grew more distant. Taking their own career paths and meeting potential partners was important for them as they entered adulthood. Still they remained close to one another when they were dealing with difficult situations.

Because they grew up with very few financial resources both women strived to attain wealth. Indeed, they are very successful businesswomen who work together on their different business ventures when they can do so. They turn to each other for financial and hands-on help. They are still competitive with one another as adults. They long to get along but have difficulty finding a balance that allows them to do this. Anger at one another for being different makes closeness tenuous and difficult, in spite of their need for connection. Neither twin has had a romantic life partner that has lasted more than five years. So in their early sixties they rely on one another in many stressful situations such as health and safety. Still fighting and critical of each other they are almost next-door neighbors.

Early memories reflect the interdependence these twins shared because they were always together and disciplined as one. Both are driven to succeed and are very effective problem-solvers. They see their differences in this way. Madeline became the more outgoing risk-taker and Vicki the perfectionist. They were highly critical of one another but always felt responsible for the other as well. The continual closeness and animosity for who the other was and still is as an individual created deep rifts and a great deal of unhappiness for both of these bright and accomplished women. Because they were not abused physically they have an easier time making their way in the world in comparison to Vince and Victor who were so tortured that life became too overwhelming for Victor. While parents create the relationship that twins share later in life, other factors such as emotional, physical, and sexual abuse can create unrelenting depression.

Adrienne and Eileen

> Adrienne: I remember being afraid to separate from my sister in kindergarten.

Adrienne's early memory foretells the ongoing struggles of living separate lives that these women experienced alone and together. While they find great comfort being together, they are very ashamed of still living together. Family input, friendships and psychotherapists have attempted to give them insight into "how to do it"—separate from each other. At 40, there is still so much trepidation about being apart that progress is very gradual.

Adrienne and Eileen were born into a middle-class family in a working-class community. Their parents were comfortable. Financial issues were not a determinant of their interdependency. However, their parents did not have the motivation or wherewithal to break their children's intense need for one another. Adrienne and Eileen developed their own special language that their parents could not or would not understand. Their younger brother was able to interpret their special way of communicating. Very shy children, both were actually afraid of people outside of the family circle. A great deal of their interpersonal interactions were with each other. Behavior that was obviously too close and dependent was permissively endorsed by their parents.

Eileen shares some of her early childhood experiences:

> I don't remember much from when we were little ... I remember always sharing a room, my bed was on the left and Adrienne's was on the right.

We would talk all night and my parents always had to tell us to stop talking. When we would get scared at night, Adrienne would always come in my bed ... never me in hers. Kinda like our relationship now, strange. Adrienne goes out of her way more.

School was very challenging for both because of their social inhibitions and their secret language which created problems communicating with others (Koch, 1966; Mittler, 1971). They attended speech therapy separately at public school for over three years, which made them feel singled out as strange by the other children. Fortunately, by third grade they were able to communicate with other children. However, they still shared friends and all their life experiences.

Adrienne: I remember in first or second grade being invited to a friend's house and not wanting to go because my twin wasn't invited. My mom made me go. I don't remember anything about the play date except that I didn't want to go since Eileen wasn't going.

Eileen: We were just always together. Once in fourth grade or fifth, Heather, our best friend, convinced me to walk home from school alone with her. Not Adrienne. Adrienne took the bus. And I remember it took Heather a while to get me to do it, but I did. We stopped for pizza and when we got home I saw that Adrienne had gotten off the bus and had literally just been walking around the block until I got home. She couldn't be in the house without me. A couple of years ago, when we were in our early forties, I went out with a boyfriend to dinner and Adrienne sat outside and didn't even go inside to eat dinner with my parents. I guess some behaviors don't change.

Adrienne: I remember in fifth grade the different classes went to a three-day camp. We went at different times. I don't remember much, but I do remember playing video games by myself in the recreation room. I did not want to come out. I guess I was not comfortable without Eileen. Eileen probably had a different experience but we didn't discuss her feelings.

Both young women attended the same Midwestern college. They had their own dorm rooms but took the same types of business classes. In their early twenties they were still very shy and unable to live separately. They recall that after college they went to Israel. At that time they were comfortable being apart on the Kibbutz. Both twins found boyfriends. Adrienne never pursued men after her trip to Israel. Eileen had many male friends and considered marriage and a family. But after that first separation on the Kibbutz they have worked and lived together. Separation has been extremely difficult for them as it creates depression and a fear of making decisions on their own. Adrienne concludes: "I never wanted to be first in a competition. It was Eileen who was the spokesperson for both of us. Together we feel like we have to agree on what we are doing."

These early memories and experiences predict the difficulty Eileen and Adrienne have had and continue to experience trying to live more separate lives. While being together is what they prefer, they are ashamed of their inability to be more independent of one another. Eileen is disappointed that Adrienne could not tolerate the male friend who was interested in marrying her. However, Eileen is aware that she was passive in this relationship for fear of hurting her sister.

Both women lack some of the basic social skills that are necessary to make non-twin friendships. They are focused on working on and developing their landscape design business. Their nuclear family and close relatives are the center of their social life. They share most of their friendships. The comfort of being together creates roadblocks to developing their own separate friends and life experiences. Deep fears of expansiveness, which would include more individual identity, are conscious and unconscious (Stolorow, 1993). Fears of being separate prevents them from attaining an identity outside of the twinship with other people.

However, because their life circumstances were nurturing of the twinship and overall identity development through education and family stability, these women are attempting to separate from one another. Developing a sense of who they are alone has not only been excruciating but shameful. Adrienne and Eileen remain intent on overcoming their fears of being apart. The anger and shame that Madeline and Vicki feel for one another is absent between them. Desperation and depression is not overwhelming as was seen in the relationship between Vince and Victor. The quality and concern of family life and resources have allowed Adrienne and Eileen to be successful as twins.

***

In comparing these three interdependent-identity twinships you can see certain striking themes or similarities. First, inadequate and negligent parenting created an over-identification between all of these pairs of twins (Ainsworth, 1974; Baumrind, 1995). Second, at different stages of their lives events occurred. In these instances life was very difficult for both twins in different ways depending on the role they played in relation to their twin. For example, Eileen was afraid to get married, while Adrienne was afraid to lose her twin. Third, one twin always was the more outgoing and the other the more of a problem-solver. Personality differences were established between the twins, not by parental intervention. However, it is possible that each twin had certain personality traits that were brought out in the twin relationship because of different interactions with their parents. For example, why was Vince the caregiver and Victor the adventurer?

There were distinct differences between these pairs. The more abusive the parent–child relationship, the more difficult physical and emotional separation was experienced. Second, while twins who are enmeshed try to be parent surrogates ineffectively, family stability or instability, and environmental resources or lack thereof are critical in helping twins develop coping strategies to navigate their life choices and experiences. In midlife, Victor's life was empty of meaning, direction and hope. Madeline could not allow her sister to be her support, but needed her at the same time. Adrienne could not let go of her twin. Eileen who wanted to marry was too loyal to hurt her sister.

Opposites Always? Split-identity Twins

Both identical and fraternal twins can manifest a split identity. Interestingly, and in sharp contrast to interdependent-identity twins who were ignored and neglected, split-identity twins received a great deal of positive attention for being twins. Their parents are excited to have twins because of the attention they receive from others, who are fascinated by twins. While parents take pride in showing off their twins in beautiful outfits or in special photographs, they have difficulty relating to them as distinct individuals. The parents are not psychologically able to deal with two children at the same time. Splits in identity such as "halves of a whole person" become reality for these children. Confusing as it may seem this is very common.

This typical pattern of parenting twins creates anxiety and anger for twins alongside closeness. An artificial split in perception of the twin attachment such as good and bad, competent and fragile, evolves. Twins babies are treated by parents as opposites in an unconscious or conscious effort to see the children as different. While the actual differences, such as bad and good or fragile and competent, are not necessarily accurate or true, they are elaborated upon based on parental projection. Eventually projections take on reality that is hard to dispel. Mom sees one twin as the bad part of herself. Mom sees the other twin as the entitled part of herself. These imposed perceptual differences become deeply rooted in the identity of each child and the bond they share.

Unlike interdependent twins who create their own sense of how they are different, split-identity twins are trapped into a superficial category by parental over-reactions. While being together is very comfortable in childhood, there are conflicts about relying on each other and shame about who their twin is in real life outside of the twinship. Estrangement develops between these pairs of twins, depending on the traumatic experiences that these twins live through together.

Here are some examples of the earliest memories of split-identity twins that reflect the roots of their conflicted and fragmented relationships. Closeness is comfortable and important in childhood, while fighting and shame are present in adolescence and midlife. In later life estrangement is more emotionally acceptable. Estrangement is more prevalent where abuse has been experienced by both twins.

Keith and Kirk

Keith: I remember being in our play pen. My brother Kirk was outside playing with our older brother Alex. I wanted to get out of the play pen to hold my brother and connect with him. My mother wouldn't let me out because it was too much trouble for her when all three of us were together. Or she was jealous of the closeness I had with Kirk. My mother wanted to stop our closeness from developing.

Keith's early memory of being trapped in the play pen at around age two dramatically illustrates his intense attachment to his twin brother and his mother's indifference to his needs for love, attention, and companionship. Making these early years more stressful for Keith, their mom wanted to replace Keith and be more important to Kirk than his twin. While a mother's deep jealousy of the twinship is not always a determinant of the direction of the twin attachment, I have worked with this dynamic before (Klein, 2012). The twin who is favored by the mother is usually the child who gets to do whatever they want to do. While the dismissed, displaced, or invisible twin is left to fend for themselves without explanation.

In Keith and Kirk's childhood gruesome abuse was used to keep the two apart. Their parents were violently and sexually abusive throughout their childhood. Screaming and chaos were normal, even though Keith and Kirk lived in an upscale neighborhood in Northern California. Their father suffered from post-traumatic stress disorder. He was a veteran of World War II who had survived the Japanese labor camps. Their mother suffered from bipolar disorder and would sleep 18 hours a day or be manic. Dad was an alcoholic who constantly had flashbacks and often he was suicidal. It was not uncommon for Keith and Kirk to see their father threatening to shoot his brains out with a gun he was holding in his hands. There was no steady income from either parent. The family lived in a home that had been left to them by their mother's wealthy father and was maintained by the father's estate.

In their childhood until age 5 a housekeeper, RoRo, cared for the boys as much as she could as their dad was not living with the family. When their dad moved into the home in Piedmont, California, RoRo was fired for asking their dad to stop abusing Keith. At 5 Keith started dressing his brother for school and found a way to collect bottle caps to make money for food, as there was very little food in their refrigerator. Life in general was very chaotic and traumatic. Keith was the target of physical and sexual abuse by his parents and older brother. Keith protected Kirk from the abuse he suffered as he was targeted as the bad twin and the caretaker. Keith took care of his brother.

> Keith: Taking care of Kirk who needed me gave my life a purpose. While the connection was in some ways one-sided, he needed me and valued what I did for him. I did for Kirk what RoRo had done for me. While I knew that my parents were critical of me and very abusive, I knew that Kirk was desperate for my concern for his well-being.

Keith painfully remembers how he has treated as the bad child. He shares:

> My mother always told me that no one would want to hold me or touch me. When she and dad were fighting, my mother would allow my father to

molest me while Kirk and Alex hid in the closet. My brothers would not let me hide with them as they knew that I was the one to be abused.

In spite of all the traumatic abuse Keith suffered because his brothers left him out of their safety net, caring for Kirk gave structure and meaning to Keith's life. Keith was motivated to learn how to make money so that they would not be hungry. Becoming entrepreneurs allowed both boys to survive the chaos in their home life until they went away to college. As they went to school they started a seed catalog business and a printing press business. While these boys were not close in that they never shared their thoughts and feelings, they did do everything together as they lived through school. Togetherness protected them from the horrors of their childhood. As they learned to live separate lives anger, fear, and deep resentment forced their separation to take place. Many years after college, after working together successfully in an auto parts business, Kirk married. This separation led to hatred and fear. Like most twins who suffer this type of abuse as children, estrangement was the only option in adulthood.

Keith was devastated without his brother and started psychotherapy which lasted three decades. Using his experience with his brother he became an entrepreneur and his company was listed for three years as a Fortune 500 company. He is now retired and never sees his twin but thinks about him every day.

Sandy and Scott

> Sandy: I remember my brother would get in bed and cuddle with me because he was such a frightened child. I felt burdened by his anxiety. I remember being relieved that my brother was in the hospital and I would not have to take care of him.

These early memories reflect Sandy's need to have her own life and not serve as the identified parent for her twin brother. Sandy says more:

> Scott had a nightmare again. We weren't allowed to go in mom and dad's bedroom anymore. We kept daddy awake and mom said there wasn't enough room in their bed for all of us. But my bed was just for one person and I didn't have enough room either. I didn't want Scott to get in, but when I said it I felt bad. He was scared. I wanted his nightmares to go away. I wanted to go back to sleep and not be squished. I told him to get in and he put his head on my tummy, and drooled on my pajamas and fell asleep. I hated it when he drooled. I stared at the ceiling and tried not to move so he wouldn't wake up. I wished we could get in with Mom. I wished I didn't have to make him feel better.

Sandy and Scott, fraternal twins, were brought up in a white enclave in an up and coming middle-class neighborhood in French-speaking Canada. They had two older brothers who were climbing up the corporate ladder. Their father was a successful businessman and their mom helped run the family life insurance business. Their mom was a possessed 1950s parent who made every possible effort to present her family as loving and close. Of course, there was a great deal of tension in the family because of the necessity to be perceived and experienced as a perfect family. In actuality the older children were off at college or ignored the twins. Their dad was absent emotionally or uninvolved. Scott and Sandy were very different. Scott was weak and given extra support. Sandy was expected to act as his invisible back up.

> Sandy: When I first started kindergarten, I was very proud of my coloring. Scott was working at another table nearby and the adults were beside him saying how great his picture was even though it wasn't as good as mine. I wanted the adults to look at mine. I knew Scott needed to be told that his was better. I knew it wasn't and I knew the grownups knew it too. When I brought home my report card Mom told me she was proud but she couldn't say it in front of Scott because it would make him feel bad about himself. I was supposed to pretend that he was better than me even though I longed for my parent's praise.

The openness of favoritism in this family was remarkable. Often favoritism is more secretive and covert. Sandy and Scott's life existed on two psychological levels. As young twins they were seen as the perfect adorable twosome who loved each other. In real life Sandy was always expected to take care of and be less than her brother. Sandy had to keep her anger to herself growing up. As teenagers they were nicknamed Donnie and Marie because of the way they easily related to others in a joyful way. Underneath this facade was deep-seated anger and resentment towards one another. Throughout childhood and adolescence, Scott was the sickly and fearful child who hated his sister's strengths. Sandy was the protector who had to do her best and pretend she was just very ordinary and almost invisible. As an adult Sandy had a hard time making decisions for herself and got involved with people who treated her like her brother.

More simply stated, Scott wanted Sandy to be who he wanted her to be and Sandy wanted to be herself. After high school they started to live in different cities. Each twin married and their partners did not get along with their twins. Gradually they lived very separate lives. Long-term estrangement began when Scott began to ignore his twin. The final straw came when Scott refused to acknowledge that his twin sister was present at family events even when she was standing in front of him.

Early memories predict anger and resentment and the necessity later in life for deep estrangement. Mixed messages confused and eroded their attachment. Was Sandy Scott's twin, or his mother, or both? What was left over from their twinship was a need for closeness with others. Finding twin replacements was very difficult for Sandy because she was afraid of what she wanted in a man. She was afraid that a romantic partner would treat her like Scott.

Benna and Rachel

> Rachel: I remember we were labelled by our adoptive parents and these labels stayed with us. I was Daddy's Little Girl and Benna was Mommy's Little Girl.

Given up for adoption at birth by their unwed Portuguese mother and father, these identical twins were first placed in foster care in a small suburb of Ottawa. After nine months in foster care, Benna and Rachel were adopted by well to do older Jewish parents. Their foster mother, when she spoke with Rachel and Benna later in life, said that their adoptive mother was not fit for motherhood. Both women describe their mother as cold and hostile and their father as distant and away on business a great deal.

> Benna: We were raised in a strange family. We had lots of money but Dad had been poor and we always were subjected to his poverty mentality. We had two homes. One was in the suburbs and the other at the lake. We spent summers at the lake and dad only visited. Our parents were dramatic and unpredictable. They never agreed with one another and yet they stayed together and almost clung to each other.

Unfortunately for the entire family, their mother was angry at her husband for the adoption and spent a great deal of time talking with her twins about how she was going to leave their father. This idle threat created a great deal of insecurity in these twins, who had already been abandoned by their biological parents. Benna was closer to her mother, who favored her. Benna became the caregiver of the pair. She would put Rachel to bed throughout their childhood. The disruption of the bond between Rachel and her mother intensified and destabilized their twin attachment. Also, the longings and emptiness that these twins felt because they were emotionally abandoned by their adoptive parents was masked and deeply buried. Who deserved more and who got more became a source of deep anger, confusion, and resentment between these children.

> Rachel: Benna was the more motherly twin and I was more of the explorer. We were very different but relied on each other for comfort and companionship. It was harder to separate from each other because we knew how much we needed each other. Benna would get so enraged with me because I got angry and depressed with our family life. I was right to be angry at our parents, but she felt my anger was too abusive. Getting through the losses of our childhood took us years as adults.

Rachel and Benna were separated in first grade. Because they had difficulty without each other they were placed in second grade together. Benna got sick and was hospitalized and fell behind in school. Rachel remained one grade ahead of Benna until they both attended private school in tenth grade. Rachel was happy to be with her sister but Benna hated feeling like the dumb twin. As these twins grew into adolescence more and more depression related to parenting came to the surface. As children they needed each other but also felt diminished by one another. This conflicted pattern of interacting followed them as they separated from each other in high school and college. Benna was more social than Rachel and found dating, boyfriends, and the thought of marriage as a life goal. Benna took up fashion design. Rachel, who was more insecure, took up adventure travel and animal research. Both women formed their own friendships outside of the twinship. Rachel was afraid of her sexuality and never got romantically involved with a man for more than a couple of months. Rachel's approach to sexuality was quite different from Benna who longed for a long-term relationship because she felt that she had to get married. Benna married at age 35 and divorced within a year.

As adults they worked hard to understand their conflicted and enmeshed relationship through psychotherapy, spiritual journeys, and grief recovery. Benna and Rachel explored their adoption against their adoptive mother's advice and threats not to stir up the past. Grief recovery helped them talk and write about their past. Rachel writes to her birth father:

> I forgive you for being the root reason I have experienced a life of mental and emotional abuse living with my adopted father and mother. They have been emotionally self-absorbed. I have learned a sense of rejection of myself. I feel like a burden to others and worthless. I accept that I will not have a loving relationship with a man in my life due to your abandonment. I feel robbed of a normal life, robbed of cultural identity and roots in this life.

With the death of their mother these women tried to reconcile. And they have invested a great deal of time and effort in reconciliation and getting over their shame at one another because of their deep attachment and deep resentments. Trying to make one another important and not losing their own sense of self has been an incredibly difficult and meaningful journey for them. Benna holds on to her sense that she is the favored daughter and should have the final say in an argument. Rachel combats her belief that her sister knows best. These women have difficulty living with each other and living without one another. Their arguments have some resolution, unlike Madeline and Vicki, because they each have a better sense of themselves as individuals. Estrangement as experienced by Sandy and Scott and Keith and Kirk is not a likely outcome because of their interest in reconciliation.

Patricia and Pauline

> Paula: Around the age of 5 I remember when my mother told me that Patty was in our bedroom crying. She was wearing jeans. She had tangled her hair with a comb. She told our mother that she wanted to be "like

Paulie." I was a tomboy and got a lot more attention for my abilities and that made Patty feel left out. It was my first clear memory of feeling really guilty for being me. Being me hurt Patty. It was that simple.

Patricia (Patty) and Pauline (Paula), identical twins, were born into a large middle-class interracial family in the Midwest. Their dad was Hispanic and mom was Anglo. The two older children took care of the twins and the baby because their mom was always emotionally upset and their dad was always working to support his large family. In reality, their dad was very remote and never much help with the five children even when he was around. Patricia and Pauline's early home life was chaotic and often violent because of their mother's instability and violent temper. Both twins report using one another for support to get through the bad times at home when their mom was out of control. Patty remembers:

> One of my earliest experiences of being a twin is our sleeping together. We shared the same room and slept in the same bed until we were 10 or 11 years old. I remember us sleeping face to face with our hands to our faces, much like we must have been in the womb, and giggling. And then my Dad came into our room looking very beleaguered and asked us to please be quiet and go to sleep. Then I remember him leaving and us giggling together again. I can't remember exactly what we were laughing about.

Sports activities were a very important way to keep their mom happy. Patty was a talented and energetic star of all athletic competitions. Winning helped keep her mother more even-tempered. Their mom also expected Paula to support Patty by never letting her be unhappy or less than Paula. These expectations which were fiercely endorsed were almost impossible to carry through without psychic pain to both children. These twins did everything in harmony. When the family moved to California the twins were around 5. Patty remembers the closeness and responsibility that she and Paula felt for one another:

> When we were 7 or 8 years old we went to Disneyland with Mom and Mr Rose. We were given permission to go out to the park on our own and we had to meet up with them back at the hotel. They saw us together on the monorail and they were so impressed. We were very responsible children. Relying on each other was very natural.

Their other siblings got involved with drugs and introduced Patty and Paula into the drug culture. These identical twins used drugs in their teenage years. Fortunately, because of their closeness, they helped one another get off of drugs as they thought about pursuing a college education. After high school both attended community college. Actual physical separation occurred when Paula attended Cal State Northridge and lived at home. Patty moved to Westwood where she attended UCLA. They still coordinated their weekends.

They did karate together, chose what they ate together, and did their laundry together. Patty worked at Kentucky Fried Chicken and Paula worked at Taco Bell. Staying on the same page was very comforting for them.

True anger and emotional separation began when Paula had a romantic relationship with one of her twin sister's best friends who was at UCLA. Both young women went their own ways and sought out their own happiness at this time. They discussed Paula's homosexual decision. The entire family accepted her decision, but Paula had difficulty expressing her preference for women because it was different than Patty's. The loss of closeness or undeniable differences led to each one of these women to suffer from a serious depression. Both sought out psychotherapy to overcome their sense of being alone in the world. Still in early adulthood they managed to keep in touch by phone and letters. Family events also brought them together. Gradually they grew into their careers successfully and became farther apart. When Paula made a strong commitment to her partner Lisa, Patty had a great deal of resentment toward Lisa. Paula sought out psychotherapy to understand her sister's objections more deeply.

Early memories predict Patricia and Pauline's ongoing closeness as well as their deep-rooted differences, which are still the basis of their adult attachment. Paula's romantic relationship with Patty's friend created an unspoken and deep resentment for both of them. Paula was just angry that her twin took over her friendship but Patty felt guilty that she had not thought about her sister's needs first. The dynamic set up by their mother and father was unrealistic and harmful to their mature and reciprocal attachment as adults. While the relationship is painful it was not as aggressively handled as the above relationships because Paula was always careful not to upset her sister and Patty was careful to stay away to avoid feelings of being less than her twin. Sexual identity difference seemed to lend credence to the reality of their differences.

***

Comparing these four sets of twins brings out important similarities and differences. First, parenting attitudes were self-serving and narcissistic. These twins were props to fulfill their parents' projections and make parenting more predictable. Seeing each child as an individual with special needs was not possible. Children were seen as halves of a whole. Attention to the twinship was superficial in nature and used as a promotional gesture for outsiders about the family unity. This unhealthy parenting attitude deeply damaged the twin relationship. Estrangement was deep-rooted.

Differences between the twin pairs were based on the quality of family life and the presence or absence of chaos and abuse the children experienced. Keith and Kirk were so seriously pitted against each other that their relationship could not survive in adulthood. Education and financial resources clearly helped overcome some of the unhappiness that these twin pairs experienced when they were together. The amount of psychotherapy and the approach of the therapist were crucial in finding peace and understanding about being a twin.

Competitive Twins: Individual Identity

Parents who are concerned about their children's long-range psychological development are aware of the importance of developing an individual sense of self in each child. These psychologically-minded parents monitor the time their children spend together and establish separate times to be with each child alone. Real differences between their twins are based on behavioral observations and interactions with their children. There are ways in which the parent is more comfortable with one child than another which also contributes to the quality of interaction. Personality differences are mirrored in live interactions. The observation of differences in behavior creates a real sense of how each child is unique. Enmeshment in adolescence and later in life is diminished greatly by the establishment of this sense of their individuality in infancy and early childhood.

Twins with an individual identity are competitive with each other and set standards for one another. They measure themselves against one another. Their relationship is based on a search for oneself, desiring a lot of what the twin brother or sister has accomplished and then reaching beyond for greater glory. Very often twins with an individual twin attachment are highly successful professionals or artists because they enjoy helping their twin develop their strengths. While they have high expectations for one another, they share a close and caring relationship. Fighting occurs, but these misunderstandings are easier to resolve or to put aside.

Parents who intuitively or out of deliberate intention establish real differences between their children respect their attachment. These mindful parents take care to not use their twin likeness for their own narcissistic needs. For example, they do not seek out attention for being parents of twins to make up for the extra work of dealing with their children. Thoughtful parents realize the downside of too much twin attention, which is not enough attention to individuality and the development of a core self. Twins who are not over-identified with each other seek out therapy in a less panicked state of mind. While they still have problems being a twin in a non-twin world, emotional confusion about "whose problem is it anyway?" are more contained and less severe. Fighting is less intense and estrangement is not all that common. Parents have effectively established the meaning of separate ego boundaries. Seeking therapy is more likely related to longings for closer relationships and disappointment in others. Closeness and caring is common in adult relationships in these types of twin relationships.

Marilyn and Janet

> Janet: I remember our legs touching one another in our crib and feeling content.

Janet's earliest memory foretells the closeness and time for harmony that these women shared as they grew into adulthood. Marilyn and Janet were born into an Italian family who were delighted to be given the gift of identical twins.

Childhood Memories of Life Experiences 27

Their childhood was reasonably stable and secure. Older parents with a salt of the earth style of child rearing, looked closely for differences between their children.

> Marilyn: My mother could tell us apart from the very beginning. She never made a big deal of us being twins. She never dressed us alike. We were not confused by other family members even though we were identical.

> Janet: My mother always put us in different outfits. Both parents carefully talked about our differences. We were disciplined and praised as individuals, unless we were double trouble.

Janet and Marilyn shared a bedroom until they were 3 years old. Toys and friends were shared if the girls could get along. Their mom gradually divided the toys into Janet's and Marilyn's. And some toys that were for sharing. From their earliest memories toys represented their special interests. Janet was a reader and Marilyn was interested in creative and artistic activities. When they moved into their own rooms they decorated them based on their own personal style.

> Janet: Having our own rooms was liberating. We still spent time in each other's room when we missed each other. We did our schoolwork together and turned to one another for advice about friends. Mom and dad did not want us to parent one another. Every night we would each have a private conversation with mom or dad about school or friends or our feelings.

> Marilyn: Janet and I were close, but she was more bookish. I wanted to paint and draw and design doll clothes. Reading was schoolwork to be completed, not something to do for fun. I loved cooking with my mom and dad and playing games. We were different for sure but cherished our time together as well.

Janet and Marilyn were separated in kindergarten. Being in different classrooms led to some stressful experiences and reactions. Janet started sucking her thumb and Marilyn could not sleep without her twin in her room. Gradually these symptomatic issues were resolved by talking about them and with the experience that time brings. The family always emphasized the development of individuality in each child. Obviously paying close attention to individuality was a lot of work for both parents. Effort given toward individuality paid off as they grew up, as separation experiences were more fun and rewarding for each child. They liked learning what the other twin was doing and gave one another advice. Closeness was always a comfort and a necessity in some situations in spite of the emphasis on individuality.

Competition was an issue. And as hard as their mom and dad tried to talk about how Janet and Marilyn were individuals, terrible and intense rivalry was a problem.

Janet: We were competitive about our grades at school, who had more friends, if mom loved Marilyn more than me, if relatives gave my twin better presents. We desperately wanted what our twin had. Negotiating about switching toys, clothes, friendship, and alone adult time became a serious part of our life.

Marilyn: Mom and dad taught us what belonged to me and what belonged to Janet. Sometimes it really didn't matter what the house rules about sharing and not sharing were. Making up our own rules about what was important became another way of competing. Instead of competing with each other we competed with our parents. All those books mom read didn't apply to us. We were double trouble when the situation called for twin power.

It is not hard to imagine that Janet and Marilyn were top students and both were involved with the student government and debate team. Traveling to Europe to study in different countries from one another (Marilyn went to Sweden, Janet went to Italy) was a part of their high school experience. Boyfriends came along, which definitely encouraged separate experiences and relationships. Because of the careful parenting they received they were respectful of one another's choices. They were always eager to discuss between themselves who had the better boyfriend. And they could accept that they saw the world differently.

Both women went to Ivy League colleges which were several hours apart. This separation was not all that difficult for them because they had enough separate experiences alone in high school. They talked to each other regularly and were able to move forward alone. Each chose a career that highlighted their strength. Janet became a psychologist and Marilyn became a financial entrepreneur. They married different types of men. Janet's husband was a professor and Marilyn's husband was a lawyer and financial manager. Their children were all unique. Marilyn had twins. She raised them to be individuals, even though she believed that there was more to her problem with Janet than just being an individual.

Early memories suggest the comfort that these women felt when they were together. While they measured themselves against one another they could cope with one twin winning and not feeling guilty or contemptuous. When psychotherapy was sought out later in life the goals were not to understand estrangement but for feelings of missing one another and the need to find twin replacements. Being a twin in a non-twin world was challenging and an ongoing issue.

Michael and Mark

Mark: I remember sharing the stroller that mom and dad fit together to take us out to play and visit friends. I felt close to my brother and happy we were going out to play.

Mark and Michael were born in a small fishing town in South Carolina to young parents and a large extended family. The family was very close and the twins were a great addition to the life of the family. Parents described their identical twins as good babies. And fortunately they had a lot of very attentive caregivers who were siblings, cousins, aunts, and grandparents. While the family was very poor and survived on what their shrimp boats brought in, there was enough love to go around. Each child was seen as special.

> Michael: For as long as I can remember dad told us that we were no different than close sisters or brothers. I think we knew that we shared a special closeness. We also knew our place in the family. We knew we were lucky to have food to eat and a place to sleep. Some families were not guaranteed these basics.

> Mark: Our mother did not want us to be stereotypical look alike twins. Because we were poor we shared clothes and toys with our brothers, sister, and cousins. There was not a lot of time or energy spent on the reality that we were twins. We were children who participated in the family chores and then we were left alone to be ourselves.

Throughout their childhood Mark and Michael always shared a bedroom with their brothers. All of the children attended a four-room school house from kindergarten until sixth grade. Even though there was not enough money to encourage special interests, both twins remember being treated as unique. Michael was closer to his mother and interested in artistic activities. Michael was sensitive and very communicative. Mark spent a lot time with his younger brother playing sports. He was prone to temper tantrums and was reluctant to express himself using his words. Michael and Mark chose to dress differently. This decision was encouraged to promote individuality and because it was more economical for the boys to share clothes with all family members. In other words, dressing differently was not forced on these twins; it just became a reality for reasons of practicality and budgeting.

When the children were in middle school the family moved to a larger community and a bigger home. All of the children in the family were then separated by grade level. Separate interests became more defined. Michael preferred literature and Mark preferred math and science. These twins shared friends and had their own individual friends. Michael shares:

> I was aware that I was more interested sexually in men when I was in Middle School but this choice was very distressing for my father and so I chose to keep it to myself. Because mother and I were close she was aware of my preference and so was my twin brother. Mother thought that I was gay to be different from Mark but that was certainly not true. We were always very different and could respect one another's choices.

Mark became more and more interested in sports and because he was a very talented athlete he often competed in out of town sports activities. Michael and Mark missed each other but also respected one another's different interests. Mark shares:

> It was hard at first to go out of town without Mike. Gradually it became more natural. We learned to be on our own and to appreciate what the other was good at doing well in. Competition was definitely present but not an overriding feeling between the two of us. I know some twins at our school who are fiercely competitive with each other. They were brought up with lots of extras and always wanted to have the most. Our modest childhood taught us to value what we have and to not long for more. Practicality was helpful in curtailing our competitiveness.

The richness of adolescent life as compared to childhood of course contributed to the excitement of new experiences with different friends and activities. Differences became more and more apparent. When college became an opportunity, Mark got a scholarship to a West Coast college to study architecture and Michael went to a local community college to study English literature. Visiting one another was difficult because of financial constraints. When their father died unexpectedly of a heart attack, Michael was able to talk openly to the family about his homosexuality. Both brothers supported one another's choices. Because their lives were so different competition was not exaggerated and criticism was held in check.

Early memories suggest that the family did not have a narcissistic investment in Michael and Mark being twins. These boys were seen as individuals and treated as individuals. There were not a lot of extra resources to go around to support special interests that developed from interactions with extended family and friends. There was not a need to measure themselves against one another because survival was the most critical issue to deal with in this family. Abusive behavior was not tolerated.

***

Both sets of twins who came from very different family backgrounds were respected for being individuals. Attention to what made each child special was very important and respected. Competition was acknowledged and dealt with appropriately. Financial resources were important as a means of developing talents and interests. Conflicts were more reasonable and less intense. Psychotherapy was helpful in dealing with the non-twin world. Sexual identity did not seem to create any emotional stress between the pair.

Early Memories Set the Stage for Later Twin Attachments

The brief life vignettes of twins presented here demonstrate the power and sustainability of the early twin attachment that is shared and embedded in their sense of self. How early memories and childhood narratives can in certain ways predict the conflicts over separation that are experienced later in life between twins are explained in these life stories. Early memories provide a structure to directions twins take as they move away from each other and develop their own sense of self through their unique life experiences. Irrefutably, what is most intractable is the intense and primary twin attachment, which changes over time but remains a foundation to personality development. The twinning bond creates special issues with separation. No matter what the family circumstances that obviously affect the life choices twins make, "once a twin, always a twin" is a certainty. Even twins separated at birth report a sense of their other twin. Twins suffer depression from their loss before knowing that they are a twin (Brandt, 2001).

Vince, who lost his brother Victor to suicide and wrote a memoir *Naked Angels*, says poignantly:

> The journey of recovering from the loss of my brother was and remains difficult. Learning how to become one after being two for the majority of your life is a continuous process which has a beginning, while the ending is ongoing, a maturing evolution of understanding and growth ... the continual constant pull to the hole of loss, to be with your dead twin, and the biological imperative to forge on, to survive to develop a new life, is a prize fight of the century which occurs psychologically and intellectually and manifests itself physically as well ... When I think about myself I will always be a twin first.

Implications for Twins

You can understand your relationship with your twin if you look at your past experiences together and alone. When you have gained a perspective on your early twin relationship based on your early memories and narratives growing up there is hope that you will have a more enlivened sense of yourself and your twin. By understanding the past and putting it into perspective you will be able to move on to a more authentic and nurturing relationship with your twin. As well, relationships with others in your life will be easier to relate to because you will hopefully know that you only have one twin.

Developing self-awareness of your identity as a twin and as an individual is a long, slow, and worthwhile process. My personal and professional experiences lead me to predict that being more honest with others about who you are will help you overcome loneliness, disappointments, and anger.

The twins that I have worked with and written about agree that being a twin is very different than what outsiders imagine it to be. Knowing that the ups and downs or joys and disasters are normal is especially freeing for twins who eventually want to keep their unhappiness to themselves because it is hard to get others to understand the pain they feel when they are misunderstood and ignored. Twin unhappiness can become a shameful secret that is hard to share as you get older. Understanding how to get along with your twin is certainly not easy. Early memories will help twins to see the depth of their attachment more clearly. The following strategies will alleviate tension that twins experience as they confront the world of non-twins.

1. Practice separation and together times and rate them. Was it better to shop alone or together? Use other experiences in everyday life. Talk about how your feelings and changing states of mind are different for each of you. Hopefully, as young children, experiences of being on your own have been established. Still, you will need to work on your individuality through discussion and experiences with your twin and close others throughout your lifetime.
2. Understand what you are fighting about and try to accept each other's differences. This is of course easier said than done. Seriously, I have spent a lifetime trying to figure out why I don't get along with my twin sister. Well, I guess I can say it takes two to tango and she has not been able to own up to her part. But I feel that trying to assert my individuality through understanding our childhood relationship has really helped me and it has helped Marjorie as well. And so I hope you will try to see and respect your differences.
3. Know your childhood role in the twinship. Develop those parts of yourself that your twin has done for you. This will take time and your twin can help you.
4. Get help with the problems you have with your twin. Ongoing fighting leads to a great deal of erosion of the attachment you share. Try to communicate and not fight if you can.
5. Understand and then know that problems with separation are normal and can be worked through in life experience and in psychotherapy.
6. Your relationship to your parents is important to your emotional well-being. Work on developing a positive relationship with mom and dad and sisters and brothers alongside your twinship.
7. Depression over the difficulty of dealing with non-twins needs to be worked through in whatever way works. In other words, talking with your twin and the person who is disappointing you will be very critical to your successful adjustment to the non-twin world. Feedback will help you process your disappointments and resentments of others. As you open up you will feel less lonely.

Implications for Parenting

Parents have children that come in all ages. Ways to approach infant twins of course will vary from how to interact with adult twins. As twins get older they are more self-reliant. Always, parents are important and mothers and fathers should be careful not to be second fiddle to their twins' relationship. While showing favoritism is very harmful to you and your children, sharing your reflections about what is going on between your children can be very helpful.

The most important take away from this chapter for parents is as follows:

1. Concentrate on seeing infants and children as the individuals who are in possession of their own personality. Value and show respect for individuality.
2. Develop unique relationships with each of your children.
3. Respect the closeness of the twin attachment.
4. Remember that twins cannot be surrogate parents successfully.
5. Asking one twin to take care of the other twin is a recipe for disaster in the long run.

Implications for Therapists

Working with twins can be tricky for so many reasons that I will not recount in detail in this chapter. In particular it is important to take away the idea of the primary nature of the twin attachment and how complicated and intertwined it can become if left to run wild on its own without parental intervention or psychotherapy. Sometimes I feel untangling a large ball of yarn would be easier than understanding what is going on when twins of any age are at war. Twins can be double trouble for parents and therapists alike. My approach is thoughtful, calm, understanding, and supportive. I don't take sides but I don't pretend that what is going on is easy to fix. Identifying with the seriousness of the argument is important.

Understanding your client's early memories is very important as these memories are the foundation for personality and emotional development. Twins do have a separate identity as a twin that can be in conflict or harmony with their individual sense of self. Hold on to this idea when you get confused about what is going on between your clients.

In conclusion, respect the intersubjective aspects of your relationship with the twin or twins you want to relate to. Observe and identify their behavior as you see it. Respect the often unspoken aspect of closeness that is shared between twins in whatever way you can. I remember how delighted I was when the mother of my 5-year-old twin clients called to tell me that Josh and Elise referred to me as Dr. Klein Bear. I was able to provide them with the comfort of their fantasy object who could understand their twinship. Feeling connected to these children in this special way was enough for me and for the twins at the beginning of our work together.

2 Parenting Issues with Twins

Strategies to Resolve Conflicts and Uncertainties

> Our bond is soul connected, we are attached at the heart of life
> Melissa

Twin Parenting Values in the Twenty-first Century

Twentieth-Century Parenting

I am reminded of my family stories of our twin birth at Good Samaritan Hospital in Hollywood, California. What tidbits of information that have been handed down are both horrifying and hilarious. In comparison to today's emphasis on developing individuality my mother was not a strategic planner and some bystanders might say she was psychologically negligent (Friedman, 2008). It is obvious from the family narratives that my parents knew that Marjorie and I were expected. Evidently there was no preparation for our arrival like you see in today's world (Diaz, 2013). When we were discharged from the hospital we were given white and blue beaded baby bracelets. Being first born, I was baby A and my twin sister Marjorie was baby B. My parents and our large extended Jewish family comprised of "more than enough relatives" had difficulty telling "the twin infants" apart. Mother kept our hospital bracelets on our wrists for at least a month. Mom often got confused about which twin she had fed because we were both always crying. And although my mother was a very smart woman, she did not consider that she was making serious psychological mistakes by confusing us. Mom was just trying to survive.

Unintentionally and because of lack of knowledge and psychological insight about twin development, there were other parenting problems and mistakes that were enacted in our childhood (Vaziri-Flais, 2014). Our older brother who felt upstaged by the attention his twin sisters' garnered was allowed to put a sign on our strollers that said "Yes, they are twins." This sign served to foster and endorse our image that we were just copies of one another. Unstated on the sign was that our individuality was not important. Furthermore, our mother was constantly overwhelmed by our infant and toddler demands. More often than might be predicted she called our grandmother, her sisters, to come and help her with us because we were crying or fighting or just being bad. When we were 8 months old we actually caught whooping cough from one of our aunts who came to visit with a bad cough. For each one of us this illness permanently damaged our vision because we coughed so hard our eyes turned in and crossed. We have each had different surgeries to correct the problem with only cosmetic success.

There are almost no reported memories that are retold from our preverbal years. Only a tattered newspaper article survives documenting our troublemaker twinship. The following newspaper story is a legacy to our childhood. At a little older than 2 years, Marjorie and I, after too much time alone together, managed to open the kitchen cabinet and drink the pretty red furniture polish. Mother found us in the act and called the ambulance. We survived drinking poison, but our life was in danger and pumping our stomachs was a hit and miss effort, not a sure thing according to the paramedics and ambulance driver. Why did this happen you wonder? Seemingly how we were parented was not an issue. We were just double trouble. But being double trouble was promoted as normal. I say this because we were dressed alike and not separated in school until we went to Junior High. We got the message that we should share friends and always be exactly alike. Unfortunately, there were no parenting manuals for mom to read. Teachers and pediatricians were not giving advice on how to best raise healthy twins. Twins were an anomaly to be gawked at and exploited. In fact, when we started kindergarten, a classmate called us the "girl with two heads." Our family thought this was funny and openly shared it with us. Fortunately times have changed. Twins are more common and knowledge about child rearing is more available. Thoughtful parents do not endorse the idea that their twin children are freaks.

Here are some statistical facts that shed light on how I and the other twins I have worked with were raised. When I was growing up in the 1950s twins were actually very rare in comparison to the birth rate of twins today. In 1950 the incidence of twin births was 20 in 1,000 births. The twinning proportion of deliveries rose 76 percent between 1980 and 2009 from 18.9 to 33.2 per 1,000 births. In 2013, approximately 33 in 1,000 births were twins. Currently, there is a reported increase of 2 percent in twin birth rates partly because of the use of fertility treatments and the rise in age of motherhood (Baby Center Expert Advice, 2015).

As twins became more commonplace, the focus on twin development changed because parenting twins became a concern. Early psychological studies of twins were focused on the relative effect of genetics as compared to the environment (Bouchard, 1994; Joseph, 2015; Segal, 1999; Schave, 1982). Since the early 1980s interest and research has been developed to understand how twin birth and development is different from the development of single-birth children. I have been working to understand twin development through anecdotal twin research and working with twin patients since 1980—over 35 years. Fortunately, so much more is known today about how to develop healthy twin attachments (Malstrom and Poland, 1999). Exploration of how twins develop a separate sense of self away from their twin reveals very difficult and complicated emotional experiences of loss, loneliness, longing for the twin, and estrangement.

Most recently, the idea has developed that twin closeness can help mental health professionals understand the serious issues that arise in intimate and deep-rooted conflicted relationships. The idea of twinship between patient and therapist as healing is being explored by modern psychoanalytic theorists (Kohut, 1977; Tancredy and Fraley, 2006; Togashi and Kottler, 2015). My interest in looking directly at "being a twin in a non-twin world" is helping twins adjust to others who are not interested in learning to read their minds or being their twin replacements. My research and presence as an author and on the internet is bringing to life the commonality of twin estrangement and the difficulties of being a twin. How to get over fighting with your twin is a goal that adult twins are very interested in achieving (Klein, 2012; www.drbarbaraklein.com).

Twenty-First-Century Parenting

Parenting twins has become a subject of intense interest for parents and families of twins and mental health professionals and educators who work with twins: how do you raise twins so that they develop an individual sense of themselves as well as a deep and trusting attachment? Infant twins are more carefully treated as individuals from birth (Diaz, 2013; Vaziri-Flais, 2014). While family members and onlookers of twins ask cutesy and meaningless questions because there are two or more children who look remarkably similar, parents know better than to promote the twin identity as if it were a circus act—a living freak show (Friedman, 2008). Parents do not allow the twins' siblings to carry around signs that say "Yes they are twins." Glaring, staring, and asking inappropriate questions that you would never ask a mother of a single child is not encouraged, but hard to stop. One mother of twins wrote a story on the internet about how she makes her husband walk behind the children to fend off obnoxious questions like "are they twins?" This story suggests that mothers and fathers are being proactive in lessening the impact of onlooker questions. Awareness of the negative backlash of too much attention to twinship from outsiders is in fact helpful in minimizing the bad side effects, which include making twins feel like they are connected in a very strange way and that they should stay closely connected. Recently I spoke with a fraternal twin in her thirties who told me that there was peer pressure growing up to be alike even though they were quite different. Indeed as children their relationship was cold and distant.

In today's world of parenting twins, the reality of the financial pressures, actual physical demands, and psychological attention to individuality is at the forefront of parents' thoughts who are striving to be effective. No one would deny that raising twins is very challenging and consuming of all types of the family's resources. The outspoken need of parents to identify a strategic plan that takes into consideration practicality and emotional and physical health is very essential and helpful. I get phone calls regularly from parents with very legitimate concerns and questions about practicalities of separation. For example, when can twins sleep in their own rooms or should they be separated in pre-school? The internet is full of how-to-parent-twins advice—16 pages of advice articles last time I checked. Mother of Twin Clubs are nationwide. Twin University is a new and updated club for families with twins.

A new problem has reared its head. Parents can become overly judicious and rigid in their approach as compared to how I was raised and how the twins I have worked with have been raised. Giving each child a sense of individuality is important, but not the entire answer. The twin attachment is a formidable issue to value and to manage (Klein, 2003). Twins are not just siblings. There is no perfect one size fits all parenting recipe for all parents of twins. Competition between twins can be scary for parents who have tried to promote individuality. Even twins raised to be individuals still have problems with comparisons like who is smarter, prettier, more popular, more athletic, and so on. Twins have to find out who they are together, with help from parents, therapists, teachers, and close others. As twins get older they will contemplate their twinship as an individual which is crucial.

Developmental Differences Between Twins and Single-Born Children

What Parents, Teachers, and Mental Health Professionals Need to Know

It is very helpful to understand how twin development is different from the development of single-birth children as it allows parents to make their own educated choices about what will naturally be shared, what can be shared and what should not be shared (Pietilä, Bülow, and Björklund, 2012). An authentic sense of self that is clearly different from the twin, or as psychologists say "ego boundaries," will develop more naturally for twins if parents understand why their twins are developmentally different than single-born children. Parents will make more effective decisions about their twin children's overall individuality and well-being if they are informed.

Twins Share a Primary Attachment with One Another

Twin attachment is a unique same-age caregiving relationship that is fundamental to twin identity. Twinship or twin attachment forms an affectional bond in utero which grows throughout childhood and into adolescence, middle age, and old age. Contemporary psychoanalysts describe an affectional bond as an emotional connection between two people that is so strong that it is irreplaceable or cannot be interchanged with another affectional bond. Closeness to the person with whom you share such a bond creates profound distress when this immediate comfort is not available (Fonagy *et al.*, 2005). Long-term separation from the twin with whom the bond is formed creates a great deal of emotional distress and even depression which is hard to live through and bear (Shawn, 2011). Twin loss creates a complicated grief reaction that is difficult to overcome (Arthurs, 2014; Brandt, 2001; Morgan, 2014). The time and quality of closeness that is shared through affectional bonds in infancy and early childhood will determine the development of individuality and the ability to create new relationships and new and expansive ideas about life and mental health throughout the lifespan. When twins are too exclusively connected in childhood they will develop a crippling fear of expansiveness which makes individual development and separations very difficult and sometimes impossible (Kohut, 1977, 1984).

As crucial as their primary attachment is the reality that they come into the world together: they share a profound attachment that directs how they deal with parents and other caregivers in their lives. Twin attachment is as crucial as parental attachment, although both attachments are very different in their functional value. In other words, parents provide direct care and nurturing for their children. Parents feed, dress, shelter, and protect their children. Twin closeness provides comfort and warmth and a sense of safety for one another. Twin attachment is as important as genetic endowment, environmental stimulation, and parenting to the development of the self or identity (Joseph, 2015). The twinning bond involves experiencing oneself as a part of the other person—the twin. A sense of self is distributed or shared between the twin pair (Burlingham, 1952). The unconscious process of partially merged identities is normal in infancy and early life in general (Schave, 1982). Twins are born married as they are tied to one another's moods, actions, and reactions. Often, twins find the other twin more calming than their parent in infancy and later in life as well. Being together provides a deep sense of security for twins.

As twins grow they develop an exaggerated sense of belonging to each other. They find immediate comfort with each other and are not as motivated as single-born children to find new friendships because they have each other. While young twins report that friendships with non-twins are not that much fun, they cannot easily describe the closeness they share with their brother or sister in words. Drawings reveal their sense of being connected. Playing with one another and fighting with each other also reveals closeness that is not experienced with new friends (Togashi, 2015).

Confusion about a clear sense of self further complicates the separation process and the development of individuality. Transitioning from being part of a pair to an individual is complicated and stressful for the entire family when twins are youngsters. Who is who without the other is a struggle that is gradually worked out in childhood and has many setbacks. For example, what task or action belongs to you is hard for young twins. It is normal for young twins who inadvertently rely on one another to complete certain tasks without the other. One twin is the adventurer, the other the back-up scout. Separation is hard as reliance on one another is unspoken and taken for granted. Separation takes place when separation experiences are lived out in the real world. Talking about separation is not enough (Baker, 1962, 2012; Ellis, 2014).

Most contemporary struggles with the twin attachment involve parents trying to intently and rigidly understand and untangle twin over-identification, power struggles, and role assignments. This process of making each child self-reliant is extremely difficult because of unspoken negotiations that twins make on their own. What is certain is that the bond that twins share creates a profound level of closeness that cannot be replaced by mom or dad. No matter what young twins are squabbling about they want to sleep together at night. Parents, teachers, grandparents, and therapists should never underestimate the power of the twin bond.

When behavioral problems at home or at school arise over following the rules, parents and teachers—all of those involved in providing help to overcome anxiety, depression, or lack of an ability to concentrate—should observe what is going on between the twin pair. Are twins just causing trouble to make some more fun? Are the twins taking care of each other too much? Is one twin too dominant? Why does one twin hate herself and the other twin is just stubborn and withdrawn? Look for clues (www.drbarbaraklein.com). For example, language delays are signs that twins are not developing enough individuality.

Twins Share Their Parents Attention and Their Early Memories

Good enough parental attention is crucial for the overall health of all children (Brown-Braun, 2010; Winnicott, 1970). Twins especially need to develop a substantial and resilient relationship with their parents if they are going to thrive psychologically without their twin. Parents will connect differently with each child. Mom is a people pleaser and finds Mary who is also more of a pleaser easier to get along with. Dad finds her twin Veronica more athletic and enjoys her company more. But both parents will attend to each child differently based on the attachment they share (Bowlby, 1973). In healthy parenting, differences in parent–child interaction are created through lived experiences rather than projection.

As much as twins need parental attention they have to share their parents' ability to nurture. Sharing parents creates a subtle competition between the two which can undermine the development of individuality. When twins measure themselves against one another continually, too much of their core identity is lost. Twins need to find out who they are without their twin as a guidepost or measuring stick (Schave and Ciriello, 1983).

Parents hold the key to their twin children's emotional health especially in childhood and then to a lesser extent throughout the lifespan. The most important awareness is found in this question. How do parents deal with fairness? Do twins always get treated to the same hug, or toy, or ice cream cone? Or do parents try to give each twin what they think they want and need? Is indulging your child a way to promote individuality or does it just promote out of control entitlement? There is no doubt in my mind that being fair is very hard to do when raising twins. Being even-handed takes thinking outside of the box—being smart and creative. And there is no one size fits all recipe on being a fair parent to twins. So many practical variables have to be taken into account when deciding how to give your child what they need. If you are overthinking what to do next with your double trouble twins, make a practical short-term decision and go from there. A new decision about who needs what will arise for you to ponder very shortly (Brown-Braun, 2012; www.drbarbaraklein.com).

Twin Power, Double Trouble, Entwined Lives

Even when twins receive "good enough" parenting, each twin is aware that the other is getting similar attention. Awareness of sharing creates a sense that each twin could be getting more and so the concept of good enough or just enough is hard to instill in twins. There is a sense of discontent with their childhood when they are not together because of the competition they live with, day in and day out. Early competition and then sharing brings out driven personality traits in twins. It is very common for twins to act out their competitiveness in school. Sometimes high achievement and perfectionism are comfortable for twins as they separate from each other and the family. If development is too entwined twins will withdraw into their early relationship (Friedman, 2014). Fears of expansiveness arise when twins do not have a core sense of themselves as an individual.

Hopefully, because it is so necessary, the mother and other significant caregivers are aware of the demands of their twin children. As hard as caregivers try to be objective and even-handed, inevitable differences in the relationship that is developed individually is evaluated by the mother and by the twins. Their mom is soft spoken and gets along better with one child than the other. Or she is direct and gets along better with her other child. No matter what harmony and real differences are established authentically through lived experiences, mothers and caregivers burn out. Naturally twins turn to one another for love, comfort, and support that they knew before birth and on a day-to-day basis. When parents are overtired, the twin attachment is intensified and double trouble begins. Parents are the outsiders when twins are outsmarting them (Klein, 2012).

Parents cannot avoid double trouble or twin power which develops slowly and often goes unnoticed until the adorable twins have figured out how to make mom and dad feel crazy. For example, 3-year-old Harry lets his 3-year-old twin Leslie climb on his back so she can turn on the stereo that mom and dad have told them is not for children to touch or play with. Maybe twins don't get together and talk about how to create problems as it just seems to come naturally. Marjorie and I did not discuss drinking furniture polish. We just were both curious and egged each other on. We were difficult in other ways. We took turns crying to enrage our older brother. We liked to work the room of double trouble-making. We would change outfits in the middle of the day to confuse our history teacher. We took each other's tests. And we are not the only twins who enjoy trouble making or will make trouble fun.

Twin power begins in infancy and is interrelated with the conscious and unconscious attachments that develop of their own volition. Parents experience twin power in different ways. Negative aspects of twin power are seen when one twin cries and the other twin cries as a reaction. Both twins want the same thing at the same time and are frustrated and outraged that they don't get what they want. One twin is fearful at school and uses her sister to hold on to so she can feel comfortable. Ongoing bickering and fighting, even biting and pushing, is hard to stop without strict time-outs and rules for separation that are followed. Positive aspects of twin power are seen when twins play with each other for hours on end, allowing parents and other family members to move on with their own lives.

Twin power is an extension of the twin attachment and the fun of double trouble that twins look forward to creating. Families have to deal with twin power plays directly if they want to maintain their sanity. If each twin is responsible for themself, enmeshment is limited, twin power is less of a force to be contended with. When twins use one another as parental surrogates confusion and anger are inevitable. The identified twin is not doing their own work but rather that of their twin. Enmeshed behavior makes true separation impossible for the weaker twin. Let's look at some examples from Chapter 1 which reflect the power of twin attachment.

An Untold Story?

Vince and Victor used their unspoken and spoken twin power to deflect their mother's anger and abuse. They were successful in surviving the turbulence and chaos of their childhood. Memories of being tied up in the closet or having their fingers burned on the stove seemed to have some comfort because they were together. But when they had to live separate lives they were both unprepared. Simply put, Vince was stronger and more reliable. Victor was more social and made plans for the pair. When Victor was lost he impersonated his brother. Later in life after valiantly fighting depression he suffered from suicidal ideation. He was overcome with hopelessness and committed suicide. Vince could not stop him from giving up by using their twin power that he had in childhood.

A Tie That Binds

Eileen and Adrienne developed a secret language which only they could understand. Although their brother was able to do some translation, mom and dad were totally left out of their conversations. At school they each had years of individual speech therapy so that they could communicate with students and teachers outside of their attachment. Sadly, they missed the needed experiences of socializing with other children without one another. Living alone and functioning on their own has been difficult because of the comfort of their attachment to one another. Although they long to get married and live separately as adults, accomplishing this separation is difficult. Giving up the power of being together seems impossible at times. Still they have not given up their dream of being on their own.

Good Enough Parenting

Janet and Marilyn were best buddies. Janet did her homework but Marilyn found it boring and tried copying her sister's. When the second grade teacher figured out that Janet was doing Marilyn's schoolwork, the teacher called their mom in for a conference. Mom and dad spoke with both children. Each child was told that they could not copy off of one another. Solving this issue took the parents time and accountability. But Janet and Marilyn learned that they did not have to copy each other's work. Each twin did their own work. And they both felt a sense of accomplishment.

A Contemporary Twin Power Problem

The following example comes from twins that I consult with who are articulate and receiving good enough parenting to overcome their tendency to have entwined lives.

Nathan and Naomi's parents were self educated about how to raise twins. From birth they established separate experiences for each child. Both twins had their own rooms. They were separated in kindergarten. These bright and active children were always in competition for mom's attention. Who got more of what mom had to give was a serious conflict for the family. Even with the help of grandparents and the school, mother was never off the hook for being evaluated for fairness by these two. Their mom was uncertain about how to reduce the competition and so was I. Uncertainty is very common when raising twins. I suggest making practical decisions when all else fails. Strictly follow your family rules if you want to overcome double trouble or twin power plays.

Identity Development and Self-Differentiation

Twins have two unique identities as a twin and as an individual. The bond that they share is exclusive and deeply rooted. If enough individuality is developed in childhood, twin identity will recede into the background in adolescence and adulthood. When parenting is inadequate twins will have difficulty separating and difficulty getting along with one another as well. Twin fighting and estrangement are outgrowths of not enough attention to each child as unique in their own right. Whether the twin attachment is too close or too conflicted there are always problems putting twinship into the background. In other words, it is hard not to take your twin's problems seriously if you are over-identified with their struggles (Klein, 2003; Pietilä *et al.*, 2012; Shirley, 2016).

I am reminded of a psychologically highly educated twin who was seeing a therapist in her community for anxiety and depression related to her twin sister. When her cognitive behavioral therapist suggested that she buy her twin sister a Hallmark card to say she was sorry that they had not talked for a long while my client realized that this mental health professional had no understanding of the depth of their twin attachment. When she contacted me for my opinion I understood how ridiculous this Hallmark card idea really was in the context of twin attachment. Twins hope to connect with one another in a close and profound way. It is a "twin thing"—it is not an ego boundary issue to want to give a personal and meaningful explanation to your twin for your behavior.

Or to decide to ignore your twin because you don't have the right words to share. Twin perfectionism and over-identification make identity development confusing in some situations for non-twins who are therapists (Klein, 2012).

Parents, teachers, therapists, and twins need to understand how sensitive twins can be to one another. Uncertainties about the security of your twin sister or brother's reactions to you, their state of mind, or their authentic affection for you, trouble twins who don't have a clear sense of what they need to give to their twin. Optimally, twin identity should not be based on rivalry and guilt. Unfortunately, guilt, misunderstanding, and loneliness are very basic to twin identity. It is a "twin thing" to feel like you need to be there for your twin no matter what. Overcoming your over-investment in your twin requires you to detach somewhat from your twin identity. What I mean by this is that you try and deal with your twin's problems with more perspective than you did as a younger person.

Twin identity is powerful and determines how twins see themselves and how they make decisions. Because attachments and memories are shared, twins see themselves in their twin. This idea may be hard for non-twins to understand but I will reveal two obvious examples from my life as a twin. First, in kindergarten my twin sister spilled paint in her hair. I cried uncontrollably because it was my fault that this happened. Second, when she returned from studying in Sweden many years ago, I was nine months pregnant and she felt fat just looking at me. She was horrified as if I were her.

Obviously, sharing a great deal of comfort and family activities, uncertainty about ego boundaries threatens the development of individual identity for young twins and can continue into adulthood (Friedman, 2014). Individual identity development is based on how parents see their twins and react to them. When parents can nurture what is special in each child's genetic differences, whether behavioral or physical, these individual traits will become a part of determining who they choose to be. Responding to difference is quite different than over-reacting to difference or creating differences. Obvious temperamental traits are apparent almost immediately. One twin is more demanding and highly strung. The other twin is slightly calmer and easier to interact with. Parents will see these differences and naturally prefer relating to one child over the other in different circumstances. Parental preference is not "bad," it is normal and expectable. If attention is given to each child for who they are, individuality will develop naturally. A caring and sophisticated mother who works as a child advocate attorney shared her thoughts on how she helped her twins develop their own personal style. Kristin states:

> I went to a parenting seminar and was presented with the question: what do you want your child to be when she grows up. Most parents answered "happy," but I thought to myself "whatever she wants to be." That's when the idea finally went in. I can't give her "happy" but I can give her independence. She wants to do things herself, and she is relying on me to help her to do those things herself. She wants to be independent. She wants to be a person.

I have four children now, each very like the others, but also very different, all growing into people. I'm growing people. That is my parenting philosophy, and I mean it seriously, since it is also my job. It's hard, because to embrace my philosophy necessarily means to examine "what kind of person am I growing in this child?" and "what does she need from me to be that grown person?" I constantly ask myself "what is the effect of this interaction on my child?" That question must be answered mentally, spiritually, emotionally, and instantaneously throughout the day. Then to act honestly with conscious intent regarding the desired outcome (for each child) takes extra time and effort. It's much easier to say "because I said so" than to wait for a child to get on board, then process the question "how can I help you?", and then formulate and articulate an answer in every interaction throughout the day, times four children. I fail countless times throughout the day, and often we are late or the laundry goes undone, and the floors unmopped. But I try not to care too much about those things, because I'm growing people.

My twins were my third and fourth children so I had had a lot of parenting experience with the older children. I knew how important paying attention to how my children were different would be to their overall growth and development. I knew that I was raising two children and that it would be harder. I was not overwhelmed by their needs and I had help as well from my husband and family. I could tell the difference between Katherine and Audrey within a couple of days. They were fraternal and looked different. But they also cried differently and responded differently to me. I doubled down on looking for individuality. I tried not to treat them as a unit. Practically I had to do things together like changing, and feeding, and bathing. Toys from our older children were available and they were allowed to make their own choices. When they started to fight over toys I talked with each one separately. Katherine was more motivated to get her way and would grab toys from her sister Audrey. I taught Katherine to use her words and not take her sister's toys. Then I taught Audrey to stand up for herself and not give up her toys. My girls play very well together. Katherine is more reserved at first. Audrey is the leader socially. I see this difference but take care not to let Audrey take over from Katherine in social situations.

Kristin had a philosophy which supported the development of her children's independence. She knew her priorities and honored them. Most importantly she saw her daughters' strengths and weaknesses and nurtured both.

Lilly, a highly successful cardiologist, had thought a lot about raising her twins to be individuals. She shares one of her concerns about raising her twin children.

I had intense very overwhelming negative thoughts about responding to differences between my boy–girl twins. I felt guilty that my son was calmer as a baby and easier to deal with. My daughter was high strung and demanding. When I came home from the office she was insatiable and I was exhausted. We had lots of help. I was angry with myself and thought that I was a "bad" mother. I did not want to have such a different relationship with each child. I felt guilty that my daughter was so certain, demanding, and hard to connect with. My son was loving and calm and easy to connect with and nurture. I was anxious about comparing their personalities and wanting to be with my son more than my daughter. But our relationships changed and my son had more difficulty with school than my daughter. I had to set limits for him as I had for my daughter. I guess that I allowed them to be who they were and who they are. Today they are very unique but also very close to each other and to me.

As I think about Lilly's parenting ideas, I believe she was concerned with favoring one child over the other. Initially she thought that she would need to treat them the same not to show favoritism. As her twins grew Lilly realized that the problem of favoritism was far more complicated. Tuning into each child's special way of reacting to the world was what was important in treating her children fairly.

Rita and John, both physicians with a highly sophisticated approach to parenting twins, called me because one of their 16-year-old daughters was anorexic (Kendler, 2001; Marmorstein *et al.*, 2007). In speaking with both parents I learned that the girls were identical and that they had been raised with the idea that they were just like siblings (Friedman, 2008). They both had their own rooms, choices about clothes and toys. They were separated in school and encouraged to make their own friends. Rita did not miss an opportunity to encourage differences and to endorse how unique and special each daughter was to the family. Caring, loving, and thoughtful parents, they were concerned if there was a problem with their daughter's attachment to each other. I spoke with Lyn, the daughter who was refusing to nourish herself, and then with Elaine who was thriving. I observed a strong bond between these twins.

> Lyn: My sister is concerned about my eating disorder. We are very close and we share many of the same friends. We play soccer together, and ride horses together. I don't want her to be concerned about me. I will overcome my problem with eating.

Her sister Elaine seemed to agree:

> Lyn is going to be able to get over her concern about how she looks. She wants to be thinner and is not eating enough. She is getting weaker and less able to play soccer and do her schoolwork. I encourage her to eat and tell her I care about her as often as I can. She has always been more sensitive than me. Maybe being the thinnest is giving her a sense of being better than me.

Rita called me and said that her children enjoyed our conversation. John and Rita were still concerned about Lyn's failure to eat and decided to put her into a hospitalization program for eating disorders. While they could have taken a less strict approach and had Lyn talk about her separation issues with her sister, these parents were set on seeing their twins as just siblings. I am sure that there were unresolved twin issues related to competition and ongoing comparative questions from onlookers that needed to be worked through (www.eatingdisorderhope.com). My advice and insight was dismissed.

Angela, a young mother who had her children after she graduated from college, had a great deal of difficulty with the challenges and the complicated decisions necessary to raise twins. Born and raised with wealth she hired two nannies to help her with her children's day-to-day care. Angela wanted her identical twins to be the same and stay the same. Angela's nanny called me for advice but I spoke directly with Angela. Angela told me:

> I want my twins to be close and to share everything they possible can share. I want them to be "almost copies of one another." The twins each have their own nanny but the nannies work in tandem so that our twins receive equal amounts of everything. My husband and I do not want to show any favoritism. Do you have any advice on how we can achieve our parenting goals?

Of course I was horrified by the entire meeting. I told Angela that twins were individuals as well as twins and should be treated as such. In addition, I said to Angela that I had no thoughts to share on keeping her children exactly equal because I knew striving for equality was a dangerous mistake. I was able to find one good part of the story. I believe it will be helpful that each child has had their own nanny and that this experience will develop their sense of individuality. I predict serious emotional issues when these children try to fit into a world where people strive for individuality. Angela went "doctor shopping" for another opinion.

The power of sharing is a gift that twins learn from conception. Loving and longing to be together is a legacy of twinship. Inner life and emotional connections are often marginalized in today's world. Technology has taken us away from who we are inside ourselves. The more aware parents are of their feelings, thoughts, and reactions to their twin children, the more likely their children will develop emotionally rich lives. The long road to finding yourself without your twin is complicated and consists of twists and turns and detours. Often parents and their twins will feel confused and defeated when separations are difficult or when anger gets out of control. Twins and parents frequently call me about how to maintain a loving bond and still be a separate, not over-identified person with their sister or brother. Keep trying is my best advice. Freedom from worrying about your twin comes out of trying to get over your overconcern, and not giving in. Only you will know when you find the right balance between your own independence and your twin's well-being.

Non-Verbal Communication and Language Developing Differently in Twins

Sharing the womb creates a deep closeness that is particular to twins. This attachment is extended into early family life and in different ways throughout the lifespan. The comfort of physical closeness creates a rare form of non-verbal communication which is always very intense, lively, often angry, and animated. My sister's look could communicate many different thoughts. Because of non-verbal communication, the need to use language with others for twins is different than for single-born children. If parents spend separate time talking and singing to each child, language will develop more naturally (Cooper, 2004).

Biological differences exist in the language development of identical and fraternal twins. How each twin uses language can be a signal of how they are different from one another (Pearlman and Ganon, 2000). Word usage can be a window to create a special bond with each child and naturally encourage their individual development. Parents have to be careful to affirm differences and not to judge differences in language skills, as this may be experienced as criticism by their children and create stress about speaking. Shared language is preferred by twins as it cannot be judged by outsiders and is used for play, comfort, and closeness (Schave and Ciriello, 1983).

Language development reflects the quality of attachment between twins and their parents. When parenting is inadequate, twin language can become overly important and slow down the development of relationships with other people who are not twins. While twin language may be humorous and cute to outsiders, it is a true comfort for twins both younger and older. Unfortunately, too much inter-twin communication can get in the way of the important socialization experiences in childhood. Language delays can foretell problems with socialization and separating in adolescence and young adulthood (Parravani, 2013).

I have worked with young twins where one speaks for the other even when both children have been encouraged to communicate and parents are adequately bonded with each child. What creates such a difference can be related to genetic endowments even if twins are identical. In other words, not all language issues are psychological but can be biologically based. Understanding the language development of your child is hard if you are not trained as a speech therapist or developmental pediatrician. If there are speech delays or articulation problems, seeking out professional help can be invaluable—priceless for the overall development of both children.

It is very common for twins to develop their own special language or idiosyncratic way of communicating that parents and teachers may not understand. Secret languages are outlets where the twinning bond lives. These communication inventions are fun and creative and not well understood as they tend to be in play more during early childhood. Secret language remains an untold story that twins share (Malmstrom and Poland, 1999). Imaginative and creative twins will use secret languages more often than twins who are not so inclined. For example, twins who are interested in physical activities or intellectual ideas may not be as interested in using special language. Still the twinning bond needs an outlet and may be seen in play with Lego or dramatic play. Allowing the expression of twin identity is very critical to emotional health and happiness. When your children are quietly or enthusiastically entertaining each other, they are thriving (Klein, 2003).

Language development is clearly idiosyncratic because of the developmental differences that I have described. This building block of personality needs to be developed. While it may sound counter-intuitive because of the closeness they share, twins often lack the ability to talk to each other as mature individuals. The ability to communicate with parents, family members, teachers, etc. can be quite limited. Learning to communicate effectively and avoid misunderstandings is a skill that can and should be taught especially to twins. My sister has always contended that we were not taught to communicate. I think the opposite is true in comparison to some twins who are afraid to talk with each other.

I am not ashamed to say that I have a communication problem which my dearest friend labeled sentence completion disorder. It is not a deliberate act to not give enough information to my listener. I can without pretense think that I have gotten my point across but really need to say more. Often people ask me why I speak in riddles. All of my twin friends and clients understand me. I often have to work on my communication skills with non-twins.

I am not the only twin who has speaking problems. I coach a set of 30-year-old twins Marnie and Linda who never learned to communicate their thoughts and feelings to one another as children. Their parents were always fighting with each other. All these children saw was anger and criticism from the adults who raised them. While they never learned to talk to each other about their thoughts and feelings, they were always guessing and projecting how the other twin was feeling and thinking to anticipate and protect one another from unwelcome attention. As they took separate paths in life they longed for closeness with each other and contacted me for help.

It actually took me many sessions to understand the depth of the problem they had with talking and sharing their experiences being together. The most reliable non-threatening form of communication was texting. When I asked them if they comforted each other when they were young they were ashamed to say no. I was very shocked to hear their lack of comfort with each other growing up. Peace and harmony were only experienced when they looked and acted the same. Because they were highly educated and determined twins, I was able to help them understand that they were separate people and that they could talk to each other about themselves as individuals without fear of hurting the other twin. This was a very difficult learning experience for them which took a lot of patience and understanding.

I have worked conjointly with many set of twins who were brought up in a hostile and unloving home environment. Abuse and humiliation was acceptable and expected. These silent types of twins from abusive homes where they were parents to one another, played together but did not share their thoughts and feelings with one another. Learning to talk to their twin was complicated but accomplished very gradually in individual and conjoint therapy.

Talk to your twins and have them talk to each other. It may sound like a simple suggestion but using your words is a way of working out disagreements which comes easily to twins. Language and communication are tools that promote understanding and resolve anger.

Social Development in Twins Is Unique

Twins are socialized through their early attachment to one another. I have said this before but I will say it again. Twins are born married. Twins rarely spend time alone in infancy and throughout their early life. As twins grow up they feel intense pain at separation and they will scream, cry, and fight to be with their twin. Having one another to keep company and play with has positive and negative consequences. Twins do not suffer from loneliness early in life but they do have deep issues with loneliness later in life (Klein, 2012; www.drbarbaraklein.com; Tancredy, 2006). In childhood, they have each other as primary playmates. Sometimes children want to have twin friends because it is fun and unusual to share twins if you are a single-born child. Parents need to be proactive in finding non-sharing friends for their children. While it is very easy to have your children play together all of the time, there are dangerous short-term and long-term problems. In the short run twins fight more if they are together all of the time, and they don't learn how to get along with other children who may seem disappointing as playmates. Twins don't develop their language and social skills, which can put them behind at pre-school and elementary school. In the long run the problem meeting others is compounded and fear and anxiety about new friends without your twin can become very overwhelming (Pearlman and Ganon, 2000).

There are no payoffs when twins are each other's best friends. Too much of an exclusive relationship intensifies interdependence and the fear of being alone and making decisions alone. Finding and developing new friendships is crucial for the development of individuality. When twins develop the ability to get along with others outside of the twinship they can be very effective at being a friend. Twins know how to share and care in a way that single-born children cannot learn. I know from my professional and personal experience that twins are gifted friends. They are loyal and kind and enjoy closeness and sharing. Getting an understanding of being a twin in a non-twin world will help twins develop new social skills. Young children need guidance making friends, but older twins who understand themselves will be able to make deep and intense friendships (see Chapter 6.)

Comparisons Between Twins Is Inevitable and Stressful

While there is no way to avoid comparisons between twins, try to eliminate comparing and contrasting as much as possible. Develop narratives about how people like to ask inappropriate questions about all twin relationships. You could say how you feel when bystanders are comparing your children as if they were intimate family members. Saying something like "It bothers me when people are so nosey. No one asked me these questions when I was young." Find out how your children feel about being compared to one another. Make the problem real and alive. Often twins like the attention from others. I did. But it can be totally annoying and tiresome as well.

Try and put a positive spin on how questions from outsiders will help, even when you can't believe in reverse psychology. Seriously, being twins is great small talk or an opening statement to engage a new listener. Twinship is instant identity in new situations. Also have empathy for the endless and meaningless questions that twins encounter throughout their lifetime. Self-consciousness about being a twin is a side effect of too many questions from onlookers.

Parental comparison has a long-range and profound effect on twins. The intensity of these judgments, the power of which is hard to put into words, is internalized into identity and personality development. While comparisons made by parents may be unintentional, these comparisons strongly and deliberately affect the twin attachment throughout the lifespan. Talking about differences as a narrative about childhood that promotes individuality will help diffuse the negative questions and judgments. For example, the parents who say to their twin children "When you were born you were both so different from each other and special to us in your own way" is affirmative. Parents who go on about the problematic differences create problems for their children. Be careful not to emphasize the negative. "You were both such a burden that we wanted to send you back at first. Then we saw the differences—Twin A was the screamer and Twin B was the hitter." This narrative is understandably destructive to your child's self-esteem. These types of messages create shame between twins and later in life will create estrangement. Keep in mind the power of parental words about individuality and sharing. Try to avoid judgments.

There is value in well-thought-out remarks from teachers, aunts, uncles, and grandparents to twins that help them become more aware of how people perceive them. For example, teachers pick up differences between twins to which parents are oblivious. When I was in kindergarten my sister and I were painting on easels. Marjorie spilled paint in her hair and I started to cry uncontrollably. Marjorie was having fun. The perplexed teacher called our mother to talk with her about why I was crying for my sister. My mother told the teacher this was normal behavior for the two of us. And of course it was a sign of a problem between my twin and I which the teacher had picked up.

A set of twins I work with were singled out by the pre-school teachers as being unbalanced in their reciprocal play skills ability together and with other children. They recommended a need for social skills development. The teachers reported that Elli was very bossy with other children and Randy was very quiet. Their way of relating to other children mirrored their way of interacting with each other. While the parents resented the pre-school teachers' opinions, the children have benefitted from their understanding and actual interventions.

When Elli and Randy started kindergarten the kindergarten teacher told mom and dad that both twins were equally dominant socially and were able to play well with other children, which was unusual for twins. So the pre-school teachers' attention to differences helped both children develop more individual strengths.

Pediatricians, tutors, occupational therapist, speech therapist, and psychologists can see differences between twins that reflect an unbalance in the twinship. These specialists will definitely help your twins develop their unique potential using comparative ideas in a useful way. Social skills groups and parents of twins clubs are also very useful and have practical advice on how to deal with comparisons. Books and articles are readily available on the internet with tried and true mom wisdom on normalizing comparisons and redirecting competition.

In certain situations twins enjoy competition when they start the competitive activity and it is seen as a game. Of course competition between twins can get out of hand, with different negative consequences than questions from outsiders. Overly competitive twins can harbor deep resentment for one another and end up estranged. Or they may be so dependent on each other for the competition that they cannot separate from each other as adults. Comparisons between twins creates some unbelievable stress and external or internal rage. Parents need to be careful to talk with their children about comparisons and develop positive narratives that they can use when they are troubled by outsiders' questions.

Still with the wealth of knowledge and interventions available to twins, the inevitable rude and intrusive questions from curious onlookers creates stress for twins who have all sorts of complicated and deep feelings about how they are different from their twin. Some twins feel guilty or ashamed that they are different. Some twins realize the long road to individuality and are proud of themselves. Twins are understandably reluctant to discuss how they are different with strangers, as feelings are too intense and personal. As they grow into adulthood, twins very often feel self-consciousness about being twins because of too many questions of comparison.

Dominance and Non-Dominance: Another Unfortunate Way to Mislabel Twins

Parents of twins and adult twins don't know about the use of this label unless they are academically inclined or mental health professionals. It is true that twins are compared in the higher education psychological research as being dominant or non-dominant on specific measurable traits or qualitative measures such as language development. I find this type of labeling reductionistic and non-productive. However, it is considered a way of looking at twinship by genetic researchers and psychologists to understand the relative importance of nature versus nurture. Twins are always amused by this idea when they first hear about this statistical methodology because it is so out of their realm of interest and identity. I have never meet a twin who gave any credence to the dominance/non-dominance criteria from a scientific or academic point of view. Twins may see differences in personality and affect, which is very different. In my view twins should not be used as experimental objects like rats to understand causality (Joseph, 2015).

When I completed my dissertation on twins at USC there was a final oral and my twin sister came down from Stanford where she was teaching to attend the presentation of my dissertation along with my children and my husband. Separately and discretely the members of my doctoral committee asked each of us who was the dominant twin. Marjorie said I was dominant. And I said she was dominant. The experience was funny and ridiculous at the same time. To this very day she holds on to her opinion that I was the bossy mean twin and I see her as the impossible and demanding favored twin who thinks she can do no wrong. Intellectually this fight between us is meaningless.

I have come to know that dominance and non-dominance are always changing and pertains to certain variables in life such as the locus of control or self-esteem regulation. There is really no way that twins can be divided so clearly into halves of a whole. Twins are horrified when they are seen as a locked unit. While this easy to ask about dynamic about power fascinates outsiders, in actuality this theoretical construct can confuse parents and undermine self-esteem in twins. Realistically twins will have different strengths and challenges but they will each be individuals in their own right who share a deep and complicated bond. Objective classification of the twin bond is not only superficial but destructive because it does not take into account what is really important about twinship—the ability to share and care deeply for another. Twins know about the joys and pains of being able to read each other's thoughts and feelings. The deep closeness that twins share is now being studied by inter-relational psychoanalysts and self-psychologists in order to heal traumatically induced psychological pain.

Thoughts on How to Parent Twins

> Stephen Hart: Read as much as you can about twins to understand twin development better and how to parent. Then acknowledge that however hard you try as a non-twin you won't—can't—get it 100 percent. But that's not the end of the world. Try to know adult twins as friends for perspective. Then work very hard to individuate the children as they grow up. Discourage questions from outsiders. Keep reminding yourself how different twins are from non-twins.

> Linda Pountney: Notice individuation attempts on the part of each twin, and look for fallout. One child may be happy to be different and the other wants to hold on to being a twin. Again, each twin is not ready at the same time. Communication between parent and child and between twins is key. This must be established early on, even though twins tend to lean into their own twinship before looking for parental support. Support groups for twins and parents of twins can be valuable for this purpose if their inclination is to learn about relationships, not just glorifying twinship.

Vince Arthurs: Keep reminding yourself that you are not going to get it right. Do the best you can. Twins are very challenging to raise. Encourage individuality slowly and then support their different endeavors to encourage their passion. Their differences will make them stronger together and apart.

Jackie Martinez: Don't treat your twins the same way. Understand that they have different needs at different times. Their twin relationship is really important. Your children need to learn to communicate on all levels not just their twin wavelength. Teach your twins to talk to each other about their own relationship and the natural ups and downs they will experience as they go their separate ways.

Dotan: For sure they should have their own room. Give them as much individuality as possible. They want to be together. Dress them differently and let them dress alike if they want to. Our own rooms were what we missed most.

Louise: Raising twins when they are young is like herding cats. You just push them forward in the right direction. When they are teenagers it is like herding mountain lions.

In today's world there is so much information on parenting twins that should be read and considered by new parents of twins and those who are struggling to feel good about their parenting abilities with older twins. Here are some helpful strategies.

Before They Are Born

Read and understand as much as you can about twin development before your twins are born if possible. Information and knowledge are power. The points made at the beginning of this chapter are important to keep in mind. Start researching, reading, and learning about how other people see the difference between the twin relationships and single-born relationships. With this new information it will be easier to make decisions about how to raise your twins to be strong individuals and trusted friends. Your awareness of how your twins are different will help you to make careful decisions about how to slowly promote individual identity and what the challenges your twins will face as they separate from one another. Make a point of speaking to other twins and parents of twins, while keeping an open mind to ideas that may differ from your own.

When They Are Born and Throughout Childhood and the Teenage Years

Make special time for each child with both mom and dad. Make these times opportunities for play, fun, and general development without making any comparison between your twins. Think non-judgmentally about how they are different. Elli likes to sing and Randy likes to read.

Acquire extra help to free you up to just take care of your twins. Having extra hands around to help is so valuable because it allows for some calm times where everyone can just be themselves. This is also a good time to separate your children at home and get to know them.

First Year of Life Through Childhood

Give your children their own clothes and toys. And also give them shared clothes and toys. Talk to them about sharing and not sharing. Remember your attention to both of them is a form of sharing. When they are alone with you they do not have to share you, which is extremely important for their separate identity and the building blocks of your relationship with your child.

Second and Third Year of Life

From a child-friendly perspective discuss their twin relationship. Just because they are twins and live this experience day in and day out, do not assume they know everything about being a twin. Teach them about how they are different from single-birth children. See if they have any questions about being twins. Help them to come up with answers to questions by onlookers. For example: "Yes we are twins but we don't like strangers asking us questions."

Value your children's time together as precious and nurturing. Help them get along. If you need help to bring some peace to your home life consult a mental health professional or go to twin support group meetings.

When twin fighting persists at any age try to get to the reason for their anger at each other. Then help them to come up with solutions that will reduce the tension between them. This will take a lot of time, but don't give up. If discipline is needed be clear that each child is responsible for the problem in different ways. Both twins have to change their behavior but in different ways.

Fourth Year of Life

Make continued efforts to encourage each twin to have their own interests and friends, without forcing this separation. New friends and activities can be a difficult task, especially if one twin's not open to the idea of new friends and fun, and the other is! It is still fine and natural to share friends or just to spend time with you alone.

If you can, set up a structure where your twins are separated with their own play dates, classes, grandparent visits, etc. Talk with your children about how they feel about being with other people without their brother or sister. Help them share their feelings with other people and each other.

Five Years and Onward

Put your children in separate classrooms in kindergarten. Talk with them about these separate experiences and develop narratives about their experiences to share with close friends and family. For example, Twin A might say that she was at first shy and reluctant to make new friends but the teacher helped her to get started. She played with her twin at recess and that also made school less difficult. Twin B could say that school separation was a relief, but she noticed her sister was sad and tried to spend special time with her. Do not judge one reaction as better that another.

Separation anxiety is normal for twins even as they grow older. Encourage separate experiences but try not to be too strict if your twins are overwhelmed by going to separate camps or separate play dates or parties. Normalize their anxiety by understanding their feelings, not your feelings.

Double trouble begins early in life and becomes fun and functional as twins grow older and more interested in outsmarting their parents and teachers. Let your children know that you are on to their antics or games. Try and find out what is behind their insistence on getting their own way. Do not over-react to double trouble which might include copying each other's work or covering up for a mistake that they want to go unnoticed. Make sure you set appropriate limits for their misbehavior. Discipline them as individuals.

Teenage Years

Talk to each child about how they feel about their brother or sister so that they know you are their ally and can accept that they don't always get along. This will help you and your child when one twin falls in love and the other one doesn't. Or when one twin wants to go away to college and the other one wants to stay home. These issues are described in more detail later in this book.

Thoughts for Mental Health Professionals Working with Parents and Infants, Toddlers, and School-Age Twins

Working with families with twins is intense and complicated because twins develop differently than single children. Their primary attachment, sharing of parental attention, and closely intimate non-verbal and verbal abilities can be hard for the therapist who is an outsider to decipher. Parental confusion, uncertainties, and exhaustion can present a more serious problem than actually exists. On the other hand, there can be very serious problems that parents are covering up with their own denial over time. Twins can trick their parents into believing that everything is fine when some dramatic issues are being ignored. It will take time to understand what is going on emotionally between twins and their parents. So give yourself time to evaluate the complaint or reason for therapy. Here are some suggestions that might help you gain a deeper understanding into what is causing emotional turmoil.

On initial phone contact try and set up at least five sessions to evaluate the twins and their parents. Try to get a direction for their goals.

1. Meet with parents first and get a detailed understanding of their childhood, adolescent, and young adult experiences including education and career choice. Find out how each of them reacted to having twins. Are they overwhelmed by their children and why?
2. What is their parenting philosophy if they have one? How has their relationship changed since the twins were born? Do they have help with their children?
3. Meet with the twins together and their parents to see how the family interacts. Depending on the age of the children ask them questions about their daily routine, fighting, sharing, and bedtime. Ask them to draw pictures of themselves alone and with their twin.
4. Meet with each child alone to get a sense through play and drawings or talk how they see themselves as twins and as single children. Try to see the similarities and differences between the pair. Are there any areas where one twin needs extra help and support? How would therapy be helpful to each individual?
5. Make a plan for treatment after talking with teachers and other mental health professionals who work on the case.

Conclusions

Without a doubt, identical and fraternal twins must be seen as individuals, each with his or her own strengths and challenges. Respect for the twin bond is critical. Undermining the twin relationship by suggesting that it is just a normal sibling attachment will confuse twins who know how close they feel to their twin even if they are still unable to verbalize their attachment. Twins know through lived experiences how friendships are different and less intense than the bond they share with their brother or sister. When you undermine the twin relationship you will confuse young twins, leaving them unprepared for interacting socially at school or in after-school activities. It will also be more difficult to introduce separate activities and friendships if twins don't understand in some way that they are different. Twins should be allowed to revere their twin identity. Otherwise they may feel like "freaks" or "the girl with two heads."

***

No matter how many books you read and respected friends and professionals whom you talk with, life with twins is never easy and calm and organized. Have fun with your twins and allow them to be close to you and the family. While the twin attachment is important for emotional growth and development, other members of the family will provide much needed support and direction.

3 When Do Separation Issues Begin for Twins?

When Do Separation Issues End?

I can't imagine my life without my twin even though our relationship can be very disappointing. I can't end my twinship. It is permanent. I have developed a fear of lack of permanence in non-twin relationships.

Stephen

Even though she infuriates me, I can never completely let go of my sister. Totally separating from her would be like cutting off my arm. And then the ghost would still remind me of our twinship.

Sarah H.

I know that I am not like my sister in looks, attitude, and accomplishments. Still, when I look in the mirror I see her image that reminds me that we were once very much alike even if now we are very different and separate people.

Dr. Klein

I don't understand how twins can decide not to love each other. My sister is so important to me the thought of not wanting to talk to her is incomprehensible to me.

Melissa

Inevitable Psychological Separations for Twins Are Challenging and Crucial

Speculatively, separation issues begin at birth based on observations of twin behaviors. Even earlier, twins who have lost their twin in utero or at birth claim that they experienced loss throughout their life time that is related to their unknown brother or sister (Brandt, 2001; Morgan, 2014; Segal, 2001). There are untold stories of twin separation anxiety because of the reality of how language develops, and the special languages, often partially non-verbal, that twins rely on to communicate with each other. Early communication between twins is often not understandable to outsiders. Stories recounted by twins and psychological theories suggest that separation can be frightening and cause serious emotional regressions at any age (Ainslie, 1997; Engel, 1975).

The separation of parts of the self—twin identity and individual identity—and the following loneliness and confusion related to this physical and emotional separation can have different outcomes. With careful attention from significant others to feeling states of twins, the journey of learning to be alone in the mirror can be navigated with understanding and a sense of closure. With inadequate attention from parents to this primary attachment, personality damages or limitations are created which are very difficult to mend and overcome throughout the lifespan (Klein, 2012). In dire situations such as serious illness and death separation will become a traumatic event (Brothers, 2008). The range of reactions to separation are explained in Chapter 1.

While infant twins scream and even withdraw when they are separated, older twins develop coping strategies to contain their anxiety about being alone. For example, twins talk and play out their painful feelings or just stick together depending on the circumstances of the separation they confront. Stories of twin loss reflect the depth of loss and confusion. Dramatic and always unforgettable, narratives of twin loss shed light on less intense separations (Arthurs, 2014; Engel, 1975; Morgan, 2014; Parravani, 2013). Many years ago I worked with Judy, a twin, who told me that she felt like she "had a hole in her heart" after her sister committed suicide. Only gradually over ten years did she begin to heal the emptiness she felt without her sister. Her relationships with her children and her own self-understanding contributed to the healing process (Klein, 2003).

Twin loss reveals the depth of closeness and shared identity that twins experience and the often treacherous path of separation. More recently I have worked with a twin Vince whose brother Victor committed suicide. As Vince left the hospital after seeing his brother for the last time, and for many many months after, he describes "feeling trapped in a vortex of the present and not having a sense of himself." He felt estranged from himself because his twin was deceased. Who was Vince the lone twin. Finding out who he is as an individual and understanding his relationship with his brother has helped Vince overcome, one baby step at a time, his fear that he cannot thrive without his brother. He has had experiences that convince him that he is not guilty for surviving, Vince has come to know that he is entitled to be alive and prospering. Valuing himself as a lone twin has been an intense journey of overcoming serious developmental arrests and a complicated grief reaction.

As well this year I consulted with Annette who told me of her reaction to the loss of her twin sister in an automobile accident. It is over ten years since her sister's death and Annette still remembers very clearly that she felt paralyzed—unable to move. In fact, she did not want to move. She feared that if she changed and her sister Joan came back to life that she would not recognize her. And Annette feared that Joan could be critical of her. Annette's first solution in a state of shock was to remain the same forever. Was she in shock because she lost her twin identity and was confused about who she was? Or was she afraid to leave Joan behind and survive without her? Would Joan approve of who she was going to become? The depth and intensity of her feelings go beyond survivor guilt and can be hard for non-twins to understand.

Can twin feelings related to missing your twin through separation or actual loss be felt or seen by outsiders to the twin pair? Or do these profound feelings of anxiety and invisible desperation go unnoticed by outsiders until twins explode into confusion, physical pain, sadness, and rage? Clearly there is an often unseen aspect of twinship which is related to psychological separation that non-twins cannot understand (Shawn, 2011; Verghese, 2009). Dramatic and real, these anxious feelings of being on your own are unique to twins. I know, and all the twins I have spoken to know, with 100 percent certainty, that it is not unusual to suffer when you do not have your twin by your side in critical situations, especially in childhood where closeness is an essential experience.

Parents, mental health professionals, and teachers see their children's or student's separation anxiety but they have a hard time grasping the depth of feelings about being alone. New psychological ideas support the importance of separation in conjunction with closeness in elementary school (Diaz, 2013). The teenage years bring out struggles to separate that can be overwhelming. Anger and fighting arise out of developing different friendships and different interests. In early adulthood new committed relationships make separation a part of life. Twins have to balance their closeness with one another with their partners' needs for attention and loyalty. Competition between twins over who is more "successful" can dominate midlife. The outsider questions that were asked unabashedly while twins were out in their strollers come to the forefront of twins' lives. Who is smarter, prettier, more talented, has a better partner and children, and so on, are debated out loud or inwardly with self-criticism. No one really wins these arguments, which leads to fighting and even estrangement. As twins grow older they begin to reflect on their relationship and refine their feelings about being a twin. While separation issues change in dimension and intensity in later life, they are never eradicated. Once a twin always a twin.

In general, throughout their lifetimes, separation issues which include longings for closeness and harmony, or deep feelings of anger and estrangement, can be very intense. And then, feeling states are redirected and twins carry on with their own lives. What a twin gets from their attachment to their twin is never easy for non-twins to understand and never easy for twins to give up. When twins get along there is a type of harmony and sharing that is hard to replicate. Twin closeness and togetherness is always deeply missed.

Sharing the womb with your twin creates a deep comfort and sense of security for twins. At birth twins are separated for the first time and observers will notice how being next to one another as new-borns is so comforting. While there are video records of interactions between infant twins, some non-verbal connectedness is experienced through physical proximity. Infant twins who cry can be settled down by being close to one another. Parents have to carefully negotiate separation issues in early life so that twins learn to tolerate being apart.

Psychological separation is absolutely necessary if twins are going to live mature and productive lives when they are apart and when they come back together.

On their journeys through separation twins often begin to develop emotional vulnerabilities related to their sense of self as an individual and as a twin. While some twins overcome conflicts and confusions over who they really are, other twins are unable to separate from each other. For some twins being peaceably alone means being in close proximity to their twin. Without a doubt, subjective experiences of separation are unique to each twin and each twin pair. Enlivening, painful, exhilarating, and frightening, each and every twins follows his or her own separate path to develop and achieve an individual and twin identity that is quite distinct from their childhood identity. Being alone in the mirror is complicated, with many different meanings (Klein, 2012).

Fears of expansiveness or fears of being too different from your twin arise out of too much closeness and concern for the twin. Will I be better than my twin? Will I abandon my sister or brother? Will my twin accept my decisions? Some twins overcome these conflicts and uncertainties about who they are alone and together. Without a doubt emotional issues related to separations are ever present in the psychological lives of twins as they journey through the non-twin world. Mental health professionals who work with twins must understand that the road to individual identity is hard won and often overdetermined. Indeed, once twins get a taste of independence and specialness, they hunger for more individuality. A mature twin who can get along on some level with their twin is quite independent and open-minded.

How do Healthy Psychological Separations Evolve?

I am defining psychological separation as moving from a state of togetherness to reaching out to be different and interacting on your own without your twin. There are different stages of separation for twins throughout their lifespan. When one stage of separation is missed, this developmental arrest will have to be made up later in life. For example, psychotherapy can gradually assist a twin to learn to be more independent from their twin if this stage of development was missed. The quality of parenting will also affect how separation between twins is handled in childhood and later in life. Twins who are not given enough individual attention will have much greater difficulty with separation. Emotional confusion, rage at your twin, competition without reasoning and logic, difficulties getting along in the world of non-twins, isolation and deep feelings of emptiness are after-effects of too much closeness or enmeshment in childhood. There is a pattern to how twins react to separation at different developmental stages. The following stages are observable and developmentally reliable.

Infancy Through Pre-School

Early life is a time when twins are extremely close to one another and enjoy being together for a sense of comfort, security, and understanding. First they are womb mates and then crib mates. And so on. It is normal for twins to be play mates and often best friends, even though they fight with each other for who gets what and when. Remarkably, at this stage, competition and then sharing go hand in hand. When parents can understand how to help their twins get along they are providing lifelong coping skills for their children. But twins have their own well-developed coping strategies of togetherness from conception onwards. Even in elementary school finding one another at recess is calming. Twins still like to sleep together at the end of the day no matter what fighting has ensued. For twins physical closeness is very reassuring.

Carefully separating twins is critical at this early stage of life. First know how your twins are different and develop their individuality while respecting their twin attachment (see Chapter 2 for parenting advice). Separation anxiety is normal for twins and needs to be expected and respected. Give one of the twins very early notice—a heads up—that their twin is going to be involved elsewhere. When one young twin is alone or left out there will be tears and sadness. Try and console the lonely twin with empathy and compassion. Redirect their attention to other activities until their twin returns. Giving in to their fears of separation will not help them develop their potential. Expecting too much separation can cause an alarming fear of being alone.

Setting up a structure in your home that allows for individuality to grow is important. For example, if possible, separate bedrooms, some non-sharable toys, clothes, friends, and time alone with mom and dad foster self-reliance and independence. Select parenting classes, toddler classes, and pre-school classes where your children can be together and practice being separate spontaneously. Social play is a very good way to understand your children's different interests. Helping develop new ways of getting along socially with children outside of the twinship is a perfect strategy that will prepare your double trouble children for kindergarten separation. Letting them go with other trustworthy adults without one another will also teach twins how to get along when they are young and solo.

On a day-to-day basis, accept and validate your children's need for each other as well as their need to be learning to be on their own. Teach them coping skills when they are separated in their own special activities. Or just talk about how they are feeling, be it happy, or sad, or frustrated. Be a part of their separation experiences through comfort, compassion, and positive thinking. Affirm their strengths when they are missing one another. Be proud of their efforts to separate and tell them about your good feelings for them. Explain to your children that they are twins and that means that they have a special attachment so that it is normal to miss one another.

Kindergarten Through Sixth Grade

School separation is important in kindergarten. School separation issues play out differently depending on the pattern of twinship that has been established. Twins should be developed enough to tolerate being away from one another during school hours. If separate classrooms are too difficult for your children, seek out help to understand why they need each other so much. Are they under-socialized with other children? Are their language skills underdeveloped because they have spent so much time talking to each other? Do they want all of their friends to understand them as their twin does? The earlier a twin problem is identified and worked on the easier it will be to solve.

It is normal for twins at first to have a sense of newness and loss in kindergarten. Difficulty concentrating on class work and making new friendships is predictable. Gradually these times without one another will be easier and separation anxiety will subside. School-age twins tell me that they enjoy being on their own during school hours. But they also look forward to being together again. I remember fondly the 6-year-old twin who told me that he waited for his sister's bus to come from camp, because he always got home first. Waiting for her to come home and play with him was very important to him and to her.

Interactions between twins at this stage of life is crucial, as some of their sense of self is entwined with their twin. Shared experiences and opinions have intensified their attachment to each other. Cognitive development as described by Piaget (1950) suggests that children of this age group are not interested in understanding the psychological aspect of their identity; rather they are interested in who they are through their day-to-day experiences with their twin, and parents, and friends. Separation anxiety is understood through missing one another and having the twin return in a predictable manner. In the stage of concrete operational thinking children believe in the importance of rules and order (Piaget and Inhelder, 1969). While they definitely question who has more or less, they still believe in fairness in spite of their complaints that one has more play time or better clothes, etc.

In elementary school separations are naturally established by teachers and school administrators. This imposed structure from outside of the family is very helpful and almost critical. Twins who are home schooled are separated by interests and friendships. Twins still rely on one another and measure themselves against one another. Who is the better reader or math whiz? Who is more popular? Who is the most attractive? Who gets better grades? However, anger and competition are more in control at this time of life because new friendships do not entirely replace the twin attachment. Help and comfort seem to come more naturally for elementary school twins. Talking about their twinship with parents and teachers and each other is extremely important to the development of self-reliance, communication skills, and independence.

Parenting that helps school-age twins thrive is focused on developing the identity of each child and the quality of their twinship relationship. Undermining parenting will most likely take on the same features that were established when the twins were young. Interdependent-identity twins will have serious difficulties with separation because they have difficulty functioning without their twin. Split-identity twins will flourish with separations because they feel more free to be themselves beyond their label. Individual-identity twins will establish a clear sense of boundaries between one another because

When Do Separation Issues Begin for Twins? 63

their parents understand the importance of separation. Elementary school is the beginning of more serious competition and arguments because of all the new relationships and complications that are not present in early childhood. Twin struggles of 6–11 year olds are nowhere near the explosions of the teenage years.

1. *My 7-year-old twins are identical but they have opposite interests and strengths. John is good at math. Henry loves social studies. On the other hand they love to play together. Is this strange behavior normal for twins?*
Your children's behavior is very normal and healthy. Treat each child as an individual. Encourage them at their high points and help them where they struggle.

2. *Rachel and Rebecca are just 8 years old. The two of them can get together and create different kinds of emotional and actual chaos in our home. When our girls decide they want to get their own way they use each other to be persistent. And they get their way. Is there something wrong with my daughters or with me?*
Yes there is a problem. All twins are masters of double trouble if left on their own too much. You need to set clear limits and strict enough consequences for each child so that they do not over-run your home. Speak separately with each child so you understand the roles they take with one another. Tell your children that you are in charge of making decisions about school and homework, schedules and food, safety and screen time.

3. *My twin children have just started first grade. Our son is high strung and has certain demands about toys, TV, and the computer that he has to have met or he has a huge meltdown in public or at home. Our daughter is high strung about different issues. She is over-eating and needs to be shopping and be with friends continually. I feel like I never get a break from these two. The teachers are complaining about their behavior at school. What am I doing wrong?*
Your children are asking for help. They each need more quality time with you. Are you too busy at work or are you depressed? Maybe you need to get some of your own insights in therapy about how hard it is for you to raise twins. Find a support group as well. Support groups give you strategies to cope with your child and emotional support that you are not crazy.

4. *The teachers see my son as less able than his twin sister. They are humiliating him by asking why he is so behind his sister. My fun-loving son is afraid to go to school. What should I do?*
This is a serious problem. Get an educational advocate for your son if the principal and teacher cannot make school a fun place to learn for both of your children. Pitting twins against each other always causes traumatic consequences for both children. There is no reason for your children to be subjected to this type of psychological abuse that can do long-range psychological damage.

5   *Katie is invited to more parties then her twin sister Alexandra. What should I do?*
Your children have different social needs and talents. Their differences are very important to respect. Now that they are teenagers they will receive different invitations and have different friends. Talk with them and be sensitive to their emotional concerns, but do not call the person in charge of the party to have the uninvited daughter invited. Tell them that for sure this will change and the other twin will not be invited.

6   *I have boy–girl twins who are 6 years old. Linda and Austin have different interests. Austin is ignoring Linda to the extent that she has told me that she wishes she were dead. What can I do?*
You need to consult a mental health professional who has worked successfully with twins. One twin is dominating or overpowering the other twin who is lost without her brother. Both twins will be burdened by this deep enmeshment which needs to be understood and gradually made less intense.

Attachment problems between twins go underground making parents unaware of the problems their children are having being separate. All of these questions reflect that parents feel overwhelmed by elementary-school twin issues. These parents need more support and understanding and strategies to understand and manage their twins. There are so many options for support groups and online counseling and support. Finding a mental health professional who works with twins will help parents resolve these troubling but normal-for-twin problems. Working to develop each child's individual strengths and help them with their challenges is an excellent way to start.

When One Twin Lags Behind

Usually in early childhood or when school begins parents notice if their twins have very different needs based on physical limitations, learning disabilities, autistic spectrum disorder, or attention deficit disorder. Developmental lags can be very difficult strategic and financial problems for family. The child with the problem needs extra attention. The healthy twin can feel guilty for being spared the disability and resent at the same time the extra attention his brother or sister is receiving. Or the healthy twin fears that they will get sick. It is natural for the higher functioning twin to want to help the less fortunate twin. Reliance on the stronger twin becomes a problem when it goes too far and the twin becomes the caretaker. When innate differences are handled with psychological mindedness, troubling crises can have benefits for both children. Real problems and problem-solving teach children about decision-making, choice, and resilience. Family therapy is a way for the twins and other siblings to talk about the stresses related to the disability.

Lagging behind is a matter of degree when twins are able to manage their idiosyncrasies. Twins develop differently even when they are identical. Hopefully with the knowledge about how to parent twins readily available from pediatricians, online, in parenting books, and through twin support clubs, twins are seen as different. The old-fashioned belief that twins should do everything alike is as outdated a wonder as bread is an important nutritional food staple. Extreme differences between twins are also common and complicate parenting and decision-making. I have consulted over the years with many families where one twin is lagging behind the other. What I have come to understand through observations and conversations with families is that the twin attachment is still very profound even if one twin is on the autistic spectrum and the other is not suffering from this disability. Or one twin may be homosexual or transgender and the other twin is not bothered by their differences, rather attachment makes for comfort at this time. At this stage of life twins can accept their brother or sister's differences more easily than the parents.

Young twins because of their twin identity help each other through their disabilities with more grace than parents and mental health professionals. Twins at early stages of life feel a deep connection to one another that has a boundaryless quality about it. When parents do their part in helping the child in need, twins will naturally do their own part and help each other. I worked with a set of 4-year-old twins where one child Karen was evaluated as gifted and the other Stacy was evaluated as being on the autistic spectrum and mute. Karen was able to communicate with her sister who eventually began to develop language. Their parents wondered how much was enough of Karen helping Stacy. Decisions were made about separation and support, with the help of all of the teachers and specialists who worked with the family on a monthly basis. The support team wanted to balance their twin attachment with their different learning needs.

Of course it is not appropriate or healthy for twins to be parents to one another. Nevertheless it does happen. As a last resort, when all services are unavailable, twins helping each other is fine. Recently I was talking with 6-year-old twins who relied on one another to get through the school day. Alan was shy and Sally was outgoing and friendly. I asked Alan to try and make his own friends without the help of Sally. Alan stared me in the face and said "well I do Sally's math homework so it is ok for her to help me." Being a twin myself, I thought that this was a good answer from a twin point of view. I did talk with their parents and teachers about teaching each child to be self-reliant.

In conclusion, there are clearly ranges of reactions that are appropriate when one twin lags behind. There is no one answer to this problem of how to be even-handed with both children when they are so different in their abilities. Separation in areas of difficulty will usually be very helpful for both children as each twin will get the attention they need. Over-reacting is not helpful. And pretending that there are no issues is also negligent. Look hard and someone will be able to help!

Seventh Grade to High School Graduation

All teenagers have difficulty separating from their families and finding and establishing a separate identity or sense of uniqueness. Adolescence is a time that is very turbulent for all teens and their parents because of cognitive and hormonal changes which create emotional instability in normal teens (Schave and Schave, 1989). But for twins and their families, the teenage years are truly double trouble. Teenage twins can be hyper-sensitive about everything that is going on around them. Moody fighting between twins is intense and confusing to outsiders. Even though the twin pair may understand some of the reasons for anger and disharmony, they may be unable to explain the problems they are having with one another in a way that parents, psychologists, and teachers can understand. For example, and common for twin teenagers unfortunately, is when one twin develops an eating disorder (Marmorstein *et al.*, 2007). The eating disorder is a way of establishing a physical difference in order to be able to demonstrate that one twin is different from the other twin. Or this is may be a way of a twin to feel in control without their brother or sister. In serious cases hospitalization may be necessary to stop the self-harm of the twin who will not eat. I believe that an eating disorder can be a symptom of deep identity confusion which is acted out to provide a better sense of self (Kendler, 2001; www.eatingdisordershope.com).

In adolescence, twins really want to be their own person and seek out different friends and interests. They begin to date, and boyfriend and girlfriend relationships further separation. Still twins check in with their brother or sister on a daily basis to get feedback, mirroring, and validation for what they are doing on their own. What happens cognitively is that teenagers are capable of thinking abstractly. This means that they are no longer rule-bound like school-age children. Piaget (1975) describes this phase of development as formal operational thinking. The major tasks of this cognitive stage are the ability to think abstractly and to look at possibilities as well as actualities. There is a heightened interest in the social environment which is also critical for expression of the self. Teenagers who now think abstractly learn to argue against the rules because they can see beyond the actual rules and come up with their own rules.

In search of their own sense of self, the teenage twin years bring in anger, disharmony, and tears based on disagreements about friends and interests. While they are finding their own paths in life which is crucial, separation is also fraught with deep and painful struggles. Absolutely essential is the extension of the development of separate friendships and interests that began early in life. In elementary school twins are more accepting of the other twin's differences than in the teenage years. At stressful times during adolescence, interactions can become non-supportive, mean-spirited, and jealousy-based. Or twins can become more attached to each other and not seek out separate interests and friends. Or twins can insist on sharing all of their teenage experiences because they are under-socialized with close others who are not their twin. Opposite identity also develops. One twin is social the other awkward. One twin is smart and the other is not. One twin is attractive and the other very plain.

Parents can definitely be confused by their teen twins' hostile antics toward one another or their over-involvement in each other's lives. Dramatic fights and long silences are predictable between teenage twins who are so emotionally overwrought by their distance from one another that they are not even capable of being aware of their out of control, unstable behavior. There is a provocative quality to twin dramatics. Unfortunately, this is a time when anorexia and cutting is common. Pronouncements about transgender and homosexuality are also discussed openly in a way that often frightens parents.

Parents and therapists should never underestimate the profound attachment that twins share as they develop more individuality. While teenage twins may consciously seem to be distinctly on their own path and not in need of each other, they are still very deeply connected on an unconscious level and will have problems making their own decisions and living their own lives. When do parents need help from a mental health professional? Troubling issues will include the following:

1. Separation anxiety from the twin or parent. For example, 10-, 11-, 12-, 13-year-old twins can be afraid of going to school and to separate classes without their twin.
2. Problems with making or keeping friendships. This might include a lack of social skills in everyday interactions—such as an inability to make small talk. Or a twin might display misplaced anger or jealousy with new people who seem better able to explain their ideas.
3. School or schoolwork fears or conflicts. Often an inability to concentrate on schoolwork in an age-appropriate fashion suggests the probability of depression or a lack of language acquisition skills related to the twin dynamic.
4. Jealousy or intense competition between twins, which causes too much intensity. Twins can be ridiculously jealous and competitive with clothes, cars, friends, and grades. Some twins need everything in their lives to be even, which is indicative of a problematic development of the twin bond. There is most likely a lack of individual identity in each twin.
5. Isolated behavior that may lead to phobias can develop when twins spend too much time with each other and lack the confidence to try new experiences alone and together. If isolation gets worse children turn to drugs and pornography on the internet.
6. Taking on opposite roles that will undermine the development of their individual potential is self-destructive but happens easily. Turning this behavior around once it starts is extremely challenging.
7. Sharing every object, event, friendship, and making decisions together will not help twins to learn how to function on their own. The longer too much attachment goes on the harder it is to change because developmental arrests occur which are hard to reverse.

Behavioral and emotional issues that I am consulted about can be very different from one phone call to the next.

1. *My 12 year old daughters are pulling each other's hair out.* This is obviously a problematic behavior that needs to be addressed by parents and a therapist.
2. *My 13 year old twins have not spoken to each other in a year.* Why would a parent let this behavior go on? Parents in these situations need insight into why they have let this situation persist.

3   *My son has a girlfriend but his twin sister is not interested in dating.* This is normal!
4   *One of my 14-year-old twins is being evaluated for being transgender. His brother is very upset and having a hard time as well. What do you think would help them?* Of course it is hard for both children and it is so important that the transgender twin is being evaluated and counseled about his decision. His brother would benefit from psychotherapy as well.

All of these questions reflect different problems that teenage twins are having with separating from each other. Identity confusion and who is better or who is right are the underlying issues that twins face as they walk their own life path. Obviously, disharmony is really intense and needs to addressed by the parents of these children. Twins will need a great deal of help separating from each other. Twin difficulties with self-definition can be frustrating for mental health professionals who don't understand the primacy of the attachment. Finding the therapist who wants to understand twin problems is crucial.

Attachment Issues with Emotionally Healthy Separations Are Apparent After Adolescence

Separation problems are normal when there is an ability for the twins and their family to work out their anger, fear, anxiety, resentment, and longings about more closeness. When twins are not treated as individuals their ability to tolerate separate lives can be compromised severely. Here are some examples of inadequate parenting that lead to an inability to separate to anger to estrangement.

Undermining Parenting Creates an Interdependent Identity and Next-Door-Neighbor Sensibility

The twin pairs Victor and Vince, Patricia and Pauline, Adrienne and Eileen whose early memories were presented in Chapter 1 did not receive enough individual attention in infancy and early childhood. Vince and Victor were born and raised in a small country town. Treated as a unit, they learned to turn to each other for comfort from their parent's rage and actual physical abuse. When life was scary they soothed each other by being in close proximity. They created different roles for one another and did not compete, being psychologically halves of a whole unit. Vince was the planner and Victor was the lead scout who suggested new adventures for his brother to consider and plan. Taking care of their roles parenting each other, they made friends in the neighborhood and were provided for by some of their relatives. Of course they got attention as twins. They remained fearful and submissive to their parents. Vince and Victor parented each other because their mother and stepfather were indifferent to their emotional needs for independence. Unfortunately parental input about individuality was dismissed as unnecessary and out of the question. Decision-making was split by the roles these children adopted. Vince was the caregiver and Victor was the emotionally intense child. Consequences of inadequate parenting were deeply destructive. Both boys enjoyed socialization with other children and school was not a problem but rather a treat for them. They kept their grades up to prevent family strife and their parents satisfied. More serious issues related to separation emerged in young adulthood. For example, Victor began to impersonate his brother by wearing his clothes and pretending to be Vince.

Vicki and Madeline grew up spending most of their childhood time together. The family was poor and moved a great deal with their father's work. A simple life where children were seen but not heard characterized their family life. Although physical abuse was not present, attention to emotional needs of their children was seriously missing. All play experiences and activities were done together. Vicki worked to keep Madeline content. Madeline protected Vicki from social situations that stressed her out or just left her feeling alone. Decision-making was complicated, although Madeline was more able to initiate separation experiences than Vicki. Madeline needed Vicki's steadfastness. There were no pre-school experiences and no preparation for kindergarten. All socialization was within the family. These children led entwined lives until they went to public school for kindergarten. The kindergarten teachers picked up their interdependence and separated them from one another. Speech problems and secret languages were attended by speech therapists in the public school system. Separation experiences created competition and anger at one another.

Adrienne and Eileen were brought up in a stable Midwestern home environment. While their parents were not wealthy, they were quite able to support their children. Unfortunately, their parents had no idea how to raise twins. And so these identical twins were allowed to rely on one another. Both women could not live without each other. Their attachment and their fear of being on their own was never addressed adequately throughout their childhood and adolescence.

Both women had difficulty separating from one another because of their deep attachment and need to always agree. While they are aware of their issues of being enmeshed, they have not been able to overcome their fears of taking their own path and of being on their own making decisions. School separations, and outsider comments, and even parental insight has had limited success.

Undermining Parents Who Assign Opposite Labels to Their Twins and Encourage a Split-Identity Pattern of Twinship and Estrangement

Patricia and Pauline were born into an inter-racial family that was totally dysfunctional. Patricia and Pauline were terrified of their mother who was a very volatile and deeply angry person. Their father was mostly absent from home life. When he was home he was not attentive to his children. Dad traveled for business which provided for the family financially. Patricia and Pauline had their brothers and sister to relate to which made them less dependent on each other in many ways. Pauline was the stronger minded twin and was told to take care of her sister who was seen as more fragile.

Interestingly, imposed differences between these identical twins, although abusive and disingenuous, gave each daughter a sense of identity inside and outside of the twinship. They were treated as distinct halves of a whole rather than a unit. And so they learned that they were different through interactions with their parents. Why these stilted interactions between parents and children developed is hard to understand, in hindsight the opposite identities did play out in a psychologically apparent identity structure. Fortunately, Patricia and Pauline did not want or need to make decisions together. Paula was the leader and Patty was the follower who needed to be taken care of. These roles were honored in early childhood. Patricia and Pauline got comfort from being together even though they knew they were different. They shared a bed until they were 11.

Even before they started school, Paula was the athletic twin who could ride a bike and play baseball and Patty was more awkward and accepted her physical limitations in comparison to her twin. Paula was the tomboy and Patty was the girlie girl. Brothers and sisters treated them as twins and as individuals. But mom and dad reinforced the strong and helpless labels which became a source of identity for these twin girls. While this form of separation was destructive to both women later in life, it allowed for different friendships and interests to evolve. In general, separation in early childhood was extremely difficult but not impossible. Patricia and Pauline did everything in harmony if they could. They were best friends but not entwined.

Sandy and Scott were born to a classic 1950s "Mother Knows Best Family." These twins were perceived as very special and entitled to extra attention from the community. In other words there was an enormous investment in the children's profile as twins. Sandy and Scott were dressed up as a little couple as young children when they went to church and family events. But Sandy and Scott were very different not only because they were boy–girl twins. They were also given roles in the family that mirrored their parents' roles with one another. Dad was passive and resentful and Mom was controling. Their older brothers were out of the house and spent very little time with Sandy. Scott had some "guy time" with them. But Scott was a fearful child and needed the protection of his sister.

The family dynamics are complicated and hard to explain and understand. Dad was ruled and over-ruled by mom. Sandy was also expected to be submissive to her brother like her mother who felt she was less than her husband. Scott was helpless and afraid and Sandy had to take care of him while also being submissive. Both twins were happy to be separated. But as children they played together and found times to enjoy one another. Going out without their twin was a relief. Scott could be on his own and make his own mistakes. Sandy could try and take care of herself instead of Scott. They were not under-socialized as they played in the neighborhood with others their age. They took ballet and sports classes and went to church regularly. Kindergarten was not a problem for either of them in terms of separation.

Scott was seen as a troubled child when he entered public school. Teachers and administrators believed that keeping the twins together would help Scott's adjustment. Keeping the children together had the exact opposite effect.

Teachers compared both children and Scott was humiliated for being less than his sister. Teachers made a spectacle of Scott's learning problems and Sandy could not protect him from this. Their mom and dad were not involved. In second grade Scott was placed in a special school for children who are different.

Young Adult Acknowledgement and Conflicts About Differences

Separation in young adulthood is dependent on the pattern of twinship that is shared. Interdependent-identity twins are too over-identified with one another to live truly separate lives. They are the next-door-neighbor twins who may fight a great deal but cannot be physically separated for long periods of time. They remain close throughout their lifetimes.

Other patterns of twinship are affected by external events such as sexual choices, marriage, careers, and children, which shape and direct how twins make decisions for themselves. Twin identity is always present even if their twin is not by their side. By the time twins are ready to graduate from high school there is some calmness between them which replaces the tensions of the teenage years. Sexual identity, which is based on many genetic, environmental, and interpersonal factors, has hopefully been explored and partnerships with non-twins formed. However, because twins have been used as tools to understand the genetic components of homosexuality which is out of context of twin identity formation, I agree with Dr. Martinez (2011) when she explains:

> To know that someone one is heterosexual or homosexual is to know very little about that person … What one can do sexually varies just as much between heterosexuals as it does between homosexuals. Couples who share a commitment to exclusive long term monogamy … have very similar make up regardless of the sex/gender makeup of the couple.
>
> Martinez, 2011: 36–7

While the blueprint of twin personality is in place, there is still a great deal of individuality that needs to develop. Understanding who you are as an individual in the non-twin world is an endless challenge. I write about this struggle in Chapter 7. New friendships and a broader sense of the world provides a structure for each twin to grow and become different and distinct from their twin. Still there is anxiety and ambivalence about being apart, because being apart means taking new partners that replace the intensity of the twin bond.

Marriage often creates deep anxiety for twins which they were not predicting or expecting. In the classic novel by Dorothy Baker *Cassandra at the Wedding*, the overwhelming and unforeseen psychological consequences of separation in young adulthood are recreated magnificently. Both twins, one gay and the other straight, who are alike in so many ways, struggle to get through the wedding of the straight twin. The reader feels the tension that both twins experience leading up to the event. But a serious suicide attempt by the twin who is observing surprises the twin who is getting married, the psychiatrist, the family, and the non-twin reader. Touching and inspiring are the psychiatrist and the groom who save the suicidal twin and her frightened sister. The novel very accurately reveals the pain of separation that twins can experience when a new partner is chosen to replace their twin.

While not all marriages create suicidal ideation in twins, there is a devastating quality to making commitments to new partners. Twin replacement is very stressful and has a steep learning curve. Understanding what you need from a close other who is not your twin is very complicated and hard to find. Relationships will fail because of too much immediate faith and hope in the twin replacement (Klein, 2003). I have observed many times over how twins are excited to get married or to take on a serious partner and career. At the same time they are also emotionally confused and apprehensive about how the separation will play out with the absence of their twin.

My own experience of separating from my sister after college was within the "normal range" for twins. Right after graduation from UC Berkeley, we both married within ten days of each other. Marjorie did not attend my wedding as she was on her way to Europe. We did wear each other's wedding dress. Or we wore the same dress at different weddings. We went our own ways. Marjorie went to Sweden with her husband the artist who had a fellowship to study sculpture. I married a soon-to-be medical student and moved back to Los Angeles.

Marjorie and I were not thinking or talking about having trouble with separating from one another. Friends and romantic partners told us that it was time for us to be on our own. College had been a time of anger and disharmony that had been previously repressed. But we still respected each other and found comfort in just going places together or discussing other people and ideas and shopping. We were still confidantes at heart. Even so, Marjorie and I argued and disagreed on how I should live my life. She was critical and ashamed of me and hoped that I would turn my attitude around and please her. I thought that it would be a relief to have her opinions in Sweden and far away from how I wanted to proceed with my life. Marjorie wanted me to be like her and I was not able to take on her intellectual or emotional interests in literature, art, and travel. I wanted her to be normal and eat like a healthy person would. But she would not listen to me. Her eating disorder helped her feel in control without me.

Freedom from each other came with deep feelings of not fitting in with other people and intense loneliness. My sister and I both suffered like most twins I have known personally or professionally when we were young adults. Young adulthood is a pivotal time to separate physically and emotionally and to grow into very different lifestyles. And yet there are feelings of sadness, loneliness, emptiness, and newness that trouble twins who may really want their own lives. These feelings of loss are so profound that even talking about them with your twin, therapist, or family members takes a great deal of time and effort. Often separation reactions of twins differ depending on the strength of the attachment. One twin adjusts better than the other twin. Or seemingly so.

Twins are often surprised by their deep problems separating from each other in young adulthood. Here are some common ways that twins are critical of one another in a self-righteous and demanding way or dramatically missing one another and suffering from loneliness. These issues reflect intense separation anxiety.

1. Social identity differences are very predictable. One twin A may feel that her sister twin B was hanging out with the wrong crowd and doing too much partying. While the other twin B feels like her sister is just a stupid loser who doesn't have a sense of adventure and hangs out with nerds and losers. This fight can go on and on about who knows the best crowd to hang out with and why. Different types of friendships are explored and criticized, and sometimes accepted and sometimes not accepted. But twins do feel lost with new friendships. They use one another to defensively justify their choices of new friends and new experiences. They don't agree and often have a serious argument. After the fight is over they do return to some old more harmonious states like shopping or going out for dinner, karate, yoga or tennis.
2. Financial identity choices vary and cause strife. Twin A wants a traditional life. A wants to be wealthy and live in a big house and take great vacations She wants to have kids who she drives around with in fancy cars. Twin B is artistic and sees money as the root of all evil. B wants to have a simple authentic life in the country. Raising her children to be community advocates is twin B's life goal. Sometimes these twins with very different goals for life just let their twin be and don't harass one another. At other times battles are endless. Disappointment and shame in the other twin is apparent on both sides of the fence. Parents and other close friends may try to reason with their unhappy child, friend, spouse, or boss, but this is to no avail. Twins fight an eye for an eye, a tooth for a tooth, at this stage of life. Questioning values like the importance of materialism is very common for twins who see the world differently.
3. Physical identity changes—weight loss or gain—creates enormous stress and confusion. When twins start living apart physical changes can quickly appear. Twin A gains 50 pounds and twin B stays the same size as in high school. Twin A dresses in casual clothes all of the time. Twin B is always dressed up strangely according to twin A. Twin A hates to exercise while twin B works on getting her yoga certification. A and B are both uncomfortable about looking different. This self-consciousness goes on and on and on. How unbearable looking different than your twin can be is hard to describe to a non-twin. But all twins agree looking different is painful and unsettling. Craziness occurs when twins have to eat the same foods so that they are like one another.
4. Career choice identity is always a point of contention in young adults. No matter how similar career choices are, there is always criticism within the pair. I worked with twin attorneys who both went to Ivy League Colleges and had very important and impressive jobs, but were always battling over who had more status. While they were able to use each other's knowledge

and experience, they were very reluctant to give the other a compliment. Competition and identity confusion contributed to their anger at each other in all areas of their lives. How to raise their children was an ongoing battle.

5   Who is the boss creates anger and confusion. New friends change the balance of power. No longer is the twin the "go to" person of choice, rather it is a friend or romantic partner. Feeling left out and second fiddle to husbands, children, wives, lovers, and bosses is a common and predictable event in young adulthood that continues on and on and on. I know first hand that it is hard not to be your twin's "go to" person. It does become a relief when you have more freedom to pursue your own life.

Young adulthood is different for each and every twin pair. And so I share these thoughts from twins who have shared their life stories with me. Melissa and Katie had a close and loving relationship as children. Their mother was careful to treat them as individuals. They separated after college. Melissa shares her experience with separation as a young adult.

> Katie and I took different course work at UCLA. She studied science and I studied finance. We met our husbands within months of one another. We both married around the same time and I moved across the country with my new husband. I wanted to get married and have my own life and so did she. But I did not know how hard it would be to not be able to see Katie when I wanted or needed to be with her. I tried to talk with her every other day because I felt intense loneliness which could only be relieved by flying across the country to be with her.
>
> I really wanted to be on my own. I tried very hard to develop myself. I learned finance and became a day trader. I traveled with my husband. I studied piano and cooking. I had lots of friends to go out with when I wanted to go shopping or to dinner and the movies. As hard as I tried I could not manage my life alone. My marriage began to deteriorate and I went home for longer and longer periods of time.
>
> I divorced and moved home and stayed with my sister and her husband and her two children. They comforted me by just being present in my daily life. After many months of living with my twin and her family, I found my own condo and moved out. I was able to live on my own.

Pauline shares:

> Patricia went off to UCSB and a semester later I was at Cal Poly. It was an adjustment not to have Patty around all of the time. But we stayed in close contact and I never really felt like she was that far away. The real separation came when I went to graduate school in New York, which was very far away and hard because I was pursuing something on my own. I

was not measuring myself against Patty. I never felt so alone in all of my life. I was pursuing a PhD and if I couldn't work things out I would bring shame to my family for failing.

I felt so very alone, and even though Patty and I talked a lot on the phone and wrote a lot of letters to each other, it was difficult to really communicate about what I was feeling in a way that made me feel connected to Patty. It was very difficult for me to find comfort in my relationship with my peers, even though I was well liked and looked to for support by them.

Sandy who had a very difficult relationship with her brother shares:

We both got married around the same time as each other. We were very different and did not need to be together. And yet, I cried in the bathroom for an hour at his wedding. I didn't know why I was so upset at his wedding. I married three months later and moved across country.

We went our own ways and grew more and more distant. I did not miss him at all but looked for others to be close with even though I was not sure of myself with other men. Scott became more and more indifferent to me. We talked to each other on rare occasions. Scott was favored by the entire family and their favoritism became more and more apparent as we took our own paths in life.

Madeline shares her separation experiences in young adulthood:

I left the house when I was 18 because I was the social twin and more adventuresome than Vicki. It was easier for me to imagine being on my own. I would get lonely and Vicki would come over and spend the night if she had to give me some extra attention. Vicki did not leave home until she was 29. Vicki went to a four-year college and became a CPA. I went to Court Reporting School and opened a very successful business. We kept in close contact and had our own friends as well. We could accept that we were different but found a great deal of comfort being with one another.

Young adulthood is a time when twins begin to realize that they are truly different from one another. Often they feel contemptuous and fearful of one another. Equally strong is the comfort they get from being together to recharge. They experience their uniqueness in interactions with friends and family and at work or at school. How they are different is no longer something that can be challenged by the other in the hope of changing them into who you want them to be. There is some cement to their individuality. Twins often seek out psychotherapy to help understand why they are alone and unhappy when they have chosen to go their own way. Fighting can turn into estrangement which is the subject of the next chapter.

Middle Age Differences Are Cemented in Individuality

Separate lives become the norm for twins unless they cannot live without each other, as in the cases of the interdependent-identity twins previously discussed. Attachment issues of earlier life recede into the background because of external life changes such as families and careers. Still the twin torch burns on with a less bright light. Twins can see that they are different and that changing back to the earlier stage of life is not possible or important. Maturity allows some twins to try and compromise in order to get along. Patterns of interacting with one another are established. Some twins will talk several times a week. Some twins will not engage with one another at all. As needed interaction and dialogue between twins is common when twins live far away from one another.

In midlife there is more acceptance of differences and more ability to tolerate separation. When family emergencies arise or serious illness or other types of unfortunate circumstance threaten a twin, the other will try and help no matter how disappointed they feel with one another. More fighting and then estrangement can take hold of the life of a twin pair in middle age. Also possible is the ability to develop a more mature twin relationship which is based on care, support, and loving. Ego boundaries are firmly established based on each twin's separate life experience alone without their twin. This slows down and stops the rollercoaster ride of wishing for childhood closeness and harmony. The twin attachment if not optimal is stable, predictable, and less conflicted. Life stories of twins confirm this statement. Typical patterns of midlife interaction between twins include the following range:

1. The ability to talk to one another spontaneously as is needed. Visiting each other's families, special events, and travel together.
2. Limited but regular communication about life events and personal problems. Meetings with family for traditional events. Clear ego boundaries that establish a structure for what is not acceptable to talk about and what is important to share.
3. Phone calls on birthdays and other events that are important to both twins.
4. Phone calls when family emergencies require communication.
5. Total estrangement with no interest in communicating.

Senior Twins Complain and Care for Each Other

> My twin sister came to my house. I was on the bed exhausted. My sister was angry and critical of me for being exhausted. She called me lazy and criticized me for being too removed. But I was tired because I had gotten up early to take her to the hospital. Why won't she give me a break? What can I do?
>
> Ann

By the time twins are seniors they have an understanding of why they do or don't get along with their sister or brother. Still they complain about each other and want more. There has been a lot of water under the bridge metaphorically speaking and this has brought acceptance of what is and of what might have been. Depending on external circumstances twins try to get along if they are not totally estranged. Physical separation and illness often determine the closeness that twins can share. In general, older twins try harder to be forgiving and empathic with their twin—their closest friend and closest enemy (Pietilä et al., 2012; Shirley, 2016). Twin loss in old age, while devastating and emotionally horrific, is easier to overcome because individuality is more rooted in the self than twinship.

The Devastation and Trauma of Twin Loss

The ultimate type of physical separation is twin loss. While estranged twins feel similar to lone twins and grieve deeply for what they wanted from their twin, intense suffering is more bearable. When a twin dies the surviving twin finds the loss deeply disorganizing and traumatic. Separation of the physical presence of the twin can lead to a complicated grief reaction for the lone twin. While memories of the twin remain, the physical presence and dialogue between the pair is gone forever. Recovery is very difficult and takes an extended period of time, family and psychological support, peer support, and the tenacity to survive (Brandt, 2001; Morgan, 2014; Woodward, 1998, 2002, 2006).

Having spoken with lone twins and read stories and novels about twin loss, it is still very difficult to put into words what is lost when your twin dies. I believe that the image of being "alone in the mirror" captures an emptiness and sadness that lone twins experience. The only way to bring back your twin is as a ghost, or shadow, or through memories and imagination (Klein, 2012). Visualizing and imagining and remembering is not the same source of feedback and support that alive twins provide. The survivor has lost an emotional part of him or herself that is hard to define. Only the survivor knows what part of his/her emotional self has been lost. Suffering in itself is loneliness, which leads to isolation. Grieving is a long and arduous process for the surviving twin.

Research on twin loss suggests that the age of the twin at the time of loss is very important and will impact the lone twin's ability to develop and thrive. Always crucial is the support of others in the grieving process. At different stages of life there are different characteristics that come to the forefront. Psychological researchers do not agree on the long-range effects of twin loss before birth or at birth. Reports of these events indicate that the surviving twin experiences a sense of emptiness and depression that is difficult to put into words and to explain to others. But this loss is deeply felt and difficult to overcome. Talking about the loss with the family and other survivors is critical to the grieving process and moving forward for the lone twin and parents.

Twin Loss at Birth

I received this note from a woman who wanted to share her lifelong pain about losing her twin at one day of life. Ann writes:

This story begins 54 years ago. My mum never knew she was having twins. We were born 12 weeks early. I survived and my brother John lived for one day ... My family told me it was better that John died. It seems I wanted more room and pushed him up under mom's ribs and his legs weren't right ... Do you know what it is like to grow up thinking you killed your twin brother? I grew up for the both of us ... I don't know what was worse, not having my brother and my guilt as a survivor or not being allowed to talk about the loss. I have lived with survivor guilt.

Survival guilt and a sense of loss that is unexplainable in words is very common for lone twins. As Ann suggests, it can begin as early as in utero or at birth. Acknowledging the loss and talking about it with others is one step toward reducing survivor guilt.

Early Childhood

In early childhood twin loss is profound. Parents and the surviving twin are challenged in ways that are hard to put into words. Parents have to deal with their grief as well as the grief of their lone twin. Parents are naturally overwhelmed and can lose perspective on their child's loss. Overprotection of the lone twin is common. Or parents can idealize the lost child and reject the twin who survives. Because of the developmental stage of life the twin may not understand the finality of death and continue to long for their brother or sister. Fearful because of this traumatic experience and loss, lone twins have difficulty making friends and achieving in school. Guilt about survival and just missing their best friend can lead to serious depression. Psychotherapy for the lone twin and the family is always important for childhood twin loss.

Adolescence

Twin loss in adolescence can be devastating because identity formation is in many ways developed by the measuring of themselves against the other twin. In addition, there is a loss of twin identity. Twins at this stage of life are very close even if they are in conflict. They still see themselves as a pair and get social and personal validation as a twin. Death creates an enormous sense of confusion and emptiness. At a time when identity should be expanding, identity is lost. Intensive psychotherapy is crucial and should not include the family, as often twins try to replace their twin by caring for their parents.

Adulthood

Twin loss in adulthood is extremely painful because the survivor knows in his or her mind what has been lost and that twin replacement is not an option. Still the surviving adult looks to others to fill their emptiness. This tactic can be helpful if there is an emotional reality to the new close relationships. Often lone twins are too optimistic and too negative about forming new friendships. Adults who lose their twin seek out psychotherapy for many years. Vince who lost his twin to suicide shares:

> Healthy separation from your twin is possible. But each twin must be conscious of the effort. Leaving one another is not the end of twinship but rather a redefining of how you will relate to one another.
>
> Too often in the struggle to be individual, without proper guidance, the fear of loss becomes amplified with what may be lost. It is my understanding since losing Victor, the intimacy of twinship without definition leads to an incomplete and un understandable confusion about who I am. What does each twin possess which the other does not? Who is stronger and in what area? How are they connected and do they have a sense of otherness or individuality? Without clear definition of all of these important issues and questions, can the intimacy of the relationship be understood, hence becoming individuals who can go on to live happy lives with other people.

Another common complication is when the grief process of losing a twin is postponed because the survivor is helping other family members recover. I have heard far too many times "I don't want my family to see my sadness because they will become more upset." When grief is not processed longstanding depression and confused expectations for others' reactions will prevail. Or more simply said, the survivor will continually twin with the others in his or her life and not accept that their twin is gone. Forming relationships that are stable and healthy is difficult when you want to just replace your twin. The possibility of long-term survival is difficult when grief is not addressed.

Unfortunately, later in life the death of a twin can be devastating if the twins were highly interdependent and shared friends and social networks. Aged survivors can be lost if too many career and family connections are shared. Recent research suggests that losing a twin later in life is more difficult than losing a spouse later in life. It is estimated that the life expectancy for senior twin loss is only two years if twins were isolated in their relationship.

I will end this section with a question I was asked in a newsletter for the Twinless Twin Newsletter:

Dear Dr. Klein,
Is there a normal time frame for twin loss to be experienced? Should it take months, one year, or many years to successfully grieve and recover from the death of a murdered twin? How can a spouse help to support a twinless twin—what role can they take?
Anonymous

Dear Anon,
There is no "normal" time to grieve the loss of your twin. At first twin loss is like having a hole in your heart. Gradually the pain will lessen as

the meaning of this loss is understood. New relationships, careers, and children also fill the hole. Twins never forget their twin. The adjustment to this traumatic loss should be dealt with in psychotherapy and the support of close loved ones. Group support is crucial. Often it is very difficult for non-twins to understand the magnitude of loss and pain. Outsiders will get frustrated and impatient. It is more helpful to talk with other twinless twins.

Don't expect your non-twin loved ones to make it better for you. This will just breed frustration and alienation. People who don't understand are not the enemy. They just have not had your experience. Be kind to yourself, there is so much trauma to process with the loss of a murdered twin.

Dr. Klein

Helpful Things to Consider When a Twin Dies

I write more extensively about twin loss in *Alone in the Mirror* (2012). Briefly these interventions are very helpful for the family, the mental health professionals, and lone twins.

1. Explore feelings of loss to start the grieving process.
2. Develop an understanding of the survivor's role in the twin relationship.
3. Support the growth of underdeveloped identity in the lone twin.
4. Assess for complicated grief reaction and post-traumatic stress disorder with a psychiatric evaluation.
5. Deal with survivor guilt.
6. Look for support groups such as Twinless Twins.
7. Develop hands-on family support to avoid self-criticism and social withdrawal.
8. Continually remind the lone twin that healing is a long-range goal with twists and turns that are not predictable.
9. Have family members talk together about the loss and devastation.

Concluding Remarks on when Separation Issues Are Over for Twins

I have never met a twin who didn't ask themselves or anyone who would listen: "When will I get over missing my twin?" Or, "When will I stop looking for a very close twin relationship like I had with my twin as a child?" My bottom line answer is most likely never! Although, in time, you can understand your longings, which will definitely help you expand your world. The attachment that twins share is primary and makes an everlasting and indelible mark on personality development and the need for the comfort of closeness, empathy, and understanding. Missing your twin is a form of separation anxiety that goes hand in hand with twinship.

Because twin pairs are parented differently, not all twins are alike. With great certainty I can say not all twins love each other and revere their relationship.

Some twins are just stuck in the mire of their closeness, their anger, and their longing for harmony. Even when twins remain conflicted and are unable to resolve their anger and disappointment with one another, they still miss the closeness the other provided. Fortunate twins who have a strong sense of themselves as individuals and are able to resolve their differences are able to support one another through difficult life situations. Twins who see themselves as individuals are resilient enough to fight and miss each other. Resilient twins can reconnect for help with their happiness or their despair. Twin attention when needed is certainly one of the best parts of being a twin—the gold ring on the merry-go-round.

The twin attachment—one of closeness and separation—teaches us about the power of human connection. Deeply felt intimacy based on the ability to identify with the other person because of shared or similar life experiences is a life-sustaining force for twins and for other close relationships. Losing this profound connection can be disorganizing psychologically for twins and leads to self-destructive behavior, negative thinking, and negative narratives. Unfortunately, twin closeness can be an enigma in our individually driven objectified technological world. Why is separation so hard for twins? This cultural and personal inability to understand the hardships of twinship is coupled with the idealization of twinship as the perfect intimacy. The important nuances and comfort of emotional closeness and attachment can remain a mystery to individuals who come from cold and distant families, and are desperately seeking attention and love. The gulf between twin intimacy and internet fantasies of intimacy is longer than the Great Wall of China.

Non-twins have great difficulty understanding missing your twin and the loneliness that goes along with this state of mind. And twins don't really understand how non-twins can conquer being alone. I can empathize with the suffering that twins feel when they experience a sense that something is missing in their relationships. Separation anxiety will diminish with age and experiences but never be taken out of the lives of twins.

4 Why Twin Fighting can Lead to Estrangement

I want so much closeness with my twin, I don't understand why we fight. Arguments hurt me so badly that sometimes it is easier for me not to engage in conversations with her.

Jackie

Please help me. My identical twin and I have been estranged for over a decade. Our estrangement has gotten worse and worse. Your writing about twin estrangement is the first time that I can feel an inner twin connection again. I miss my twin. Thank you for understanding.

Joanne

Recovering from twin estrangement is a long and unforgiving path which requires positive emotional support and determination. You have to keep trying and negotiating if you can. Sometimes if there is a great deal of physical and emotional abuse it is hard to reconcile.

Dr. Klein

Dr. Klein,
I am a 53-year-old identical twin and my sister and I have been embroiled in constant fighting as adults. We love each other dearly, but it has just become easier to ignore each other than end up in the same old arguments. I feel like my sister sees our differences (and there are many) as a personal attack. At the same time, I know I have let her down many times. Can you offer any insight/help? We shared a very difficult childhood. Our mother was schizophrenic and we were abused (sexually and my sister, verbally) by extended family members. I feel like many of our issues are surrounding this. For me, I confronted these issues in counseling and have made peace with my past, except for my sister. She has been angry at me for something our entire adult lives. At the same time, I love her so very much and want desperately to re-unite. The sad thing is we are both very successful adults, separate of each other. We have happy marriages, wonderful children and grandchildren. Our kids love each other and us dearly.
I am at my wit's end. I'll do anything to fix this, but I just don't think I can.

Jane

Strange? But True! Twins Fight a Lot

Images of harmony and seamless closeness permeate our cultural and popular mythology, video presentations, film, television, internet, and scientific understanding of twins. What comes to mind quickly for most non-twins is the deep and loving relationships that twins share. Metaphorically speaking, twinship has been used to portray the duality of human nature by using their extremely strong and primitive alliance to illustrate good and evil as opposite images of emotional experience. Only recently have novels and memoirs been published that explain the pain and animosity that twins can share and are forced to tolerate in one another. The dark and disconnected feelings that twins experience are very alive and real for countless twins (Lamb, 1998; Parravani, 2013; Verghese, 2009).

With great certainty I can report that twins who don't get along or who are actually estranged from one another wish that they could get along, in order to know that they have not been abandoned by their twin. Estrangement truly creates a deep sense of loss. To make twin despair more intense, disconnected twins are burdened by the feeling that they are seen as "not normal" twins by onlookers or non-twins who see twinship as a perfect state of intimacy. The reality of harmony and disharmony between twins is in my experience a difficult one for twins to live through and for non-twins to understand. Superficially explaining the twin relationship to others who are curious is very challenging to impossible (Lanigan, 2016). While twins know through their lived experiences that getting along with your sister or brother can be filled with pain and anger and reconciliation, talking to non-twins about this on and off again harmony is stressful. To add confusion, conflict and reconciliation cycles will begin again and again in an almost endless spiral (www.drbarbaraklein.com).

Understanding and then accepting why twins fight and that twin fighting is natural and different than sibling fighting is basic if you want to get along with a twin, marry a twin, raise twins, or work with them in psychotherapy. Twins share everything—parents' attention, love, and nurturing. Even in infancy they are aware of their twin and what they are receiving or not getting. Twins learn to measure themselves against one another. Who got more food, toys, play dates is the beginning of a life of measurement. There is also an over-identification between the pair that intensifies competition. This simple struggle to get what you need begins perhaps in utero where one twin has more space to grow then the other. At birth twins react to hunger and attention and feeling safe and warm together. Do twins get fed together or is this too much trouble for the mother? What is necessary to make twins feel like they are both special and that favoritism is not possible? There is no one size fits all answer to these rhetorical questions. Mindfulness about validating special traits in each twin and avoiding favoritism is a critical attitude for parents and other people who are close to twins (Schave and Ciriello, 1983).

Twinship is fraught with many identity struggles that can play out in deep rage and disbelief at one's twin. Shame about "who your twin has become" or "who your twin wants *you* to be" is very common. Twin estrangement is often an outcome of deeply conflicted twin relationships. Estrangement based on a lack of adequate parenting creates despair and loneliness for twins. The depth of despair that comes from twin estrangement is hard for close friends and family to understand, unless they happen to be twins. And twins who get along have great difficulty understanding the depth of this estrangement that twins who are at war feel toward one another.

I am a twin, so I can tell you from my experience that intense disagreement and then not being able to work it out—being estranged from your twin—is very hard, painful, and lonely. I would say that estrangement from your twin can create a sense of serious loss and unhappiness. While twin estrangement is not as painful as twin loss, unending conflicts are very difficult to accept as you get older. I have found that when twins talk with other twins about their loneliness that is based upon estrangement, their anguish is diminished and less frightening. Talking with other twins in groups who have ruptured or are ready to rupture their relationships often helps to heal despair. In some instances, twins will reconcile. In other cases, twins learn to accept their differences and move on. Having an audience for anger, fighting, and estrangement will heal loneliness and desperation. Straightforwardness about your deep disconnect can also heal the twin attachment that has gone astray (Klein and Martinez, 2016).

Patterns of Twinship Predict Fighting and Estrangement

Patterns of twinship give structure and definition to understanding the severity of anger, fighting, and estrangement that twins contend with throughout their lifespan. In general all twin fighting is natural, given the primary attachment that is shared (Fonagy and Target, 2003; Tancredy and Fraley, 2006). Obviously twin anger is more intense than sibling anger. Siblings fight with one another with more detachment because they don't share elements of their identity. The intensity of twin conflicts is very strong, and based on a division of power and roles in the family. Twins fight with each other as soon as they can as a way of defining themselves as individuals. Play between twins can be of a competitive nature and healthy or self-destructive. The quality of parenting that is available when twins are overwhelmed with one another will be a strong determinant of the health of their interactions. In situations of parental neglect one twin can fail to thrive. When parents impose or ignore the development of individual identity twin fighting and later estrangement is a serious consequence (Klein, 2012).

Interdependent-Identity Twins

Fighting between interdependent-identity twins can range from mild arguments over food, clothes, cars, money, and friendships that resolve easily. Confusion between the pair over who is responsible for being the caretaker and who is responsible for interacting most directly with the world can lead to more serious arguments and some violent episodes. Interdependent-identity twins will use impersonation of their twin when they are having difficulty separating. For example, they will wear each other's clothes and pretend that they are their twin to emotionally connect and cope with their loneliness and sense of loss. When child abuse and mental illness are part of a twin's identity too many separations can lead to suicide (Arthurs, 2014; Klein, 2003). The lone twin experiences the most intolerable form of estrangement (Morgan, 2014).

In general, fighting between interdependent-identity twins is mild in comparison to split-identity twins because interdependent-identity twins have an enmeshed relationship and deeply need one another to approve of them and help them make decisions. Childhood fighting is coupled with differences being established between the pair. One twin is the adventurer the other is the protector. Keeping these roles in alignment—the caretaker twin and the worldly twin—is more central to their emotional well-being than any differences of opinion that may arise. Fighting can be resolved through closeness in physical proximity. In their teenage years and young adulthood these enmeshed, very close to one another twins will fight and be critical of one another. Here are some examples.

> Vince: I had the worst fight of my life with Victor over a broken Christmas tree stand. I told Victor not to be so forceful with the screw driver. He didn't listen to me and Victor broke the Christmas tree stand. I screamed at Victor who screamed at me that I owed him 35 cents from 10 years ago. And then the fight was over.

Eileen and Adrienne have had great difficulty being apart. There most serious arguments were over Eileen's male friendships.

> Eileen: I got so involved with an old friend John, and our friendship turned to romance. Adrienne tried so hard to tolerate my time away from her. But she became concerned that he was not the right person for me. Adrienne would text me 20 times an hour. She could not stop texting. She was so panicked and John realized how intense our twin relationship was and left me. I was devastated and ashamed. But I could also accept that Adrienne needed me and I thought she might be right in her concerns about John.

Benna and Rachel fought about everything and then agreed with one another because they couldn't find a life alone or tolerate being separate.

> Rachel: The worst argument we ever had involved a Spiritual Counselor that Benna was working with who told her not to see her sister. We had a huge fight over who was responsible for the other's happiness. Benna did not see me for an entire year. I was so terribly lost and devastated that I withdrew into a world of my own. When mother got ill we reconnected. Benna has not done this again.

Madeline and Vicki have a much more combative relationship than other twins I have worked with. Amazingly to me at least, they always compromise.

> Vicki: I have tried to help my sister recover from her health problems by encouragement, giving her financial support, and even finding therapists for us to work together on our twin issues. Madeline is stubborn and rejects my concern about her business issues and stress level. When I get too close to her or our therapist tries to talk about her anger and defensiveness at me she retreats. Her first and seemingly last action is to find fault in me and the therapist. She calls me a perfectionist, cold, indifferent sister and withdraws into her self-destructive behavior. Madeline refuses to see our twin therapist saying that she does not understand how abusive I am to her. And then she will back down and try again to be amicable with me.

Tolerating separation is hard for over-identified twins and usually these entwined twins are living close to one another as they grow older. How issues are resolved between these pairs is of course idiosyncratic to their relationship and lifestyles. In my experience depression is common when there is too much separation for the weaker and dependent twin to tolerate. While each and every twin and twin pair have their own anger issues, the following fights are common and recur time and time again, depending on the circumstances of their lives:

1 You are a self-righteous hateful know-it-all who cannot see my point of view.
2 You are a pathetic loser who needs to be more like me.
3 You are not being assertive with your boss. I would be more direct.
4 Your boyfriend is a loser. I have made better partner choices than you have.
5 You don't know how to run your business. Your interpersonal skills are totally inappropriate.

The fighting that goes on is painful and scary for both entwined twins. Fighting is resolved with time. Fighting issues will begin again throughout the lifespan of these very close twins. A fear of expansiveness which includes being different from one another runs deep and makes adopting more separate lives very psychologically difficult. Fears of being abandoned by your twin are intense and keep closeness essential.

Split-Identity Twins

The split-identity pattern of twinship creates deep anger and resentment between twins as they begin to make different choices for themselves. As oppositely labeled twins separate from one another, deep confusion and shame arises about their brother or sister because of the hidden mixed messages that they have received from their parents about who they are alone and together.

Parental reverence for the twinship is exhibited to friends, family, teachers, and onlookers in general. Privately, these twins are seen as opposites of one another and responded to as such. These parental messages are literally crazy-making. When you go out to dinner with family and friends act in harmony and equality. At home the good girl does what she wants and the bad girl gets in trouble. Both children are in a double bind.

With split-identity parenting projections become more important than the actual uniqueness of each child. In other words, twins are praised for their similarities but attended too differently for their perceived and projected separate identity. When opposite twins are together they are harmonious as children. Separately, the good twin is encouraged to be their own person and the bad twin is criticized for being inadequate. Because of all the parental mixed messages there is a great deal of anger and shame about one another when they are apart. Fighting can be very intense over who is right and how a decision should be made. In my life my sister could not accept that I was not going to do what she said I should do. Later I gained more leverage for my opinions. In the end we both modified our expectations of one another. Still that is our biggest stumbling block. Who is right?

I have heard many life stories of twins who began as teenagers to physically fight with one another and pull each other's hair out in a rage for not being in agreement about who got to wear the better shoes, coat, dress, bathing suit. Later on these are arguments about who is making a better decisions about life. Twins who fight so badly with one another can end up not talking to each other. This deep estrangement begins in anger and feelings of shame about the twin. Shameful feelings lead to humiliation and an inability to be together. Being and living very separate lives seems to relieve the hatred and self-loathing that twins feel for one another.

Split-identity twins get real comfort and enjoyment from one another in childhood because of the attention they receive for being twins. Fighting and the beginning of estrangement, some report as early as 6, grows as twins make their own friends and find their own paths in life. I remember at the age of 23 being in psychotherapy to deal with deep feelings of loneliness. A light bulb in my mind—an insight came to me that changed my life forever. I realized that Marjorie and I were expected to be alike. We were rewarded for being clones of one another. But in reality we were treated differently and we were very different in our interests and friendships. She was the favored twin and I was the loser. We wanted to be separate because on some level we did not really like each other but being together was comfortable and also an expectation.

Thankfully we saw the world differently and went our own ways. Getting through my seriously damaged self-esteem took countless hours of psychodynamic psychotherapy. Psychotherapy was extremely valuable to my sister as well. Fighting with my twin was so painful and at first confusing that it was difficult to contend with my feelings. Marjorie was ashamed of me because I was fat when I got pregnant. Or she was embarrassed that I married a medical student and appeared to be materialistic and empty-headed. She was embarrassed that I didn't finish my master's degree. On and on it went. And when I became a doctor she was disappointed that I could not rest on my laurels while she caught up with me. Gradually we got further and further apart, which was such a relief. All along, we needed help to understand that we were different.

Typical fights that split-identity twins have are intensely focused on right and wrong, good and bad. Fault is always the core issue of an argument and most likely an unresolved issue from childhood.

Keith and Kirk needed one another to survive their traumatic childhood. Keith was the troublemaker who was unfairly abused and protected his brother and actually nurtured him. As children into early adulthood these twins confronted life together. They shared business adventures and found solace in knowing the other's presence. As adults Kirk fell in love and married a woman who did not like Keith.

> Keith: Kirk's new wife saw me as the root of all of my brother's problems. She was like my mother blaming me for everything that went wrong in our business. She encouraged Kirk to leave the auto parts business we shared and start his own. Kirk's business did not work out. We grew further and further apart.

Deeply attached and deeply at odds with each other, Keith and Kirk fought all of the time but never split up until age 25. Keith needed to take care of his brother to give his life meaning. Keith shares: "Having grown up is such a neglectful and abusive home is the reason we spent so much time together. We had no one else."

Sandy and Scott were coupled together by their mother as the most adorable twins. They were relieved to be apart. Family favoritism of Scott and needing to take care of him was painful and burdensome for Sandy. Scott needed to be the important twin given his own emotional limitations related to fearfulness and a deep sense of inadequacy.

> Sandy: Every Christmas we would have a family party. As the years went by Scott pretended more and more that I was not at the party. I was literally there but to him I was invisible. The last Christmas that I saw him, he actually totally ignored that I was in the room. It was so embarrassing in front of family and friends. I have not seen him since then. Even though it was a silent fight it hurt me so deeply. I am afraid of men that they will hurt me like my brother.

Patricia and Pauline were buddies as children and teenagers. As they grew older and developed new friendships in college they began to fight.

> Paula: I remember that we were screaming and yelling and crying. Patty started by saying that I always got to drive the car and I was the dominant twin. She had uncommunicated expectations of me. She said that I was

responsible for our special twin bond and that I was not honoring our closeness with enough care. It was clear to me that it was my job and not her responsibility to make her happy. We had so many fights about her expectations of me that I was relieved to go away to graduate school.

Sarah and Elizabeth, like many twins who are raised in emotionally abusive home environments, were never close communicators as children. Still they got comfort from the presence of one another. Their mom wanted to twin with Elizabeth and favored her. Sarah was the bad twin and Elizabeth was the good twin. Sarah says that her sister always saw her as lesser. Sarah felt that she was not as pretty or popular as her sister. As children they did not fight about these arbitrary and untrue distinctions as both accepted their labels and roles with one another. Both grew up to be attractive and outgoing, although Elizabeth was certainly more of a risk taker.

> Sarah: Our biggest fight occurred when our father was hospitalized for seizures and suffered some brain damage. Elizabeth called me on the phone and screamed at me that Dad was not going to get better because I encouraged him to not take the medicine. His ongoing illness was my fault. She was so angry with me that I could not talk with her. I was afraid of her anger even though I knew that it was our mother's decision to ignore the doctor's request that our father had to take his medication. Once again my mother and Elizabeth ganged up against me. I was devastated and I sought out a therapist to help me understand why my sister upset me so intensely.

There are some common themes in split-identity twin fighting:

1. You are not good enough to me. Change now as I need more attention and devotion.
2. I need more help and attention. You are heartless. You have abandoned me to your own life goals. I feel left out and abandoned.
3. You are being so stupid about X. If you had finished college I wouldn't have to be embarrassed about your low-paying blue-collar job.
4. You are so fat and ugly. I don't know why you can't find a diet and a stylist. I cannot bear to see you looking like this. You are a mess.
5. Your success enrages me. Why won't you leave me alone so I can see myself as the accomplished twin. Remain invisible. Don't bother to share your success with me.
6. You are a total loser. Please stay as far away from me as you can or I will try and hurt you.

As you can see, the intensity of the anger and animosity between split-identity twins varies. The more abusive the family life the more intense anger and violence is expressed and experienced by the children. In terms of mental health and the ability to make your own life, split-identity twins who are able to overcome their serious personality limitations based on traumatic life experiences are better off than interdependent-identity twins. Twins with a singular sense of self outside of their twin identity are able to expand their world more fully. Still the fighting twins who are opposites of one another in the twin part of their identity go through horrific emotional devastation which can lead to estrangement. Talking about injustices can be helpful for both twins, but talking can also lead to more alienation. Too much fighting can be very destructive in young adulthood. In midlife there is more acceptance of differences and embarrassment may be diminished. Later in life split-identity twins may try and get along on some level in order to share the burdens of their senior years.

Individual-Identity Twins

The attention that twins who are seen as unique receive from parents helps them to contend with their competitiveness and fears of being different from one another and learning when and when not to share. Parenting that takes into consideration individuality and the depth of the twin bond helps to prevent identity confusion between twins and fighting that on some level is meaningless and can be very destructive and toxic. Appropriately raised twins will fight and compete with each other, and be able to let go of the fight. Twins who have had good enough parenting are different than interdependent-identity twins because they can stick to their own point of view and do not give in to their twin or just react as if there was never a problem. The intense self-righteousness of split-identity twins is toned down and put into perspective because they are not functioning as parents to one another.

Twins with enough sense of self can be reasonable with one another. Not over-reacting to problems is a strength that has been validated by parents. Twin pairs have learned from their parents to accept that competition is not a do or die event. Rather competition is a natural dimension of twinship that has some validity in an objective context. While separation experiences can bring out anger in one another, realities of life are also taken into consideration. For example, that Melinda gets to go to Europe and Lisa has to stay home and finish college is difficult for both but not overly important because of the reality that they are different people with different responsibilities. Enough experiences of being on their own dilutes the pain of feeling different. Acceptance of your twin as a special person who is different from you is possible. Separation anxiety from the twin is tolerable. Fearing your twin's reaction to your decision-making is much less intense.

Still twins with a strong sense of self fight and compete over who is right and who is wrong. But they do not hold on to their anger. Often they use their twin's ideas to improve upon what they are being criticized for to begin with. They trust each other. Lisa shares her struggle with her sister:

> I wanted Karen to go back to work and stop being so reliant on her husband's income. I wanted to teach her day trading. I set up her computer

system so we could work on my internet business together at my house and her house. But our plan never worked out. We could not work together as business partners. We both agreed that it was not a realistic idea that could be implemented.

In general there is less intensity between twins with enough individual identity. Intensity that is shared is more positive and based on the security of knowing that they are able to work things out.

> Janet: My sister Marilyn and her husband were a little provincial for my husband who was more of a show off than her husband. There were always disagreements about where we should go to dinner. Once my husband said if we can't go to the four star French restaurant we might as well go to McDonald's. Of course my sister's husband was irate as they lived a more modest lifestyle. We could accept that we had selected different lifestyles by our choice of husbands. We did not want to change each other.

Separation anxiety, competition, fighting, and fears of expansiveness are apparent in twins with good enough individual development. Working to overcome being different than your twin is a manageable goal of psychotherapy.

You Are Not Your Twin

What Fighting Means to Twins

Fighting is a way of establishing that you are different from your twin. Fighting can be normal and healthy and most of all inevitable. Fighting for young twins can be fun at first, almost a game. But there are real identity issues that are involved in disagreements and differences of opinion and too much sharing. The pattern of twinship that is established in childhood from the type of parenting that is available will determine the quality and intensity of fighting.

Twin fights change as twins grow and develop. Disagreements are always an important form of communication between twins. Unresolved anger issues are deep-seated in a primary attachment and they are very different than siblings fighting. The shared identity between twins—the twin bond—has to be understood and shared or eliminated through estrangement. Even twins who are estranged know that they are a twin who can't get along with their twin. There is always pain and disappointment when twins fight.

The Twin Bond Makes Fighting More Intense, Serious, and Frightening

Over the last several decades I have gotten many many phone calls and emails from adult twins who are learning to live separate lives. Separate lives can lead to emotional confusion about who you are as a twin and as an individual.

Getting along as very different people is often a serious problem for twins. Sometimes a twin asks about fighting with their twin or disappointment with their twin, but the core issue that twins ask me about is always related to how they can get along with their twin.

I have spent a lifetime trying to get along with my twin sister. Sometimes I have been successful in accepting her way of dealing with me. Sometimes we have been successful getting along. And at other times I have had to distance myself from her. There are no easy answers to creating harmony between twins that I have found as a twin and as a psychologist. Without a doubt, twins have conflicted and complicated relationships because of the power of their bond. Non-twins cannot understand their deep pull toward one another and their deep resentment. Smart parents are certainly in the right when they take separation of their twins as crucial to their children's happiness and social–emotional well-being.

From my perspective, the first thing that you have to do to get along with your twin is to understand that you are each individuals who share a deep bond. YOU ARE NOT YOUR TWIN. No matter how identical you and your twin appear to be, you are each special and individual. Each twin within a twin pair sees the world through his or her own eyes even though twins share a very deep and primary bond. Fortunately, twins usually have different interests and want to live separate lives. It is natural and healthy for twins to have their own friends when they are feeling self-confident. When life gets tough, twins want the comfort of their twin identity. They may turn to each other for support in times of crisis. Closeness can and will lead to arguments when emergency situations are resolved (Klein, 2003).

Strategies to De-Escalate Fighting

Fighting is a result of too much closeness and too much need for mutuality. You and your twin do not have to agree with each other. Essential to a non-combative relationship is respect for one another. Saying this is easy, but holding onto who you are and how you are different from your twin is hard to do. You try to be supportive and understanding, but you can become frustrated with your twin interaction. From my longstanding interest in twin development and the many people I have worked with over the last 30 years, here are some tips that can diffuse the deep entanglements that twins experience.

For Parents:

1. Carefully develop a unique attachment to each of your twin children when they are born and as they grow.
2. Talk to each child about how special they are to you as an individual and as a twin.
3. Respect your twin children's deep attachment by giving their relationship space to grow.

4   Discipline the child who misbehaves, not the twin pair.
5   Encourage close helpers such as grandparents, teachers, and nannies to treat your twins as individuals.
6   Gradually separate your twins, being careful to talk about how they feel being separated. Teach your children ways to cope with missing one another.
7   Put competition between your twins in perspective by using a narrative to explain that the reasons for competition are time limited.

For Adult Twins and Their Therapists:

1   Try to understand your anger at your twin and put your anger into perspective. For example, your twin sister is too busy to help you babysit your children because of her own life. Accept this explanation and get another babysitter.
2   Respect your twin's differences. Your twin loves someone who is really not your type. So why would you like the same person?
3   Have an objective and subjective understanding of how you are different and similar to your twin. Continue these conversations as often as necessary until they are embedded in your mind.
4   Identify areas of harmony and disharmony. Obviously some activities may make one twin unhappy and the other twin happy. My sister loved to travel and listen to rock music. I was not a good traveler and liked classical piano. Respect each other's differences.
5   Look at your anger or feelings of estrangement as a temporary state of mind that can change with time. Maybe your sense of estrangement won't change overnight but in the long run understand why you are so angry.
6   Value the harmony you have with one another and try and make that the focus of your adult relationship. Develop twin rituals like hiking, or shopping, or family dinners and make sure they happen on a regular basis.

Detoxify Your Twin Relationship

Onlookers to twin relationships can idealize the closeness and companionship that twins share. For instance, twins sometimes are envied by people who suffer from loneliness and depression. Indeed, for those seeking the perfect mate, twins are supposedly excellent role models, to be admired and copied for their capacity for understanding and empathy. In actuality, twins can suffer and be stifled by one another. While the twin attachment is strong, enduring, and very close, the twin bond can also be fraught with competition, obligation, fear, anger, and resentment. Twins learn to take care of one another from birth. Hands down, they are deeply attached. Sharing parents, life experiences, and memories promotes a deep and indestructible early twin identity. Separating from your twin can be traumatic, liberating, and tricky. As each twin develops a unique identity, both twins may feel excited and frightened.

Unfortunately, enmeshment and resentment can poison the twin attachment. Twinship can easily become toxic when clear boundaries between twins are seriously confused and the unique individuality of each member of the pair is not respected. Twins can feel betrayed by one another, ignored (even invisible), or deeply disappointed in their sister or brother. How to have a healthy relationship with your twin can be totally mysterious to twins in the throes of fighting with each other or having difficulty living separate lives. The following ideas will hopefully help the reader unravel and face the stress of drawing clear boundaries with their brother or sister. Not over-reacting to your twin's problems with school, friends, food, clothes, children, and partners/spouses is very difficult. NOT taking on your twin's problems can be almost impossible at first. These strategies will help you detoxify your relationship (www.drbarbaraklein.com).

Establish a Non-Discussion Zone

Twins like to evaluate one another's decisions, which can limit the development of individuality. When certain topics, such as friendships outside of the twin relationship, are not up for discussion, the possibility of critical and anxious input from your twin will be avoided. For example, your twin gets a job that you think is not right for him. Instead of sharing your concern, you could say, "I respect your decision." In other words, don't share every thought and feeling you have with your twin. Privacy is very important to the development of a mature attachment.

Establish a Non-Comparison Zone

Because twins are natural competitors, comparisons between twins can be endless—whether the comparison originates from your twin or an onlooker asking inappropriate questions about who is smarter, richer, prettier, etc. I suggest trying to eliminate areas of comparison because this will limit enmeshment and issues of identity. To onlookers or your twin you could say: "Measuring ourselves against one another is something that I think should be avoided." If you respect your twin you will be able to accept what they look like, what they want to be, who they want to be a partner with, and so on.

When you compare yourself to one another you are regressing back to a younger age than you are at this time. Share if you have more with your twin. If not, let it be. You are different people.

Make some People, Objects, and Ideas Non-Sharable

Fighting over what belongs to whom begins with young twins and can move into adulthood. I advise parents of young twins to give each twin some toys and clothes that are not sharable as well as some personal possessions that can be shared. Drawing the line or setting a boundary about what belongs to each twin exclusively is critical to eliminating fighting and general confusion over ownership. This lesson when learned will help the twin relationship mature.

The worst thing to share, in my personal and professional experience, is friendships. This is a no-win situation for everyone involved. The twin attachment will be treasured in spite of an important new interpersonal relationship. By this I do not mean that social interactions with twins and new friends are bad. What is destructive is when twins do not respect the privacy and importance of their twin's new relationship.

Fighting and Rampant Anger Are Destructive to the Twin Attachment

Try to calmly talk to your twin about what is bothering you. I have heard crazy stories of twins pulling one another's hair or actually being physically aggressive. Yelling, mean conversations, and attacking each other accomplishes nothing of positive value. It is better to get distance from your anger if you cannot control it. Anger can burn the bridges of attachment that twins share in adulthood, and while divorce is not an option, anger can destroy twin attachment, which can be very difficult to rebuild.

Don't Go Down with Your Twin / Hold Up Your Twin

Drowning in your twin's problems is a sure mistake based on your lack of ego boundaries. Try to help your brother or sister keep their head above water when their problems are very serious and complicated. Hold out your hand and help them swim to shore. If you totally ignore your sister or brother you are at risk of alienating your right-hand "go to" person. If you drown there is no hope.

Focus on Empathic Interactions

Understanding and kindness can begin to heal the most tormented relationships. Taking the high road is always better for twins because of the depth of their attachment to one another. Just reflecting on your twin's pain is a start to reconnection. Go slowly in giving advice to your adult twin.

Do Fun Activities

Being together in companionship is something that twins do well. Hiking, going to museums, concerts, traveling, and non-competitive shopping are all activities that twins can really enjoy together. Loving family time can build the attachment between adult twins.

***

Adult twins have different relationships than young twins. Getting along with your twin is not as easy as it may look to an uneducated onlooker. Twins always have highs and lows. They love being apart and then they miss the other. Try the strategies I have suggested. These ways of thinking about getting along with your twin have helped me and helped the many twins that I consult with (www.drbarbaraklein.com).

Parenting Style is Critical to the Twin Relationship's Maturity

Fighting is a serious issue for young twins, parents of twins, and adult twins. Twin fighting is a style of interaction and a part of identity development that grows out of the twin bond and lives on and on as small children develop into adults. Competition is one acceptable and understandable form of fighting. Twins always measure themselves against one another. Who is the best? Who deserves more brownies? Who has the trendiest Lego? Who has the coolest boyfriend? Who has the best car? Disarming competition can be extremely difficult and troubling for everyone close to a twin pair. Brothers and sisters, parents, grandparents, aunts and uncles, teachers, and psychotherapists can become overwhelmed and confused by predictable and sometimes understandable twin fighting.

Let's look at the complexity of the twin attachment or bond, which some psychologists might label as overdependent or a form of enmeshment. Competition is rooted in the twin bond. Twins are born "married." Twin closeness is based on a primary attachment that is irreplaceable, much like the parent–child attachment that is the footprint of identity. Nurturing and interdependence between twins is deep and all-encompassing in infancy and childhood. Personality development and the need to be competitive is established and based on twin attachment. Separating out and finding individual differences between twins is a serious and important struggle for parents and their twins. Emotional health and an ability to see the serious side effects of fighting are based on each twin's individual development.

It is critical to keep in mind that co-dependence, interdependence, and over-identification are not sharing but forms of a psychological merger. Sharing and harmony, often idealized by twin onlookers, grow out of an acceptance by each twin of differences. Telling twins to respect one another is a meaningless task when twins share too much of their identity. Practical ways to foster sharing and eliminate competition are based on developing individuality and unique interests and gifts in each of your twins or clients. Yes, twins are individuals even if they are very similar. Twin sharing is a way to limit individual development and intensify competition. Parents who want their twins to really get along will seriously limit sharing, both overt and covert, that goes on between twins. Therapists should do likewise. Adult twins will establish firm boundaries about what objects and thoughts are sharable and what are off limits.

Teaching twins to share or learning to share with your twin should be orchestrated. In other words, parents and twins themselves need to see their individuality and respect their uniqueness. In order to teach twins to share you must let them experience "real" sharing. One way to encourage sharing is to teach them the difference between mine and yours. For example, designate some important objects in the non-share zone. Parents can see which toys, clothing, and friends are special and keep them as separate. Other toys, friends, etc. can be shared and labeled as such. Adult twins know not to share but they can tumble or fumble into sharing everything, including opinions and advice and "too much information." Adult twins need to learn to respect their twin by not being critical. From first-hand experience I know that keeping your unsolicited thoughts to yourself can be very difficult because twins see themselves in one another. Unfortunately, sharing critical thoughts is destructive to the health of the twin attachment as the aging process takes hold.

Young twins, teenage twins, and adult twins need to have exclusive no-sharing zones. The following strategies will make psychological room for the no-share space between twins.

1. As a parent or a therapist, know and talk about differences between your twins.
2. Be aware of sharing behavior and try to understand why it is necessary. Ask yourself: Do your twins need more individual attention?
3. As a twin, understand the times when you are co-dependent and why?
4. Talk about what you would like to share and what is private and respect these boundaries.
5. Remember, you are not your twin.

Thoughts and Strategies for Therapists to Contain Anger Wars

> *Dear Dr. Klein,*
> *I am suffering from a severe twin problem. I am married and I have three wonderful children. My twin sister is single and she has never had children. I am so upset and angry with her for not finding a man to marry and have children with. Her lack of direction and support is an unbearable situation for all of us, and it affects my marriage ... Our relationship is complicated and competitive but this situation is a climax of it all. I cannot be happy if my sister is unhappy and alone. What does this mean for the rest of my life. Can you help?*
> *Susan*

This internet question reveals the following issues that therapists can work on with their twin clients.

1. No matter how old your twin clients are it is important to keep in mind that sharing that is based on the wrong reasons such as convenience or the neglect of identity definition will lead to serious fighting and entanglements. Help your client understand this issue and implement a non-competition and non-sharing policy. Or help your client see that it is really very healthy for twins to be different.

2   Work slowly to understand the twin dynamic that is creating fighting as it is always complicated and can change easily in younger twins. In teenage years fighting is acceptable but should be limited. Adult twins should limit their unleashed anger if possible through individual therapy.
3   Try to establish a structure for your client that allows for time apart from one another. Too much time together at any age will lead to anger and fighting.
4   Sharing friends is always a problem for twins as alliances with others are confusing. Try to avoid friend sharing if possible.
5   Significant others will have problems with your twin client's twin. Never underestimate the extent of these ongoing problems and the need for your client to develop independence from their twin.

When Fighting Leads to Estrangement

Defining Estrangement

Estrangement is a subjective emotional experience that makes twins afraid to be together or actually unable to be together because of deep hatred. Parenting style creates the development of estrangement (Klein, 2012). Estrangement also causes deep shame because twins are supposed to get along. These dark feelings seem to be deep-seated and often have a traumatic element to them. Estrangement—serious avoidance of one another—between twins can be permanent depending on what triggered the darkness. Estrangement is most likely if twins have been sexually abused by parents or had an incestuous relationship with one another. Also, if one twin sleeps with their brother or sister's romantic partner and their twin finds out, these enactments will lead to problems in reuniting. Abuse in childhood is acted out between the twin pair. This dynamic is of course hard to understand. In my experiences working with twins, if the anger between twins is not acted out through serious death threats but just fought about, twins will take long breaks and come back together over serious life-threatening situations.

I have worked with twins who are deeply estranged from one another after many years of heart-felt fighting which turns in some cases to enormous fear or hatred of their sister or brother. Tension cannot be resolved. There is no compromise that is acceptable to both. There is no available negotiator or therapist that can deal with this deep and entrenched bond that has been fractured. In my experience psychotherapy cannot effectively reunite twins. Often twins seek out individual therapy as adults to feel better about themselves as individuals. Insight into your estrangement from your twin is a very healing possibility if the therapist understands the idiosyncrasies of twin development.

Twin estrangement is found in the split-identity pattern of twinship. Opposite labels—good/bad, competent/helpless—create anger and embarrassment, as well as confusion about why they have received mixed messages about being twins. Split-identity twins are treated as different and then the same. Understanding and entangling their relationship is extremely difficult and very emotionally painful for the pair who are placed in these confusing psychological circumstances. There are different ways that estrangement affects twins.

Loneliness Is Almost a Certainty for Estranged Twins

Loneliness is a side effect of estrangement. Loneliness is a very hard state of mind for a twin to experience, which is why twins fight so hard not to be alienated from one another. Loneliness can be physically painful. Loneliness can overwhelm and depress the twin who is more vulnerable to criticism. In my own words I would describe my experience of loneliness thus:

> For me loneliness was frightening. I first felt the emotional panic of loneliness with a boyfriend not my twin sister. When I fell in love at 16, I would wait for my boyfriend to call me. If he was a minute late in calling the loneliness started. I was missing him and felt like I would be totally lost and would come unglued if he did not call me. I imagined the world ending. Thankfully he did call. As might be expected, my brother and sister had fun teasing me about the strength of my reaction.
>
> I took my symptoms very seriously. I worked very hard to avoid the panicky feeling of being lost and alone at all costs. Keeping busy helped keep the loneliness away. Boyfriends and back-up boyfriends, academic success, marriage, my two loving children, trying to get along with my twin, writing books, becoming a doctor, and my own psychoanalysis were all outlets to diminish my sensitivity to missing someone or longing for understanding. Gradually over many years I was able to stop running away from my fear of being alone. I learned that the world would go on if I felt alone.
>
> Painful losses of my parents, my long first marriage, and the hopeless state of my relationship with my twin made me realize that I would survive if I was missing someone. I actually admitted to myself that I would get over my missing problem and deep loneliness which was painful and scary. As I started talking about the loneliness problem, I felt less afraid of it. Talking and writing about being "Alone in the Mirror" (Klein, 2012) helped me. The love of my children, friends and second husband have eased my pain of being alone in this world. Working with twins in individual and group therapy has not only given me a platform for my ideas but it has created a new circle of twins to identify with and to help. Feeling connected to my identity as a twin has brought meaning and companionship to my life. While I wish that I had a stronger connection with my sister, my loneliness is diminished because of the work I have done understanding what it means to be a twin.

I work with an identical male twin who reported that the pain of his loneliness can be seen in Edward Munch's painting *The Scream*. Stephen feels that Munch's painting reflects his state of mind when he feels loneliness. Stephen reports:

> I have experienced what I would term "loneliness" for much of my adult life. My loneliness is a powerful yearning, a longing, a craving for a profound connection with another human being. I have felt incomplete in hindsight since I was 18 years old when my brother and I went our separate ways.
>
> My loneliness has a strong physical element—a warm pain in my chest which is not related to heart disease.
>
> At worse this loneliness is an excruciating psychological experience, which dominates overwhelmingly everything I do. On such days I feel really desperate. I do know now that it will eventually subside only to return again. The loneliness is unfathomable. The mornings are always the worst. My ongoing divorce has exacerbated these feelings but has not created them.

Stephen is aware of his loneliness and identified it as a problem that needed to be understood. Fortunately, he sought out cognitive behavioral psychology help to decrease his symptoms of physical and emotional pain. Group and individual therapy with a focus on his twin development has helped Stephen accept his "loneliness pain" as a part of his unresolved feelings of separation anxiety from his twin brother.

Sandy agrees with Stephen that loneliness is a physical pain in their chest or heart:

> I have experienced true loneliness through isolation which I impose upon myself. I was ostracized by my twin and my family took his side. My husbands were useless as they were unable to provide the emotional connections that I longed for so deeply. I made my own pain worse. I lived in a foreign country where I couldn't speak the language or make friends. I wanted to be isolated. I didn't want to feel my loneliness. And I wanted to protect my parents from my loneliness.
>
> When I finally fell in love I was in my late forties. Connecting emotionally with a romance took me a long time. We started out as friends who shared an interest in nature. We were both members of a Naturalist club. As our relationship turned into a romance, I loved being in love. And then it was over in three months because his mother did not approve of me. Almost a year has gone by and I am missing a long-gone romantic partner. At first I was totally heartbroken and overwhelmed.
>
> I found a therapist to help me understand what happened to me was related to my relationship with my twin brother. I am better at understanding why I was so hurt. But often I feel an overwhelming pain in my heart like a migraine. I start to cry and I can't stop. It is funny but taking aspirin will help the pain subside. I have learned in individual and group therapy that this loss mirrors the loss of my twin brother which I have never grieved over. We are estranged from each other and prefer to leave our contact as such.

One year ago Sandy sought out psychological help at the end of her first true love relationship. She now understands that the way she has approached relationships with men relates to her estranged relationship with her brother. She is extremely fearful of deep commitments with men even though she would very much love to have a partner to share her life with.

Sarah feels the pain of loneliness in her whole body:

> My sister and I were not close twins. We didn't talk to each other that much because my sister was so close with our mother. Mom and Elizabeth acted like twins sharing thoughts and feelings. I was the outsider. Still we walked to school together and shared a car and some friends. When we each got married and had our separate lives I began to have very strong feelings of loneliness. After a huge fight which lasted five years with no contact, I looked to therapy to understand what had happened between Elizabeth and me. The best way I can describe my confusion and despair is the image that something is missing. I feel it as a burn in my heart. It is a childhood feeling. I imagine holding my daughter as a baby and this visualization seems to help the pain to go away. My other coping strategy for dealing with deep loneliness was to keep my distance from other people so I would not be hurt by them. I did become isolated. And I had to learn to make friends but I always feel disappointed in them. I want to find a friend who I can really trust. Group has helped me feel better about myself because everyone in group is a smart, kind, warm, and supportive twin.

Sarah has worked tirelessly to find friends that she feels can be there for her. Sarah tends to take care of everybody and then feel some resentment and loneliness. This conflict is a reflection of her deep loneliness for emotional connection. Her husband, children, and work as a school librarian have helped her to feel better about herself. And now she feels OK with saying no to other teachers and principals who want to take advantage of her intellectual strength and persistence.

Pauline suffered from overwhelming loneliness which turned to depression and suicidal thoughts when she was separated from her twin sister as a graduate student. She shares:

> I don't know when I started to see isolation and death as a solution to my loneliness which was very intense. I believe it began one day when I was sitting on the bleachers at the gym. I noticed an exit door to my right. I had never really seen that door before and at the moment that I consciously recognized it as a door I had the feeling of walking through it and leaving forever. I imagined myself getting up, going out the door, walking away and never stopping. I did not recognize that my thoughts were of leaving this world as an alternative to living. But they continued to torment me in other forms of isolation and feeling trapped or encased.

In my late forties after many years of thoughts of being in a situation that led to death, I have realized as I have worked on my identity as a twin that this feeling is related to the loss of the closeness I had with my sister. Knowing that I am a twin has helped me accept and understand that I need to be close to people who understand me deeply, as close relationships reduce my feelings of loneliness. Still I am careful about getting involved with other people and ask for help. I need to feel in control and in charge or every detail.

Pauline came to understand the deep connection with her sister has changed over time. Because both of them have taken different roads in life to find themselves as individuals, they needed one another in different ways. A mature adult relationship had to be developed. Seeing that over-trying with everyone was a symptom of unconsciously feeling lonely for the connection she had with her sister, who she took care of no matter what, helped Pauline overcome her role as an emotional servant to others. Patty is still working on accepting that Paula cannot improve her sense of self.

Keith like Sandy never sees his brother. When his brother got married their deep animosity grew into warlike anger. His brother's wife distrusted Keith and blamed him for "everything that went wrong." After a huge fight which ended with his brother threatening to shoot him, all ties were broken.

> Keith: I began to see a therapist to talk about my loneliness. Even though Kirk took my mother's side against me and made me responsible for his well-being, I needed him for my sense of self. He was my room mate and business partner. I had spent my whole life with him. I was totally lost and I sought out psychotherapy. I worked with this kind and compassionate psychiatrist to overcome the loss of my brother. I was devastated by his absence. I attended sessions twice a week to get over the shame of abuse I suffered as a child but to also let go of my brother and deal with my loneliness. I still miss him and think about him every day. I am beginning to understand the connection to my twin identity.

Twin loss presents a more intense form of loneliness. In my twin estrangement group we have discussed the differences between losing your twin to fear and hatred as opposed to death. Both are painful in a deeply psychological way, but different. With estrangement there is always hope, which actually may be false hope, that you will rekindle your relationship. Some people manage to work through estrangement as adults. But there is a great deal of disillusionment and depression that is connected to a loss that you cannot really grieve. With twin loss you have to hold on to your good memories to survive your grief and move on. Vince shares the loneliness he felt as a result of his brother's suicide:

> Victor and I shared a world of enmeshment, which was a result of severe childhood abuse. Intermingling of our personality and disassociation from

emotional and severe pain was common but necessary to our survival. Understanding who I was after my loss became paramount to my own survival as a lone twin.

The loneliness I felt in the first six to eight months was all black and all encompassing. Gradually my fear of loneliness subsided and became a sink hole that I would carefully walk around. Holding on to my good memories helped me stay out of the blackness. Some days it was torture to not fall into the sink hole of loneliness. Did it take me too long to stay away from the darkness? I will never be able to answer this question.

Six years have passed since my loss. I survived my own suicide attempt. I found strength to persist, move through the overwhelming emotions of anger, hate, depression, hurt, betrayal, related to his disappearance from my world, our world. I don't hold on as tightly to the memory of my dead brother's face in the emergency room.

The days of profound loneliness are less frequent. New experiences, relationships, support in therapy both individual and group, have helped me to heal and understand myself better. My healing has provided light where *the night of darkness with no stars once existed.*

In this reflection Vince is alluding to loneliness of loss as being related to pure darkness. He survives by slowly finding a way out of this dark, bad, painful state by talking and writing about his experience of loss in a memoir *Naked Angels*. Friendships bring light back to his life. Staying away from the triggers of darkness are also healing. Understanding the devastation of twin loss by connecting with the Twin Less Twin Organization has promoted his healing and survival.

Linda who lost her twin sister in an airplane accident shares her thoughts of loneliness. Linda says:

When I was able to acknowledge the depth of my twin loss and start my grieving, a pervasive loneliness accompanied me everywhere. As my healing journey unfolded, the loneliness was ever present, intensifying on birthdays and anniversaries. Its gradual lessening gave me more comfort in the world, as it appeared to be replaced by a searching for another perfect match, a piece to be original pair. ... I remember the horrible pain that accompanied my feelings of aloneness, probably made worse by not being able to share this strange pain with another human being. After meeting other twins who experienced the loss of their twin, I began to feel supported and not so alone. The word "loneliness" never matched the feelings because I was not feeling lonely, but drastically, and unarmed alone, a totally foreign feeling in my world as I knew it.

Like Vince, Linda suffers a profound loss and struggles to find her own way. Her work with other survivors of twin loss has helped this community of twins and helped her to contribute to others who have suffered like she has.

Having an identification with others who have gone through what you have experienced has helped Linda heal herself (Brothers, 2008; Togashi, 2015).

The loneliness of estrangement and twin loss looks different or has unique manifestations or enactments in different pairs of twins. Still the underlying security of self-connection with the primitive twin relation in utero and throughout childhood creates painful feelings of loss, depression, emptiness, and alienation. Fortunately, not all twins will go through this dark and confusing experience.

Common Questions About Estrangement

Dear Dr. Klein,
My twin sister and I live in Quebec at opposite sides of the city. We are 61 years old and we have both lived successful lives. Our mother just recently died and I am experiencing irrational anger at my sister which is not very attractive or understandable at our age. I am having difficulty being with her. We both read your book Alone in the Mirror *and fit into your split identity pattern of twin ship. I was the good twin and she was the bad twin. I have been in therapy for many years thinking that we were normal twins. Since mother's death I realized that I have never separated from my twin sister Jean. When we went to scatter our mother's ashes I was almost unable to contain my anger with her. My anger feels so new and I am afraid of my twin sister. I really don't want to be estranged from Jean but it seems like my only option. Any words of wisdom?*

Karen

Dear Karen,
Thank you for your courage in sharing your painful thoughts with me. I do agree that estrangement is very much an end of the line action you take when all hope is gone. Estrangement is hard for both twins. I have experience working with twins who are totally enraged with each other. Understanding and acceptance of estrangement is the best outcome. I cannot promise a happy ending.

Dr. Klein

Dr. Klein,
I am a fraternal twin and I cannot get along with my twin sister. We are in our fifties and I can't believe we have not settled our disappointment with each other. We get along and then there is a horrible fight. I miss her but I am afraid of her. I have been in intense psychotherapy to understand my divorce and get on with my life. My therapist knows nothing about twin relationships. I gave her a copy of your book on twins and she asked if she could read my underlinings. I was troubled by her indifference. Can you help?

Arlene

Hi Arlene,
I am hoping that what I know about twin relationships in the adult years will help you feel more accepting of the ongoing struggle with your sister. I am very aware that most therapists are not as educated as they might be

about twin issues. It might be helpful to work with someone who knows more about twin development.

Dr. Klein

Shame and Humiliation are Side Effects of Twin Estrangement

Judy: I am embarrassed to share that I am a twin when you and I lack a mutual caring, reciprocal, and responsible twinship. I long for that relationship and have been hurt about it for years. I cannot accept that my behavior is the reason. A relationship is built by two people. There has to be room for both of us to discuss what triggers the blaming and shaming that goes on between us.

Amy: I try to maintain a positive relationship with Judy. Her screaming and yelling when I was in the hospital woke up the neighbors and embarrassed me. I prefer that our fights are kept rational and the words spoken are said at a reasonable tone. When she comes to visit she is on the war path and mows any one down who is in the way. Shame and humiliation is the price I pay for her help.

Twins want to get along. When they just can't, for all of the reasons I have gone over and over, they feel ashamed of themselves. I have spoken with so many twins who feel like misfits in this world because they experience distance and distrust with their twin. Twins want to be "normal" twins who get along and can't wait to see each other. I recall in my long fighting stage with my sister how embarrassed I felt about not getting along with her. At first I pretended not to be a twin as we were living in different parts of the world. When my secret came out mostly everybody I met made me feel like I was not trying hard enough to get along. I should be loving and concerned about my sister. I wrote a book called *Not All Twins Are Alike: Psychological Profiles of Twinship* to show the world that getting along was a fantasy not a reality for all twins. While this project of self-disclosure and qualitative research was effective, it did not take away the deep despair I had within me that I could not get along with my twin.

What is so interesting for me is that twins who get along cannot understand the twins who don't get along. I have met twins who are horrified that my sister and I are estranged. But twins who can't get along understand what it is like to fight over and over about who is right and who is wrong, who is smarter and prettier, and who is richer and more mature. It can deplete a relationship. Guilt over what one twin needs and what the other twin should give can be torturous for both. For example, twin A needs protection and twin B wants her freedom. Both are unhappy and fight about how they are being taken advantage of by the other. Unfortunately, too many decades of fighting and resentment will lead to estrangement.

Explaining your intense feelings of estrangement to outsiders is almost impossible. In sharp contrast twins who are estranged want to talk with other twins who are having similar issues. When twins read my books or articles online about estrangement and call me, they are thankful that someone understands. My twin estrangement groups provide support, solace, and insight to twins who can't get along. As estranged twins learn that there are other twins who have experienced conflicts, their emotional pain is easier to tolerate. Knowing that you are not alone with your feeling of loss and disappointment is truly healing. Self-confidence and self-esteem is developed in groups for twins who cannot get along. Here are some issues that we work on together:

1 Setting boundaries for how much time you will allow yourself to be preoccupied with the disappointment of your twin relationship.
2 Understanding why estrangement is not your fault.
3 Understanding that estrangement is normal if you were raised as split-identity twins.
4 Ways to go beyond your original twin identity.
5 How to develop a more expansive sense of self and find new significant others.

Conclusions

Feelings of anger, animosity, resentment, traumatic fear, or deep-seated anxiety in early life can become a part of the twin attachment and live on throughout the lifespan. These primitive or even preverbal experiences create a twin bond with toxic features. While careful parenting is totally essential, no one can protect children from the unknown stressful events in life which causes scarring to the psyche and affect the development of a positive and expansive sense of self. Twin loss or serious illness can alter the nature of the twin attachment in dramatic ways. One twin's pain will direct the other twin's journey. While life journeys will cross paths, they should be separated.

Twinship has been idealized but not investigated. Understanding that the twin attachment is very complicated is the first step in understanding the twin relationship which has a variety of faces from love, harmony, and balance to anger, jealousy, and deep disappointment. Fighting is a natural aspect of being a twin and needs to be accepted by parents, close caregivers, therapists, teachers, siblings and spouses. Estrangement happens and can be understood as a part of some twins' experience in life.

Self-awareness and understanding from others is the only way to heal the deep pain that twins feel when they are at odds with each other. Judgements such as that twins have "ego boundary issues" are handed out quickly and are confusing for twins. A counter to this unwelcome attack would be as follows. "You are rigid and lack empathy for others who depend on you." Of course twins rarely use this as a reply to uninformed critics. In my experience, twins cannot really understand their vulnerabilities to being judged by others, but they are hurt by such judgments. More understanding of twin issues will shed light on intimacy from a subjective point of view.

Undoubtedly it is natural and normal for twins to get along and be secure and happy with each other especially in childhood. Separate experiences can lead to anger, disappointment, bickering, and fighting. In many twinships fighting is disarmed in middle age. However, when twins have been raised as opposites of one another estrangement may go on for many years or forever. When twins understand deeply that they are different than their twin and need to make their own choices, fighting will be reduced and more understandable.

Questions for Twins and Their Parents, Teachers, and Therapists to Explore in Order to Curtail Arguments

1. Is this point of contention worth the time and stress it will create or should I ignore it?
2. What is my objective in fighting with my sister or brother?
3. Is there a better way to get my point across?
4. Is there a pattern or trigger to our arguments?
5. What can I do to calm down our power struggles?
6. Why am I so threatened by my twin's actions or decisions?
7. Why do I feel guilty that I cannot solve my twin's problems?

5 The Lives of Adult Twins

So, when you were talking about setting boundaries and basically drawing a line in the sand, I immediately pictured a fence. I was standing close to the fence but not right next to it—I was surrounded by green grass, wildflowers and apple trees. The sun was shining and I had a flowing summer dress on. I felt relaxed, at peace with myself and my surroundings. I had a contented smile on my face as I gazed towards my sister on her side of the fence. I didn't really picture anything specific on her side—I knew she was there and I was sure she would be fine but I was now on my lovely side of the fence and contented with just being me in this beautiful space.

Sarah H.

When we are on the same side of the fence …
We used to have fun together on the same side of the fence. It used to be easy, she used to have the sun shining on her face, happily dancing in the wildflowers, looking for the next rock to jump off. But this sunny time together feels superficial now. Looking back, she really never was that connected to me, now that I think about it—we were "us", a fun force to be reckoned with but she was always looking somewhere else, to the view just beyond the trees. I feel like I used to observe her and follow her in the fun and joy she created but our connection was somehow never that deep, maybe. She seemed to be drawn in another direction, searching or worried or unsatisfied with the moment—I don't know. We had more fun in the past on our same side of the fence, but now life has turned more serious and the deep connection I thought we had seems fake now. The sun is not shining very brightly now, the clouds have come, there is a cold wind and we both stand there not far from each other but in our own worlds—some *imaginary wall (the twin identity?)* is keeping us from really connecting.

Sarah H.

Boundary Issues: The Struggle of Adult Twins

Cementing the separation experiences and unique identities that have been established in baby steps and giant leaps in childhood, the teenage years, and early adulthood is the stressful difficult developmental chore of adulthood. In order to truly separate from one another, adult twins consciously and unconsciously seek out twin replacements. The emotionally driven need for identity is stronger than any intellectual understanding of separation in early adulthood. The intensity of motivation for unique life experiences and new significant others is very different from what siblings experience when they go their own ways. The primary attachment that twins share is being added on to—rebuilt and restored to a more up-to-date mature attachment. The "remodeling" of the twin bond is necessary, but a long-range problem that adult twins have to work through alone and together (Klein, 2012).

The quality of the attachment that is shared shapes how much independence is actually achieved in adulthood. Interdependent-identity twins well be less intent on replacing their twin, although they will try to make new personal experiences for themselves. Talking about new friendships with your enmeshed twin is difficult. Often, over-identified twins avoid these conversations for fear of displeasing their sister or brother. As adults, gradually the stored up anger and resentment shared is expressed and processed slowly. Split-identity twins will seek out twin replacements feverishly at first without being aware that they are driven to find a new complement to themselves. Discussion about the new partner that is coming into or between the twin relationship will be analyzed with a great deal of certitude by both twins. Usually, split-identity twins come to accept but not embrace their twin's partner. In contrast, individual-identity twins seek out new relationships that are intimate and intense naturally. While competition is a cornerstone of their relationship, they check in with each other about the quality of the relationship they are beginning to seek out and to make a commitment to others as well. Fear or hostility is less intense for twins who have a strong sense of themselves as individuals.

New Partner Issues

Adult twins are eager to find new partners to build their lives with. Unfortunately, they do not have as much emotional experience with non-twins—singletons—as they need in order to separate without the risk of traumatic consequences. Lack of lived experience leaves twins at a disadvantage because they have too many expectations for deep understandings that are verbal and non-verbal. Still to this day I often imagine and wish that the other person could read my mind or finish my sentence. To further complicate new relationships there is a juxtaposition of high hopes and a need to take care of the new significant other. In general, when twins leave the gate that physically separates them from their twin they are at a serious disadvantage. Desperation can grow out of their eagerness for love and companionship. Even adult twins who have had some experiences with other partners are blindsided by the lack of input from their twin and the hard-to-take reality that non-twins are very different kinds of partners. New partners might love them but not understand them as quickly or deeply as their twin. Sad but too true, in new relationships twins can be lost and wild at the same time. Confusion on the part of the new love object is bound to appear and be extremely disruptive to the future of a relationship. In other words, new boyfriends or girlfriends can feel totally overwhelmed by the expectations of a new twin partner.

In adulthood when new relationships don't work out for whatever reason, twins turn to each other for advice, comfort, and solace. Finding the next non-twin relationship can be hard because of the serious disappointment in the previous non-twin relationship. Interdependent-identity twins often just give up looking for new partners and rely on one another with a great deal of devotion. Whether these twins live next door to one another or a city away, the physical presence of the other is critical. Commonly, when children and husbands do make it into the circle of trust that twins share, they have to take the backseat to the twinship. Maintaining a primary closeness between interdependent-identity twins is not unusual in adulthood. Whether or not they fight or work side by side closeness seems to be critical to their well-being. Psychotherapy is useful as a third eye in the twinship.

Split-identity twins are better seekers of new relationships because of the underlying or unspoken shame, anger, and resentment that they have for one another. Still, opposite twins turn to each other when adult non-twin relationships fail to develop into strong commitments. Using their twin as a restorative agent to overcome disappointment, they seek out other friendships that turn into partnerships. Usually, conflicted twins find deep relationships after several unsuccessful relationships. In addition and as important, opposite-identity twins find twin replacements in their children and other close friends. Often they become driven about the quality of their relationships and their careers. Perfectionistic because of deep narcissistic injuries they received, there is a great deal of difficulty accepting what life brings to them. Accepting their accomplishments is confusing as they are programmed to only be half of a whole. Fears of expansiveness are interlaced with a quest to be the "best" they can be. Seeking out psychodynamic, interpersonal, or attachment therapy will be essential to the development of their true self as an individual (Brothers, 2008).

Individual-identity twins are often very disappointed by new partners or marriages. They naturally turn to each other for support, insight, and deep understanding. Because they love each other deeply they have a more understandable amount of trust depending on their twin as they search for a new partner. In other words, they will listen to their twin's opinion and not just take it or react against their advice. Twin replacements are usually found with partners, children, and work responsibility. An over-investment with work or finding the perfect partner can also become a life obsession. Raging anger and estrangement are not common with twins who have developed enough individuality. However, perfectionism trying to relate to others is common. Psychotherapy can be very helpful.

Disappointments, Conflicts, and Moving on

For almost all twins, twin replacement takes on different struggles and conflicts. The side effect of a search for intimacy is deep loneliness. Fitting into a new world of closeness with others and sharing your twin is totally tricky. Often one twin will feel left out or lag behind. Compassion for your twin's struggles is important. Learning how to "not go down with the ship" that your twin may be drowning in is a horrendous and complicated journey that requires insight into how you function in relation to your twin. Being yourself when you think you should be taking care of your twin is hard to do and can only be accomplished with baby steps.

Real differences in lifestyle will spark competition. One twin is richer, more successful at work, or healthier in comparison to their brother or sister. Resolutions of differences are hard to predict but they are always based on understanding how twins are different from one another. Changing the childhood twin identity into an adult twin identity that is mature and pragmatic takes a lot of devotion and work. In most instances one of the twins is more outgoing and stable than the less stable and more negative twin. The stronger twin usually initiates the maturing of the twin attachment and the use of psychotherapy.

Patterns of Twinship are Determinants of the Quality of Independence in Adulthood

Patterns of twinship create a structure that can predict the viability and the extent of individuation in adult twins. While there is a great deal of variation within each pattern of twinship, certain limitations related to the capacity for separation are evident. The capacity to psychologically deal with fears of expansiveness becomes obvious, as this development is related to the stability of the core self.

Interdependent-Identity Twins

Closeness and the need for emotional and physical constancy in spite of anger and humiliation are common for twins who share an entwined attachment. Fighting which can be very intense is not acted out in estrangement because a loss of the twin is a loss of the self, given the merger of their identities. Interdependent-identity twins can lead successful lives when they are in close proximity to one another. Let's look at how the adult lives of the twins from Chapter 1 unfolded.

Vince and Victor

As adults Vince and Victor were driven to live separate lives. Leaving home after high school graduation without any financial or emotional support for college from their family, they both managed to go to nursing school. Vince completed more nursing training then Victor and took care of him financially when it was necessary. They each had their own friends and they shared friends as well. Strident members of the gay community in their small home town in Canada, they also performed as drag queens in their late twenties with a great deal of success and a strong group of devoted followers.

Their will to live separate lives allowed them to manage to live their own separate lives in different cities at certain times in their adulthood. Victor was more adventure-driven than Vince and often got himself in deep water financially. As well he would miss his brother and dress up in his clothes and impersonate him. Vince tried to ignore his brother's impulsiveness and neediness and bailed him out as if he were his parent. When Victor developed bipolar disorder, family support was not available. Victor, who was treated with medication, psychotherapy, and hospitalization, decided he could not survive in this world. He left behind a large life insurance policy for his brother. Vince had to deal with the horrific reality of suicide through many years of psychodynamic psychotherapy and support from dear friends. Vince survived by keeping his good memories of his brother alive. Victor survived in Vince's memories and provided him with hope and love.

Psychotherapeutic Interventions

Victor was treated by psychiatrists with medication, psychotherapy, and hospitalization when his bipolar episodes became disruptive to his well-being in his forties. Treatment was not successful and Victor terminated his life by jumping off the roof of the apartment building where he was living.

Vince sought out psychotherapy after his brother's suicide. His first therapist was unable to understand the depth of his pain. The therapeutic lack of atonement led Vince to attempt suicide by overdosing on medication. His attempt was unsuccessful. Vince sought out psychotherapy with a psychologist who was familiar with twin issues. Doing twice a week psychotherapy for many years slowly allowed Vince to overcome his despair. He wrote a book *Naked Angels* about his journey through this loss. Vince was a part of a twin estrangement group that was also very healing.

Madeline and Vicki

Madeline left home at 17 to explore the world of new friends and career choices. Vicki did not leave home until she was 27. Most interesting during these ten years, Madeline would call Vicki on the phone and ask her to spend the night at her apartment when she was lonely or feeling lost and rejected. Vicki would immediately come and comfort Madeline. Anger and disappointment with one another always came to the surface when they were together. Whether or not these twins were fighting, they were able to comfort one another in deeply felt ways as they went down their own paths in their own different and separate lives.

Vicki was more social than Madeline. Vicki dated and had many friends to spend the weekend with. Vicki went to court reporting school and started a very successful court reporting business. Madeline went to college and became a CPA. Madeline went into business as well as doing accounting and she also did interior decorating. Vicki had several close relationships but never married. Living in the same neighborhood, they discussed their romantic lives and business ventures.

While they pursued different careers, both were concerned with financial stability because they grew up with very little extras. Family illness and death of their father and brother was stressful for both women. Fighting over who was responsible for caregiving was ongoing. Madeline who was always the more fragile and needy twin complained that Vicki could not understand what she was going through—how stressful her life was compared to Vicki's. Madeline was critical of Vicki for being perfectionistic and intense. Frustrated with Madeline, Vicki continues to try and help her sister to be more positive.

Fighting over who was going to make the decision about what to do next is ongoing. And then arguing was put on the back burner when financial stress seemed more serious than their anger at each other. As they grew into middle age, Vicki and Madeline worked together to be strong financially.

Psychotherapeutic Interventions

Vicki sought out psychotherapists to help improve their relationship. "Counselors" could not understand the depth of connection that united these women. Working with therapists without the understanding of the twin attachment always ended abruptly in failure. Psychotherapy with a psychologist who worked with twins was slowly successful and very difficult. Vicki and Madeline were seen together and separately. Psychotherapy was effective in that the process helped them to reduce their anger at one another. Accepting that they saw the world differently allowed them to get distance from their shameful feelings of being different which is what led to their very serious arguments. Saying this idea differently, psychotherapy helped because the therapist was an observer who accepted that these two successful women were different and would naturally respond differently to life problems. Having an outside observer reflect back to them their identity as individuals and as a pair established new ground for them to get along. Both women tried to tolerate the idea that they were different and the actions that followed allowed them to solve problems differently. The power imbalance between the pair was never corrected. Vicki remained the caregiver and Madeline remained the more fragile twin.

Adrienne and Eileen

After college graduation Adrienne and Eileen went to South America and lived on a farm. They were separated from one another and each twin made their own friendships for the first time. Their time and experience was liberating, but short-lived. When they returned home to the Southwest, the distance they had created gradually grew narrower. As they developed career interests and identity they began working together. Unlike Vicki and Madeline they did not fight with each other. Shy and lacking in experience with other people without one another they had difficulty living their own lives. Both women felt ashamed that they were so close to one another and sought out the help of different types of psychotherapy which opened the door to their problems being apart. Relying on one another was so natural that they were not aware of how dependent they were on each other.

Talent and an ability to work together allowed them to develop a decorative furniture and art business that was upscale and lucrative. Adrienne was more outgoing and engaging with clients, while Eileen took care of the financial end of their business. These twins painted together almost every day. Besides their business, both women traveled together exploring the world. They had shared friends that they met up with in their travels. When Adrienne and Eileen were on the road they were not ashamed or self-conscious about being together. Insight into why they felt more adequate when they were out of the country was never gained in psychotherapy.

Adrienne longed to have a child, a home of her own, and a husband. But her first concern was always about how her twin sister would manage without her. Whether they made the decision consciously or unconsciously, to avoid meeting new people and speed up the separation process, they undermined their independence from one another. Against the advice of parents and friends they went out to sports bars together with different groups of shared friends well into their forties. They never pursued computer dating for fear that other people would see them as inadequate. Family life with parents. siblings, friends, and relatives became the way that they socialized. Establishing friendships together and working together kept them from getting serious about romantic partners. Finally, Adrienne fell in love with a high school sweetheart. Eileen had great difficulty letting go of her sister for fear that she was involved with the wrong man.

Psychotherapeutic Interventions

A serious rift between these twins was opened when Adrienne was rejected by her romantic partner who felt second in line to Eileen. Both women sought psychotherapy for the third time to deal with their disappointment that they were not married and still together all of the time. Previously different therapeutic approaches were experienced by both women to deal with their apprehension about independence. Getting the courage to be more separate was the goal that was always considered most important in every type of psychotherapy that was pursued.

A theme of all psychotherapy was separation and taking actions toward independence. In addition, it was very difficult for Adrienne and Eileen to get angry with one another as it threatened their sense of emotional security and ability to make decisions. Family and friend support helped them to take small steps toward independence. Their journey is ongoing. The ability of the therapist to accept the pain of separation that these adult twins experienced was critical to their independent behavior. At times these women seemed to be 5 years old emotionally when they thought about not being together. These regressions were hard to understand but very real.

***

There are similarities and differences that developed between all three sets of interdependent twins. What is similar is the need for closeness, companionship, the ability to forgive, and eventually acceptance of each other's life struggles. Shared memories and lived experiences provided a deep connection that could not be destroyed in life. The deep roots of their attachment provided meaning and structure to their lives. Difficulty relating to non-twins was a common thread and will be discussed in Chapter 6.

The amount of disappointment and shame about being twins or about their twin was different between the pairs. Environmental stability varied from one pair to another. Differences between the pairs was related to the abusive nature of their childhood. Vince and Victor suffered continual physical and emotional abuse. They were treated as a burden to their family. Arguing between the pair was very limited because it brought up fears related to the abuse they had suffered through together. Victor's mental illness and suicide led to a complete separation from his brother. While suicide was a form of disappointment in his twinship and childhood in general, it was not done to enrage his brother. Suicide was an act of mental illness and desperate impulsivity.

Madeline and Vicki grew up with very strict and unempathic parents who were not tuned into their needs to be treated as individuals. They took care of each other and in many ways they were halves of a whole. Their interdependence led to anger, fighting, and shame about the other twin. Vicki was too perfectionistic and Madeline was too depressed. Still they could not really totally separate from one another because I imagine that they felt a part of one another and giving up on one another was giving up on who they were as individuals.

Adrienne and Eileen were brought up in a family with financial and educational resources. They had advantages in school to deal with their twin language and shyness. In hindsight there was a great deal of self-consciousness and shame that these women experienced during the three years they received special services which might have contributed to their sense of not fitting in with others—of being damaged. Their parents were not psychological minded enough to help them go their own ways. Arguing was much less intense between Adrienne and Eileen who sought out psychological advice and psychotherapy to separate. Adrienne and Eileen always wanted to live separate lives and kept trying. Enough love in their home life and enrichment helped them strive for new relationships. As they add new people in their lives, they are hopeful that they will become more autonomous.

In conclusion, the twin relationship that included deep over-identification with one another created a need to be close by and available to one another. The quality of the relationship varied depending on the amount of actual resources that these twins received from the world around them growing up. Twins attained strength and resilience from others in their world through learning how their relationship with their twin was different than relationships with other friends and associates.

Psychotherapy was helpful because it introduced a new set of eyes. The therapist was in a sense the third twin who saw a way out of entwined predicaments that trapped personal growth. For example, often black and white decision-making was used to make a plan. In all therapy with interdependent-identity twins learning how to look at a situation, using present details of life was a critical way to help them grow apart comfortably. Actual action plans were very helpful. For example, Adrienne and Eileen needed to know that walking around the park without one another was a way to begin their separation. Madeline and Vicki had to accept that they were different from each other. Vince had to learn that he could survive without his brother.

Split-Identity Twins

Closeness and profound sharing of thoughts, ideas and experiences are characteristic of twins who are seen as opposites of one another in childhood. Reliance on one another is common even throughout the teenage years and the tumult and unleashed anger of that time in life. In early adulthood different paths are explored freely, unlike interdependent-identity twins. While split-identity twins check in with one another all the time and fight with each other on a regular basis, the intensity of their anger often over-rides any forgiveness that might be related to keeping their attachment ideologically pristine and emotionally intact. In other words, because split-identity twins have their own limited self-identity these twins do not totally rely on what their sister or brother wants or expects. Knowing that they are different because they have been treated differently by their parents allows them to take their own point of view more seriously than their sister or brothers. Anger and disappointment are commonplace. Sometimes these angry and conflicted twins can become estranged. Let's look at the split-identity twins that were introduced in Chapter 1.

Keith and Kirk

Keith looked for help from neighbors, emergency room doctors, police, teachers, and coaches. When he spoke of the abuse going on in the family no one believed him. Sadly there was no one for these boys to turn to, they had to rely on one another. Keith realized that, in order to go to college, he and Kirk would have to apply for scholarships. Keith being the caretaker twin got Kirk and himself into Cal Poly where they lived in the dorms. Keith remembers that the cafeteria food was plentiful and for the first time in their lives they were not hungry.

The first year of college they spent a great deal of time together sharing friendships. By the second year in the dorms they were growing apart because Kirk would not share his friends with Keith. Keith felt lonely and isolated and he would hide in the halls when he was afraid to be without his brother. They maintained their auto parts business and their relationship was based on running the business.

These twins lived together until they were 25. Kirk fell in love and married a women who did not like Keith and blamed him for everything that went wrong in their auto parts business. The business was split up and Kirk moved four hours away from Keith. The woman Kirk married was violent and an alcoholic like his mother. Keith tried to help his brother but got only rejection and anger.

Psychotheraputic Interventions

Keith started psychotherapy when his brother married to get over the loss of his brother's presence in his life. Therapists tried to explain to Keith that his brother was a sociopath and he was not responsible for the harm he was causing to his children. Psychodynamic psychotherapy was initiated and continued twice a week for 35 years. The first seven years of therapy were used to help Keith feel safe and worthy of attention. Disassociative thoughts began to arise and then forgotten memories of abuse that had been repressed from his childhood were revealed.

Sandy and Scott

As it was in childhood, parental favoritism for Scott was endorsed in adulthood in a very determined and remarkable way. Sandy and Scott grew apart without talking to one another about their rage with one another, which centered on Sandy being the competent caretaker and Scott being the frightened and helpless underachiever. The silence between them in adulthood was unusual for twins and predicted their estrangement later in life. Sandy remained in contact with both of her parents, although there were serious battles of the wills over decision-making. The family could not give up their connection with Sandy, even though they favored Scott.

Scott went to college to become a teacher. Sandy did not go to college but had a successful job in real estate management. Scott married in his early twenties to a teacher. Sandy remembers crying uncontrollably at his wedding without knowing why. Sandy married a month later to a man who did not like her brother Scott. The deep and silent wedge between Scott and Sandy started to develop.

Over the years the interactions between these twins dwindled down slowly. Sandy developed her business talents and computer expertise. She divorced her first husband and remarried. She worked and traveled throughout Europe, visiting home and her parents. Scott taught elementary school and had two children which he did not want his sister to meet. No one in the family would tell Sandy what she had done wrong that made Scott so determined to ignore her. When Scott refused to acknowledge his twin sister's presence at family events, Sandy decided to not attend family celebrations. Other members of the family took Scott's side and Sandy was left to feel bad about herself in a very painful and confusing way. My guess is that Scott needed to be the center of attention and Sandy's presence and ability to be effective took away from his stature. However, no one really knows what happened. Leading successful lives, Sandy and Scott who are now in their middle fifties never interact with one another.

Psychotherapeutic Interventions

Sandy sought out psychotherapy in her thirties to help her understand the direction her life was going to take. This treatment was somewhat successful and Sandy climbed the ladder of success in every work environment. Sandy never understood her empty feelings regarding her marriages, but accepted her loneliness. Being alone was less confusing for her than trying to relate to a man. Sandy fell in love for the first time at age 50. When this relationship fell apart Sandy became seriously depressed. Her grief over losing this lover was related to the loss of her brother.

Sandy contacted a therapist who understood twin estrangement and who believed she could help her overcome her sense of loss. Sandy has begun to look at how her relationship or lack of relationship with her brother has determined her life choices with men, and her fear of being hurt and abandoned. Insight into how being the bad twin has isolated her from others has been crucial to the development of her good feelings about herself. Sandy has serious issues with entitlement and sees expanding her sense of herself as valuable. Reconnecting with Scott is very unlikely.

Benna and Rachel

After high school graduation both women began to take separate paths. They went to different colleges. Benna studied marketing and Rachel studied environmental sciences. Benna made a career in the fashion industry. Rachel worked in adventure travel. Spending time together in early adulthood was restorative but always seemed to end on a bad note. Separations were based on anger and disappointment. Because Rachel was treated as the bad twin, she always felt less important than Benna and was more withdrawn into herself. Rachel was quick to see her sister as better than her and she suffered from depression and poor self-esteem. Benna was more grandiose then her twin and made superficial but lasting relationships. Benna fell in love and was married for a short time. Rachel predicted that Benna had chosen the wrong man just to get married.

In their twenties and thirties their anger and resentment at each other would get out of control, and these women would actually be estranged from one another for long periods of time. And then they would make up and travel together to faraway countries. Because they were adopted, their need for one another was intense and confusing not only for both of them but for friends and family. Spiritual guidance was sought out and practised. Yoga and a striving for balance in their lives was pursued with great fervor.

Their lives took a different direction when their mother became very ill with terminal cancer. Both women decided to explore the Grief Recovery Process to understand how their adoption had affected them directly. This therapeutic process brought them closer together. After their mother died they inherited enough money to start over finding themselves as twins. They moved in together for over two years and worked on their relationship and creating a business in spiritual interior design.

Psychotherapeutic Interventions

Psychotherapy alone and together was effective in helping these women get over their shame at one another. Shame was based on being different. Understanding that it was not shameful to be different did not instantly eradicate their shame, but gradually it helped. Rachel believed that the therapist and therapy gave her space to be her true self in the relationship with Benna. Being more grandiose than her twin, Benna had difficulty seeing her part of the problem which centered on criticism of her sister and her need to get her own way.

Determination to work out their twin relationship was crucial and effective. Different therapeutic approaches were used. Benna and Rachel were unable to separate and so they ended up working with therapists who could accept their decision to live together until it felt safe to separate. Making sure that their new improved relationship was equal and one of them was not favored was a serious focus of adulthood. Their conflict-laden journey is still in process. Problems other than twinship are related to their adoption and foster care which created deep feelings of insecurity that seemed to be quelled by being together.

Paula and Patty

As adults Paula and Patty went their own ways after college graduation. Separation was difficult for both of them in different ways. Getting over the demons of their childhood took many years of individual psychotherapy for each twin. Patty had to develop her sense of competence and self-esteem. Paula had to accept that she could not possibly always be the very best in every situation and still be less than her sister. Confusing as this must sound to outsiders, Paula's need to be the best was in conflict with her need to take care of her sister's self-esteem, which is very common in split-identity twins. The responsible twin is always placed in a double-bind situation. This was apparent with Benna and Rachel and Scott and Sandy. Paula rebelled against this unspoken and confusing directive less dramatically than the other split-identity twins that I have worked with,

Both Paula and Patty suffered from different types of depression which was related to the emotional abuse they suffered in childhood and the lack of parenting that they experienced. Thankfully they each had coping strategies that they got from doing yoga and karate together. These physical activities kept them feeling connected to one another. After graduating from UCLA Patty lived in Los Angeles. She was upset with Paula because Paula had an affair with her best friend. Paula was guilty about this for over 20 years. Patty finally accepted her sister's actions but could not get her sister to understand that she forgave her. What was important to Patty was that they always remained twins together. In other words Patty wanted Paula to maintain their childhood relationship, which was always for her to be the most important person in the world to Paula. Patty was shy and reluctant to make friends. Patty was angry with Paula for being seemingly more successful in life because she was going to graduate school. At first Patty worked in hospitality services and climbed the ladder of success. She landed an excellent job in Silicon Valley as a financial consultant. Patty dated a man for three years but never married or had any more long-term relationships. Years of psychotherapy helped Patty to feel better about her abilities and success at work. She developed a more positive sense of herself.

Patty with less fervor in adulthood and continued to feel that her sister was more important than her, which made her angry at Paula. Diffusing Patty's anger was, as Paula saw it, a significant part of their relationship as adults. Paula was overly ambitious and became a high achiever in graduate school. Paula came out of the closet in early adulthood with romantic partners. In her first serious relationships Paula always worried about the other person as if she were Patty. Feeling disconnected by non-twins who took advantage of her giving nature, Paula became seriously depressed. For many years she thought about herself as worthless and undeserving. In the midst of this depression Paula managed to get her PhD in communicology and is a professor at an esteemed university. Colleagues introduced Paula to a woman, Jean, who was to become her soulmate, and later spouse. Paula was able to receive love and attention from Jean. Patty had a great deal of difficulty with Jean as she felt left out of the relationship.

Psychotherapeutic Interventions

Paula was afraid of her twin and elicited the help of a psychologist who worked with twins. Paula and Patty worked together in therapy to overcome Patty's uncomfortable jealousy with Jean. Paula found solace in psychotherapy and developed slowly and carefully a more realistic sense of herself. Unraveling Paula's perfectionism and overachievement was successful because the relationship with her therapist was based on deep identification which promoted validation and mirroring that Paula needed to grow into her own happiness.

Patty had long-term therapy that was successful in helping her overcome her "less than" childhood identity. Patty learned that she could be as successful as her sister. Paula learned that she could be herself and not worry that her accomplishments were hurting Patty. Paula and Patty have an adult relationship which is supportive of who the other is in a mature way. While they are not as close to one another as they were as childhood and teenage twins, they can get along and support one another from a distance. And they can be together for short time periods, taking care of their family life events. Psychotherapy helped these women not to revert back to childhood behaviors. The goal of therapy was to promote the development of an adult twin identity.

***

There are profound similarities in the personality development of these three sets of twins. The most prominent similarity is that they were treated as halves of a whole or opposites of one another which helped them separate from one another and feel comfortable living separate lives. Although very close as children and taking care of each other against their abusive parents, these twins wanted their own lives. The shame and resentment they felt for one another and for themselves as twins came to a head in adulthood. Estrangement and serious fears of expansiveness were prevalent in their lives. All sets managed to live separate and successful lives.

Differences between the pairs are striking as well. The quality of parenting and the resources available for growth as an adult colored their ability to succeed in a world so different than their childhood experiences. Scott and Sandy who were treated as a little couple in childhood and adolescence, parted happily as adults. Anger and resentment at one another were fueled by parental favoritism for Scott. When separated from his twin sister, Scott wanted to be the center of attention to his parents and brothers and to his wife and children. Being with Sandy reminded him of how fearful and less than he felt as a child. Pretending that he was not a twin was his solution to his relationship with his sister. Sandy was totally relieved to be free of taking care of her brother. Although she was hurt by her brother's absolute rejection and the family's favoritism, freedom was what she wanted and lived for as an adult.

Benna and Rachel were also split-identity twins. Adopted by wealthy older parents, Benna was the favored important twin and Rachel was the ignored and not favored twin. They accepted these roles as children and as teenagers. They were happy to separate but came back together because they needed one another to restore their good feelings of just being together. Harmony and estrangement punctuated their adult years. After their mother's death they tried to rework their childhood twin relationship. Seeking out spiritual and psychological help they were able to come to a better understanding of who they were in relationship to one another. Their father's wealth provided them with resources to accomplish a better relationship. Still there is always a sense of competition between these women and a longing to get along better. The loss suffered in foster care and then adoption was difficult for them to overcome. The security that they felt in each other's presence as infants and toddlers holds them close to one another as adults.

Paula and Patty were opposites of each other. Paula like Sandy was the caretaker twin who had to be successful but less than her sister. Patty, much like Scott, was the more helpless child who was enraged at her sister for being so much more effective than she was. Both of these women were driven to be successful because that was the family expectation. Individual and couple psychotherapy helped these women develop a way of getting along which was distant but not as remote as the relationship between Scott and Sandy. Paula and Patty's relationship also lacked the dramatic and overly competitive adult relationship that Benna and Rachel shared.

Getting along in a non-twin world was difficult for these split-identity twins. Confusion over emotional boundaries or expectations for others and from others was coupled with fears of expansiveness. Individual identity was developed slowly but surely. Chapter 6 addresses the issue of being a twin in a non-twin world.

Individual-Identity Twins

Twins who have been treated as individuals and as twins have the best chance of developing a unique sense of self that is not in competition with their twin. Because their parents have responded to differences between them instead of projecting differences onto them, they are less vulnerable to identity confusion found with the other two patterns of twinship. Naturally competitive with one another and emotionally measuring themselves against one another, they are still able to accept that they are different from one another. Parents have made significant efforts to develop what is unique about each twin. Parents have not capitalized on the superficial aspects of their identity as "the twins." Rather they have respected their closeness without favoring or labeling them as non-dominant and dominant. Most importantly their efforts have paid off, for their twins who can get along as adults.

In spite of all the positive efforts that are made in parenting which require time and psychological mindedness, individual identity twins have issues being twins in a non-twin world. The intensities of their problems separating from each other and their vulnerabilities or insecurities are more manageable. They use the benefits of being twins—attentiveness and concern—with more grace than other patterns of twinship. Let's look at some examples from Chapter 1.

Marilyn and Janet

Capable of being separated from one another for long periods of time, these women married, had children, and established separate careers after going to different undergraduate and graduate schools. While they were competitive with each other about who was richer, prettier, had better children, or a better husband, a better house, or a better career, these comparisons did not create tensions and resentments that grew into huge walls of anger. Rather they seemed to care for each other in terms of who needed what from whom.

They were always aware of their boundaries as individuals. Nevertheless, if money was an issue, Marilyn would pay the extra as she had more money. If time was an issue Janet would do the extra as she had more free time on her hands. These acts of generosity did not grow out of guilt or identity confusion.

Janet was more serious then Marilyn and she studied psychology and became a clinical psychologist. She married Andrew, a prominent attorney who was very successful. Unfortunately, the relationship did not last because Janet felt misunderstood. Less interested in wealth and the extras that accompany it, Janet felt disconnected from her husband. Andrew felt that Janet was too involved with her sister and always felt left out. After their amicable divorce Janet went to live in the same town as her sister. Janet went into psychotherapy to understand her "over involvement" with her sister. She came to understand that Andrew was not the right choice because he was too entitled and too driven to be married to a twin.

Eventually Janet met the love of her life at a social work meeting. Benjamin was not as interested in wealth as her first husband. Benjamin was focused on his work and his desire to have children. They shared a psychotherapy practice and lived modestly but happily with their three children. Their younger sons were twins and Janet tried to use the same approach as her parents had followed. While there were family problems that arose, Janet was able to get help and support from her husband, her associates at work, and her twin sister.

Marilyn who was the more playful twin had more romantic relationships than Janet as a young adult. After she received her BA she went into psychotherapy to understand why she always felt disappointed in non-twin relationships. Unlike her sister she was not at all interested in psychology. She studied business in graduate school. After completing her MBA she joined a financial investment company and did a great deal of marketing for their computer division. She met her future husband Steve at work. Steve was serious like her sister and very shy in large groups of people. Marilyn and Steve complemented each other without being too entwined. Both Marilyn and Steve were successful financially. They had several homes and were very interested in travel. They postponed having children.

Janet and Marilyn discussed their different lifestyles. Janet was concerned that Marilyn was not serious enough, too involved with Steve's work, and that she should have children. Marilyn was concerned that Janet was too serious and never had any fun. Their concerns for one another were debated openly. However, anger at one another for not listening to their advice was quickly overcome. Each twin respected the other's choices and decisions. Marilyn had one child when she was 38 and this child was a welcome part of Janet and Marilyn's family. If investments were in question Marilyn's husband was in charge. Education was left to Janet's husband. If travel plans were being made, Marilyn did them with her husband. Family parties and events were divided as fairly as possible. Dialogue was valued but final decisions were made individually.

Psychotherapeutic interventions

Marilyn and Janet both worked with therapists individually to become better advocates for themselves. Although they were very different, saying no to others was hard for both of them, Janet had to set limits for her children. Marilyn had to set limits for her husband. There twin relationship was never a source of unhappiness or emotional pain in that they could let go of their anger at one another.

Michael and Mark

Michael and Mark were following very different life paths when they started college. Mark was given a scholarship to study architecture in the Pacific Northwest. Michael was already involved with the gay community, and he wanted to stay close to home. Studying literature at a small liberal arts college in South Carolina he began to pursue a career in academic literature. Both young men were very interested in aesthetics and they could understand one another's educational inclinations. They were close to one another via phone calls. Mark came home to visit as often as was affordable. Proud of one another for being the first in the family to go to college further contributed to their deep attachment and respect for each other. Adjusting to a world that was bigger than their sequestered childhood was challenging for Michael and Mark in different ways. Mark had to learn about the sophistication of life outside of the South. Michael had to learn about prejudice against gay men.

Mark left home with a mission to be the best architecture student in his freshman class. And while he had the determination, his schooling had been less than perfect. He had not been exposed to as many ideas as other students from more metropolitan areas. Making up for "holes" in his education reduced the amount of time that he had to meet new friends and to socialize as a freshman. Mark in many ways relied on his twin brother for companionship over the phone. Michael was understanding and able to help his brother through some lonely times his first year away from home. Mark gradually adjusted to city life. He sought out psychotherapy to help him connect to this very different world without his family and his brother.

Mark fell in love after many rollercoaster relationships with Joan, a classmate at his college. After being together for three years they married. Michael and his gay boyfriend John came to their wedding. There was no tension between the families of the bride and groom. Joan and Mark opened an architecture firm together. They had two children. In many ways Joan was a twin replacement for Michael.

Michael was a very serious student and a high achiever like his brother. He was extremely intense and sensitive to the criticism of the community about his gay lifestyle. Michael had a long-standing relationship with John who was a professor at the college he attended. As they became more committed to one another they travelled across country to meet with Mark. Unlike split-identity twins or interdependent-identity twins these twins and their mates all got along and accepted one another graciously.

Michael and John decided to adopt a child to complete their family. Michael wanted the warmth of children. He remembered fondly playing with his cousins. Michael wanted to have a child who could get to know his twin brother's children. Mark and John decided to move to New York City to get away from the gay prejudice they were experiencing. Michael got a scholarship to NYU and John got a professorship at Columbia University. The move was stressful and Michael turned to Mark for support in his new role as father and adjusting to city life. Mark was extremely helpful, having lived through these experiences himself. The move to NYC was very successful as Michael became a successful writer and John flourished as a professor at Columbia University.

Psychotherapeutic Interventions

Mark sought out psychological help in college to deal with making new friends and adjusting to a very different lifestyle than he was used to. This short-term therapy was very effective in conjunction with his brother's support. Michael relied on his brother to get through difficult situations with other people and events. Michael found support among his writer's groups and later in life did some psychotherapy to challenge his potential. Both men were psychologically- minded and able to work on defining their individual identity and their twin identity.

***

Both sets of twins were able to remain in contact with one another and support each other when necessary. While competition was an issue, measuring themselves against one another did not lead to anger and estrangement. Rather, seeing themselves in each other's eyes helped them to develop their own unique sense of self. They were able to learn from one another's mistakes and triumphs.

Common Issues of Adult Twins

There are common developmental milestones that twins experience as adults no matter what type of attachment they share.

1. Separation both emotionally and physically is more difficult than adult twins have imagined. Overcoming these painful and confusion emotional experiences takes time, understanding of the problem, and experience tolerating being on their own. Twins and their family and friends have to be patient with this transition. Frustration and dogmatic direction is never helpful in the long run.
2. All kinds of new relationships—romantic, career, and children inspire, motivate, and confuse twins. Developing a new sensibility about non-twin

relationships takes effort, time, and some hard knocks. Understanding the problem intellectually is not enough. Insight into what is appropriate to expect from others is a good start. Experiences with new people no matter how trying is critical.

3. Understanding the different psychological boundaries you establish with friends is a long and bumpy journey. Learning that friends are not as able to understand you like your twin is learned through experience. Being able to actually evaluate the good and bad about new relationships is a useful tool.
4. Mind reading like you had with your twin is not found with other people. Bottom line: non-twins won't understand you like your twin. And working hard to explain yourself is for the best in the long run. Developing close relationships to replace your twin intimacy will take time.
5. Your twin may want your life or you may think that your twin wants your life. You will have to learn that you are separate people and not interchangeable with one another. As ridiculous as this sounds, twins often feel like they should be interchangeable. Sharing as adults is not possible and will only lead to unhappiness and anger.
6. Adult twins will experience loneliness which is inevitable and can lead to emotional confusion, depression, and being overwhelmed. Non-twins will not understand the depth of your loneliness which will only gradually fade into the background as you make new friends and get engaged in life without your twin.
7. Defining adult identity as an individual is a long and curving road. You will face competition and hardships along the way. Support from your twin will not always be available, which is most likely for the best. Find a therapist or a good friend who will understand your pain and happiness. This is when the search for twin replacement begins.
8. Defining adult twin identity is an important process which means getting over wanting to feel like young twins who only have each other to care about. Mature twin identity is caring but also limited to the reality of the different lives that are shared from a distance. Being an adult twin means knowing you are a separate person.
9. Searching for twin replacements is important and tricky. Twins can be overly hopeful that a new twin replacement has been identified. Often what seems like it will work out in terms of closeness and intimacy does not last. But it is better to try and learn from your mistakes.
10. Learning to respect your twin and not be critical of their decisions is extremely important. Twin estrangement is based on a lack of respect and understanding.

Advice for Therapists

Working with twins can be difficult and confusing if the therapist does not understand the profound nature of twin primary attachment. Actually, it can be shocking for non-twin therapists to try and take seriously the commotion that is created when twins fight and then make up. Working with adult twins will always be easier if you understand the importance of the following issues:

1. How twin development is different than the development of a single child. And the ensuing effect on personality development because twins share their parents.
2. The pattern of twinship that is shared will determine to some extent the degree of separation that adult twins can handle from a psychological perspective.
3. A twin's sense of self is qualitatively different than a single-birth individual. In young twins some aspects of personality are shared, which makes young twins develop their own language and non-verbal communication. Shared aspects of personality, twin identity, has to be navigated into individual identity in adult twins.
4. Twins have expectations to be deeply understood when they invest emotionally in another person. The therapist will need to set limits and expectations so that idealization and devaluation are minimal.
5. Immediate and close understanding are expectations twins have for therapy. The therapist has to keep this issue at the front of his or her mind.
6. Therapeutic goals should be established with the therapist so the patient does not become distracted by what their therapist thinks will work out.
7. The therapist will be a container for the patient's loneliness but not a twin replacement that is required to function in day-to-day life.

Conclusions

Adulthood struggles go on and on. Twins will work through their conflicts with each other if they try to develop a mature twin attachment. Clearly this is not an easy thing to do. Sometimes getting along for twins is impossible if traumatic events and abuse have dominated childhood experiences. A commitment to respecting yourself and your twin is a basis for establishing a strong bond in adulthood with your twin.

6 Being a Twin in a Non-Twin World

Images of Twins: Realities of Twinship

Prejudicial and idealized images of twinship portray twins as icons of intimacy or as dramatic bad/good opposites of one another (Klein and Martinez, 2016; Lanigan, 2016). Popular culture takes these images from biblical stories, books, and films and turns them into spectacles of similarity or good and evil. In contrast and in reality, there are literally countless untold stories of the lives of twins. These memories, chronicles, and novels suggest that twins know, see, and feel something about intimate relationships that single-born children are unaware of in interpersonal situations (Arthurs, 2014; Morgan, 2014; Parravani, 2013; Shawn, 2011; Verghese, 2009). Indeed, being a twin is complicated and misunderstood by non-twins. In extensive interviews with twins over the last 35 years of studying identity development in twins, I have come to the conclusion that the positive and negative aspects of twinship are misunderstood. Twins with unexplored psychological lives and untold stories are at risk in the non-twin world (www.drbarbaraklein.com).

Unconditionally good forces and the energy of twin identity, are always alive, even when they are deeply buried within a twinship (Schave, 1993). Their primary attachment that is deep and nurturing can propel twins forward and helps in the healing of painful events (Fonagy *et al.*, 2005; Shirley, 2016; Tancredy and Fraley, 2006). Twin attachment can teach single-born people about the power of attachment and companionship (*A Phenomenology of Twins' Same Careers: Exploring the Influences of Adult Twins' Relationships on Their Same Careers*). The intimacy that is shared through early memories and closely lived events and validation creates a deep enduring bond of closeness. Being soulmates in childhood creates a drive in twins to find the perfect partner in adult life—a twin replacement.

What can go wrong for twin identity is a lack of attention to individuality and the effects of the glamour of being a twin in childhood. When twinship becomes invisible in adulthood twins are deprived of their twin mirroring and validation from one another as well as the attention they get for being twins (Lamb, 1998; Pogrebin, 2010). Adulthood brings freedom for self-exploration but loneliness from their twin and misunderstandings from non-twins. The following pages will point out the struggles that twins face in a non-twin world.

The Struggles of Being a Twin in a Non-Twin World

Understanding what it means to be a twin in a non-twin world takes time, patience, and a belief in the meaning and importance of psychological insight. In my experience twins who understand their twin issues and identity have worked hard to do so. Although depression related to the loss of companionship can torture twins, understanding that this loneliness is to be expected is soothing and provides solace. The introspective twin can use their own self-knowledge to live happier and more fulfilling lives. There are certain familiar paths that twins that I have worked with take and then respond to being a twin in a non-twin world.

Twin Invisibility

There are hidden aspects of the twin attachment that put twins in a minority position with singletons (Lanigan, 2016). Twin invisibility is a strange phenomenon, filled with remarkable contradictions and confusion. As infants, toddlers, and children, there is way too much attention and even celebrity in the spectacle of twinship—of looking alike (Cooper, 2004; Diaz, 2013). Idealization by onlookers who believe that mirroring and validation are very important parts of twinship that they long for in others is hard to explain from a negative perspective. Understandably, the downside of closeness is often ignored by onlookers. Painful loneliness and invisibility become the side effects of adulthood separations. Individual identity can be ignored, confused, or overdetermined by parents. Finding a balance between your twin attachment and your individual identity is a serious challenge.

Even though I missed Marjorie every day for many, many years, I remember the relief at 21 that I felt when my sister and I were separated when she went to live in Sweden with her new husband. Naively, I concluded that her invisibility gave me the right to not be a twin. I divested myself of my twin identity. I attempted to be a non-twin or singleton in my twenties and early thirties. This was a simple-minded attempt to not be a minority in everyday life. I wanted to pretend that I was "alone in the mirror." But she was still a part of me no matter how different our haircuts, husbands, children, and outfits were. I was never really alone in the mirror. I always saw her and could not explain this phenomenon to other singletons. Many many years of psychotherapy helped me understand the depth of our relationship.

In reality, being a non-twin was hard because I was actually a twin even if no one saw my sister. The problem of her being invisible was troubling. I didn't really relate all that well in superficial situations. Small talk was something that I had to learn the hard way as an adult. I wasn't a "foodie" who loved cooking. I liked offbeat clothes. I liked dance classes because I didn't have to talk with other people about things that didn't interest me. I couldn't make the perfect little cookies that moms and doctor's wives served at parties. I felt like I was sort of a misfit. I was a well-meaning misfit with a kind heart and a problem-solving mind but still a misfit. Maybe even a fish out of water longing to be swimming again in her own choppy sea. I got over my delusion of being a non-twin gradually. I tried to understand my invisibility with other twins.

Stephen explains why unknowingly he pretended that he was not a twin and how it led him to loneliness:

> The first problem of living in a non-twin world was that I was in the minority group as a twin. But I didn't realize this. I started to seek real individuation in my late teens/early twenties, I often unconsciously downplayed my sense of twinship and emphasized my identity as a singleton. Being an unknowing minority within the singleton world was consequently very challenging for me. First, I suspect that many twins unconsciously expect that singletons will think and act like them—why would they not? Unfortunately, singletons generally do not think like twins. I did not realize this as a younger person.

My twin sister Marjorie shares her strong feelings about how much trouble there was involved in facing the non-twin world when we went to college:

> As children we were twins in a world where twins were only a tiny minority, and that made relationships with non-twins sometimes difficult and confusing. Unknowingly people make comparative observations and judgments that hurt. Together and alone we felt alienated from single birth people.
>
> Now in our sixties we are not as close to each other as we were in childhood and throughout the long process of separating from each other. As I only have one twin sister and no other friends that are twins I am not sure that the distance between us is typical. We see each other infrequently because we both have busy lives. I feel like we are in the minority among twins.

Dave shares a little different perspective on the issue of invisibility. He points out how onlookers see you only as twins growing up. Your non-twin identity is mostly dismissed when you are together. Dave's thoughts are provocative and illustrate a different aspect of invisibility. Dave suggests:

> When it comes to twins, there is always a way that you say their names: i.e. Dan & Dave—NEVER Dave & Dan. Steph & Sam—NEVER Sam & Steph.
>
> Is this just names? Or is there more to it? It is in my personal experience that I would have to lean more to the latter. I was always second in the "name phrase" and in return rather unintentionally, I was almost always put second when it came to taking turns: in school, on the swim team, in arts auditions, interviews, appointments, etc. [May be worth mentioning, that I was also the younger twin, hence the question always asked was

"Who wants to go first?" followed by: "Oh I know—Which one is older?"] Now don't get the wrong idea, I didn't grow up with this deep sense of competition nor resentment towards my minutes-older brother. Quite the contrary actually, I came to just assume he was going to "go first" and I was going to go second. This was never to say that I was worse or that he was better, in fact that was often not the case, but it was a mere set way things were carried out.

Why I think it important to note is that I do feel it came to affect my personal development as I got older. I think I came to rely on him going first, speaking first, perhaps making decisions first. At which point I could disagree or contrast with his first choice, but I was reliant on him making that first choice whereupon I could then base my choice after. Now in my young adulthood as our differences have revealed themselves more clearly to one another, our dependencies on each other have revealed themselves just the same. I think as the one who was most often second growing up, I feel perhaps I have an even stronger desire or will to prove myself as independent and individually decisive. I feel a stronger sense of accomplishment now when I choose my own path and own successes, applauding my ability to act without relying on assessing his action first. That does though come possibly with a stronger sense of guilt (and sometimes even regret) if I act on something or make a decision without him knowing.

For Dave, invisibility is a double-edged sword in a non-twin world. He cannot get over his brother's presence even though no one else can see his brother. His mindset is that he is second and less important. Still he wants to be first and to overcome his reliance on his brother and over his guilt for wanting to be first.

Heather adamantly feels the pain of not being a loving and happy twin. She shares:

> I always want to find other twins like me who have crazy twins. I feel so invisible as a twin because my sister and I can't get along. And she is crazy. I am sad, disgusted, and scared. I can't help her. Everyone pretends that there is nothing wrong with my sister. I need to find some other people who understand what I am going through.

Keith who grew up taking care of his brother as a way of dealing with the serious abuse and neglect of his childhood shares his pain of being alone at college:

> I was terrified and I wanted to be invisible as a single person. I was so afraid of being on my own that I would hide in the hallways between classes if I was not with my brother. My parents had always told me that no one would ever like me. I believed their threats. Invisibility was my

first way of being without Kirk. Very very slowly I learned to be visible. I learned from new friends that I was a kind and caring person.

The difficulty and surprise of being in a minority position after being the center of attention is clearly challenging for twins. Adult twins are relieved to have someone listen to them about being invisible and being in the minority. Talking honestly about your misgivings about your twin sister or brother's emotional stability is a huge life-affirming relief. Knowing that twins are not alone with their misunderstood identity in the world provides them with comfort and strategies to help them feel in control. Looking for a strong individual identity also seems to help twins fit into the non-twin world.

Misunderstanding About Expectations and Boundaries from Non-Twins Is Difficult for Twins to Experience and to Accept

What is an appropriate personal expectation for singletons is very different than what twins will expect from other people. For example, twins want to form immediate connections with new people and old friends. They are often disappointed that new acquaintances and old buddies can't read their minds or finish their sentences. Outsiders to twins enjoy the warmth and intuitiveness of twins and get hooked into their web of closeness. As easily as singles connect they can disconnect because too much closeness is expected by their new twin friend. Frustration is also felt with the twin. Adjusting to a lack of loyalty from non-twins is a serious problem.

> Sarah H.: My sister has misunderstood me and instead of relying on me, leaning on me when she felt weak and tired, she has been threatened by my success and strength. She is so proud and stubborn that she takes my offer of help and support to mean that she is too weak or incapable of dealing. I wish she could just see that I have no intention of fixing her, no intention of taking over her life, quite the opposite. Why can't she see that I love her and am here for her. She doesn't need me to believe in what she believes in, my non-believing is not a judgment, it's just me being me. She doesn't need to interpret my being a supportive sister as a judgment of how she deals with her life. It is just me being a sister.

Vince shares his feelings of being misunderstood by outsiders:

> How you fit into a world that has very different boundaries for closeness than what you share with your twin takes time and patience. Once you begin to understand non-twins you can exist in their world. But their world will always seem less. They are not a twin. You will sometimes understand with great insight their problems and not be able to explain what you see to them. And with frustration you will have to accept that twins understand

issues of intimacy more deeply than non-twins because of their closeness and shared boundaries.

Janet: When I need deep understanding I turn to my twin. I think that you can't have such total access with a husband or a friend. Often I feel less visible with other people. Something is missing with other close relationships. And maybe my expectations for others have kept me back in learning to reach out to others for insight, understanding, and support.

Jackie: I've always responded anxiously when various therapists have talked about boundary issues. I've always thought there was something very wrong or bad about me when I felt them insinuate, and sometimes say straight out, that I had boundary issues. Boundary issues are different for twins and non-twins. To hear a therapist identify boundary issues seemed like an admonition that I was wrong, bad, too dependent, or didn't have a strong enough sense of myself. It always felt so cold to have this person I went to help dismiss what was so natural to me as something I was doing wrong. Even to this day, when I think about having boundary issues I feel diminished.

Stephen: I blamed myself for my inability to find a soulmate. I believed that I had serious, personality defects or unreasonable behaviors. I could have gone my entire life repeating the behaviors associated with the fruitless "quest for a soulmate" time after time without ever coming to the correct conclusion that no human being can provide the level of psychological connection and nourishment for which many twins yearn on a daily basis. It is entirely possible that many twins will eventually die still not having even begun to grapple toward understanding of some of these psychological realities. In some cases, the cost of this lack of understanding may well be years of psychological problems and depression, as the twin lives out a relatively unrewarding, spiritually and psychologically bereft existence that rarely realises the very high levels of expectation of connectedness, empathy, understanding, trust, and loyalty that twins often look for in their relationships with others.

Ego boundary issues—what you can expect from others—is clearly a problem for twins who perceive non-twins as withholding or limited in an emotional way. Misunderstandings between twins are common because their shared attachment creates power struggles over right and wrong. Twins can be treated as defective because of their ability to understand others easily or be too close to their twin. All of the twins that I have known personally and professionally prefer twin ego boundaries to singleton ego boundaries. Twins want intensely close relationships. Adult twins have to learn that all relationships are not close and nor do they need to be. Twins seek out twin replacements that make their sense of being alone more tolerable. Misunderstandings are hallmarks of adult twin identity development.

Frustrations Are Common and Challenging When Twins Separate

The experience of frustration that twins feel in non-twin relationships is hard to explain to non-twins who seem to want to be close but are ultimately a disappointment. All twins will agree that non-twin relationships can be very lacking in a sense of deep attunement. Here is what my twin clients have to say.

> Stephen: This pattern of excessive expectation may well also be apparent in the twin's relationships with friends and associates. Twins often, I suspect, expect levels of openness, transparency, courtesy, respect, and loyalty from friends that is far in excess of the levels that singletons often expect from friends. As a result, they often find high levels of disappointment in their personal relationships with friends.

> Jackie: The primary issue of being a twin in a non-twin world is a very deep one. You have this really close relationship with your twin since birth which leads you to expect that you will have this deep connection with everyone. I learned that this type of intimacy was not attainable as an adult. There was always a sense of disappointment lingering behind the scenes of my public self. But frustration with others based on high standards for understanding from others are set so early in life that I couldn't get rid of them.
>
> Being a twin in a non-twin world is hard. Living in a non-twin world means learning to be satisfied in relationships without feeling deeply connected or understood. The connection and understanding I have always had with my twin has just seemed normal and ordinary. Only now, well into my adult life, have I recognized how so much of my frustration with relationships has been because I expect to be able to connect with and understand others like I do with my twin.

> Linda: As I got older I came to recognize that other relationships would have different functions in my life. Business friends were interested in my professional abilities not my understanding. My husband wanted a partner to share his life with but did not need as much continual closeness as I had had with my sister.

Sarah H. presents another aspect of frustration that twins feel:

> I am frustrated that when we are together she often prefers sitting on social media then actually being involved or invested in the people physically around her. I am frustrated that she is so angry and resentful at our mother, putting her through massive fits of her childish anger. I am frustrated that she waits for me to take charge of projects related to our mother and then resents me for taking the lead. I am frustrated that she is jealous or resentful of my success in life.

At the beginning of your separation process I felt immediately hurt. I did not know that you felt like you had to be a different person around me—that you had to wear masks to feel loved and accepted and to fit in. The imbalance in our relationship made me frustrated because you could never be a team player but always wanted me to take the lead. Now you are upset with me for being too dominant. You have xxxxed me out of your life for a crime I did not commit. Blaming me for everything is not the answer to the problems in our relationship and your life.

There is a great deal of frustration for twins as they learn to function in a non-twin world. Twins are disappointed and discouraged with one another as well because they are over-identified with one another. Explaining this idea is difficult and requires individuals who want to understand twin identity on a deep level. As twins become aware and accept their different ways of relating to others and each other as adults, their frustration seems to diminish. Clearly looking into yourself is a choice that has to be made. It is a difficult one that some twins will not choose. Accepting the remoteness of the adult world is very hard for twins who long for the unspoken friendship and attention of their childhoods.

Shame About Not Being Like Your Twin Can Plague Twins as They Come into Contact with the World Alone

As much as twins long for their individuality and freedom, they also feel ashamed that they are different than their twin. It takes courage to talk badly about your twin because the issue is so private and so complicated. Admitting differences to outsiders creates a great deal of self-loathing and emotional discomfort on many levels. Admitting to yourself that you and your twin are different can bring up intense shame. Looking different from your twin is the strongest trigger to the shame of being different. Eating disorders are very common in twins for this very issue (Kendler *et al.*, 1993; Marmorstein *et al.*, 2007).

My twin sister shares:

> I was ashamed of my twin because she was too emotional. She fell in love and was crazy about her boyfriends. In college I was a serious English major and she studied history to be with her boyfriend who was an athlete. My boyfriend Joey was an artist and we had serious intellectual and artistic values. Barbara was very conventional. She married a medical student and was embarrassingly not hip. I was ashamed of how fat she got when she was pregnant. I thought we would always be alike. But I had to suffer the humiliation of her misjudgments and how different she was than me.

Sandy: In recent years I really have forgotten that I am a twin for long periods of time.

When my twin identity comes up, I am reluctant to discuss it because as soon as I do there is instant judgment. People are curious about the twin experience and naturally assume stereotypes are true. It is bad enough when normal siblings or other family members are estranged, but twins! People respond with shock and questions. Immediately they pass judgment. I feel so ashamed of myself for not getting along with my twin brother, even though he has not talked to me in 25 years. I am actually afraid to be with him because to him I am invisible in a very scary and humiliating way.

Nancy: My sister can't manage to keep a job. Her relationships are so superficial. She seems disinterested in making a stable life for her child. I am ashamed of how she lives her life and yet I feel sorry for her and try and help her as much as I can. I can't seem to resolve my negative feelings toward her.

Vicki: Madeline can't seem to manage her business and her personal life at the same time. She is critical of me for being a perfectionist. And I am downright ashamed of how she looks going to work and she gets along with her employees.

Madeline responds: Vicki is out of touch with how hard I work and how well I do get along with my co-workers. She is very obsessive and has to do everything her way. She has made mistakes but can't admit to them. I am ashamed of her uppity attitude and need to be so self-righteous.

Shameful feelings create anger and mistrust between twins who want to be in harmony with one another. Fighting over being disappointed and ashamed fades in and out of importance as twins age. Older twins can feel ashamed of their sister or brother, but the intensity of shame earlier in life is much more serious because of the over-identification between younger twins.

Confusion About How to Fit into the World as a Twin and an Individual Is Normal

It is confusing to try and figure out how to deal with non-twins, whether or not twins want to admit to feeling confused. This confusion is hard to explain to outsiders. Here is what twins have shared with me about their confusion.

Vince: First you feel like your relationship is forever and then one day with clarity you realize that what was clear is cloudy and the closeness of your bond has changed. These feelings of loss are confusing and overwhelming.

Patty: My experience of being a twin in a non-twin world is summed up very well by one word: confusion. Having a twin, with such a sweetness of connection and deeply established bond, leaves me completely confused with non-twin relationships. I have a very strong tendency, if I like someone, to seek connection at a very deep level.

> Sarah: Being a twin in a non-twin world makes me feel self-conscious and awkward, I often feel on guard—fearful that someone is going to notice that horrible blemish of not really knowing how to behave in a twin-less world. I often wonder if I said too much too quickly. Have I selected the "right" person to have a conversation with? Often it is much easier to melt into the background and become a wallflower. Being a wallflower is safe—although realistically I know that this is not practical.
>
> Sandy: I grew up with my twin and so I connect with people differently from non-twins. I see the world through two pairs of eyes. Knowing this makes it easier to navigate relationships, and much less confusing and stressful. I feel a lot less vulnerable and better able to look out for myself. I don't expect non-twins to understand. They may think they do. They may think that they have been there too, but they haven't. And that is OK.
>
> Sarah H.: My sister is confusing but she doesn't see it. She has become a spiritual guru and sees the world in her own terms. My twin blames everything on me and is unwilling to see my point of view. When we were children we got along so much better. I could talk with her and not feel totally overwhelmed like I do now.

Feeling overwhelmed and confused by your relationship with your twin is very normal and natural in adulthood. Twins need to learn to communicate with each other and understand they are different. Saying this is easy, getting along and accepting your differences is very hard to do indeed. Maturity in a twin attachment is hard to come by.

Social Anxiety Is an Expected Problem for Twins that Takes Time and Experience to Overcome

From my own life experiences I know how hard it is to fit in socially, whether or not people know about your twin. As a younger person I often felt like I did not really fit in everyday social situations. I missed my way of relating to my sister. I felt like other people were superficial. Other people thought that I was too intense. I learned the meaning of small talk later in life. Working with twins has taught me that other twins feel this way.

> Mary: Relationships work best for me where there is a defined context. At school, at work, or in activities where people come together for a common experience or goal (such as the Karate club Jen and I belonged to for many years), I am able to interact with people effectively and nurture the relationships if I have *a context*. But without that context, I don't know where to start, where to land or where to go. This has been a lifelong challenge that, again I was aware or from a fairly early age. Now, as I approach my 50th year, I can tell you that I still feel lost.

Vince: Being a twin in a non-twin world affected me on a deep level. Growing up Victor was the spokesperson for the twinship. When I had to stand on my own without my brother's support or back up I felt self-conscious because I had not stood on my own for a long time. Actually I don't like being alone in the limelight. I get very anxious on my own in a group of people.

Stephen: As an adult I found non-twins to be less giving and less patient than my brother. I am a patient and emphatic person. Sometimes I feel that other people don't really appreciate what I give. I get angry when my colleagues or supervisor don't appreciate what I am giving and contributing. I can feel disrespected and withdraw into my work. I have worked in my twin group and that has helped me understand non-twin boundaries. Social situations exhaust me.

Sarah: My husband makes friends with such ease. I often feel like a small child still stumbling through the correct steps in "how to make a friend." At the end of the night, I often rewind the conversation in my head. Did I say the right thing? Are they going to find me odd? If they call back and want to get together again, I often wonder what their problem is. Why would they want to spend time with me? I am getting better with this and practising to be less serious and less hard on myself. But often that little voice still persists when I step out of my comfort zone to meet new people.

In order to function in a twin-less world as an adult, I have made most my strides with baby steps. I know I will never have a roomful of people flock towards me due to my charisma.

Karen: Because my sister was always the one to initiate relationships, as an adult I have difficulty taking the first steps to form a friendship and often remain skeptical with why they would befriend me. When a friendship is formed, I sometimes become disappointed with the superficiality of it. Ever since I can remember, I always dreamed of a soul sister—someone I could tell all my secrets to and know that I would never be judged in a negative way. The girl in my dream was never my biological sister but someone else who I hoped to soon meet.

Jackie: I'm beginning to understand my ability to connect with and understand another person as deeply as I do my twin as an asset that creates specific challenges in the non-twin world. But I need help learning how to make my capacity for connection and understanding work for me rather than against me. For example, all my life I have learned to pay as close attention as I can to other people and use everything I can observe to make our communication better. I've worked very hard to cultivate connection and understanding with others. I've been extremely frustrated in these efforts. I've become an excellent communicator in the process, but

I've often been left feeling empty for my efforts and have felt like, "what's the point?" This world (non-twin) can't offer what I know is possible, so why bother, why go on?

Social anxiety is a side effect of being a twin. Even outgoing social twins feel awkward if they are honest with themselves. Looking forward and thinking expansively helps. Finding a twin replacement, having children, loving your work and fun all make social anxiety less meaningful to you because you are happy and not thinking about it. Negativity and wishing that your life was different does not help. Dealing with social anxiety is a lot of hard work and takes determination to find peace.

Summing up the Struggles of Twins in a Non-Twin World

Twins know things about relationships that non-twins cannot understand because they have not shared the womb and their childhood with another person. Twins are born married. Naturally, they know how to tune into a relationship and how to share. Individuality in childhood is developed. Sharing is how twins go through their infancy, childhood, and teenage years. Because sharing is natural and learned in the womb, sharing and togetherness have a primary and primitive importance that cannot be aggressively taken away without serious consequences. Young twins experience the importance of what they get from their twin that mom and dad can't give and friends don't even understand how to give.

These deep psychological issues are difficult to explain in words and create a deep undertow of enmeshment. The actions of young twins shed light on the importance of the twin attachment. Infant twins need to be near to one another. Toddler twins look for the other when they are brave enough to separate. School-age twins like to sleep together, no matter how serious their daytime disagreement may be. Staying together is a comfort in and of itself. Reliance on the twin closeness is unique and so it is easily misunderstood.

Since I wrote my doctoral dissertation on twins in 1982 I have been in contact with twins about how they feel about being a twin, and how they cope in a world where they are in the minority. Listening to the words of others expands my ideas about being a twin in a world of single people. Now after many years of reflection, countless confusing moments, and yes, serious disappointments related to my need for closeness, I realize that there is one valuable way to describe the fear and panicky conscious and unconscious experiences of being a twin in a non-twin world. I look to the story of *Alice in Wonderland*. I imagine that if twins had the ability to talk about their life as a non-twin they might describe it as Lewis Carroll did in his book. Alice is falling down the rabbit hole and has extraordinary adventures in this strange land.

> Alice went after the rabbit who went down the rabbit hole. The rabbit hole went straight on like a tunnel for some way, and then dipped suddenly down.

So suddenly that Alice had not a moment to think about stopping herself before she found herself falling down what seemed to be a very deep well.

Well thought Alice to herself after such a fall as this, I shall think nothing of tumbling down stairs! How brave they'll all think of me at home! Why I wouldn't say anything about it, even if I fall off the top of a house.

There were doors all around the hall, but they were all locked; and when Alice had been all the way down one side and up the other, trying every door, she walked sadly down the middle, wondering how she was ever to get out.

(p.90)

The Alice books are about the child's experience in an adult environment and the process of growing up and finding a mature sense of self. Alice meets up with all different kinds of strange creatures as she wanders through Wonderland. The world that she explores is contradictory, brutal, and fanciful, interesting and strange. Twins as they venture far away from their sister or brother into a non-twin world may feel like Alice. Being in a non-twin world is very strange and unfamiliar. There are places with unusual people and rules as they learn how to deal with the non-twin world. Alice wakes up from her dream. Twins just learn that they are in an entirely different world. Twins may feel other people are like the Red Queen screaming "off with your head", or Humpty Dumpty suggesting "might makes right", or even like the just outrageous White Rabbit who rants on and on about being late. Naturally, sometimes it is just a relief to be back with your twin where you can understand the rules for non-verbal and verbal communication. The transition from twinship to a world of single people is very strange and overwhelming for twins.

Problematic Issues that Need Understanding when Seeking Out the Right Therapist to Work with a Twin

A thoughtful and reasonable patient called me for some insight into his twinship. He reported that his childhood was chaotic and he had had over 25 years of psychotherapy to deal with surviving traumatic abuse. In all of his years in therapy he had never discussed in depth the effect of his twinship on his life path. I was quite surprised. I worked with him on his twin issues, which he found very helpful for his own peace of mind and to put some bad memories behind him as understood. I have experienced this type of remarkable and shocking fact far too many times. It is common that other therapists do not see the way that twinship has affected their patient's life journeys. Parent–child relationships, traumatic events, overwhelming loss, alcoholism, depression, and situational stress, to name a few subjects, are always discussed in therapy. Twinship can be marginalized or ignored, as if it was not a special and critical effect on life decisions. I wonder if this reaction is an artifact of being a twin in a non-twin world? Is this because twins are seen as close siblings? Or is the intimacy twins share frightening or categorized as not worthy of reflection by non-twins? Lack of understanding of the force of twin attachment has not helped twins live fully engaged lives.

Because I see and write about the twin attachment as a crucial aspect of identity development, I get phone calls and emails from twins who are looking to find a therapist to help them with their relationships with their twin and their relationships with others in their life. All of the phone calls and requests I receive are for referrals to therapists who are twins or who specialize in twin issues. The twins who I have encountered as a researcher, writer, and therapist have talked with me about how it is easier for them to work with twin therapists.

Finding a professional to work with in therapy who is a twin is not always possible for practical reasons. My experience tells me that twins often do not have a clear sense of the range and depth of their problems developing individuality and relating to non-twins. While twins may feel lost, empty, and moody, they may also be very unsure about what they hope and expect to get out of a therapeutic encounter. In first therapeutic interactions, developing a dialogue that allows the twin patient to talk about themselves to another person who is trying to understand will be helpful. The beginning goal with first-time twin patients is to make a connection with them and encourage the development of their individuality.

As twins get older and have some experience in the world of their own, finding the right therapist is more complicated and difficult. It is best to find someone who has worked with twins and is trained developmentally and psychodynamically. An understanding of the intersubjective aspects of the therapeutic encounter are crucial. Also taking time to assess the connection between the mental health professional and patient over a trial period will be very helpful. Shopping for a therapist who is interested in twins and wants to understand your unique attachment is a must.

Matching the Therapist and the Twin: Matching the Twin and the Therapist

As I lay out my ideas and strategies about finding a match between therapist and twin, I realize that my ideas and theory may be of limited practical value and just a framework for both mental health professionals and twins in search of developing identity with non-twins who don't understand twin ego boundaries. My ideas are not rules. Having been on both sides of the fence, looking for help with my own emotional struggles and trying to help twins find some peace of mind, I know that attachment issues are different for twins in therapy than for single people. I have described a variety of different attachment problems in the proceeding chapters. What follows is a list of issues that patients and therapists should consider as they begin to seek out and make a therapeutic connection.

1 Does the therapist have a working knowledge and in depth understanding that twins have very different developmental issues and personality structures than single children?
2 Does the therapist see that the twin attachment and the parent–child attachment are primary and fundamental to personality development?

3   A twin's sense of self is qualitatively different than a single-birth individual. In young twins some aspects of personality are shared, more diffuse, and less defined. This can be seen in twin language usage and non-verbal communication. Has the new therapist had any experience with self-development in twins?

4   Because of their early and deep bond, twins have expectations to be closely understood by others when they invest their emotional energy into another. They will become attached to the therapist in a very unique way. Talking about limits and expectations for the therapeutic encounter should be ongoing when possible. Both patient and therapist should take responsibility for working on attachment issues. The transference will be affected by these attachment issues.

5   What is normal for a single person is not "normal" for a twin. For example, while it is normal for twins to want immediate closeness and understanding from a therapist, it is not "normal" for non-twins to expect instant insight and compassion. Therapists who have never worked with twins will find this transition from non-twins to be challenging.

6   Behavioral and psychological goals that are shared by the patient and therapist will insure that expectations and disappointments are recognized, talked about, and in the process of being understood. For example, the therapist may have the goal of trying to understand their patient's experience as a twin. The twin patient may take the therapist's interest and empathy to mean that they have become a twin substitute. Both patient and therapist can become frustrated because their goals are in serious conflict. If goals are not clarified, disharmony can undermine the therapeutic alliance and the transference. Therapy will be at an impasse. For example, for twins understanding can become an invitation to a psychological merger. Understanding for the therapist is just a good practice to follow.

7   How to establish a close relationship that is not a recreation of twinship needs to be attended to by patient and therapist. Discussion of the issue will in itself create a new bond for the lonely twin. The therapist by clearly pointing out that he/she is not a twin substitute will hopefully avoid being idealized and devalued. Often the twin patient has no understanding of what the therapist is trying to convey in psychological terms. Explaining the importance of ego boundaries can become a slippery slope for the therapist.

Instant Advice for Therapists

Just for fun, like my piano teacher used to say, here are some opening ideas to keep in mind.

1   The undertow of twin attachment is serious, which means you will have to make many many more recommendations for not overcaring and not oversharing than you could ever imagine would be necessary.

2   The twin dynamic is as critical to understand as the parent–child dynamic.

3   Suggest small goals and see what works. Build on that success.
4   Listen to the detail of twin fighting carefully.
5   Focus on what works for your patient not what the books say.
6   Frustration is not helpful for twins in therapy. Be patient.

Instant Advice for Twin Patients

Be very careful to appreciate your therapist's perspective. Here is how to do this.

1   Pay attention to the questions they ask you.
2   Is the therapist natural or rigid in their demeanor?
3   How confident does the therapist seem to be?
4   Do you feel a connection and a warmth when you are explaining yourself?
5   What experiences has this professional had with twins?

Twin Groups

Twin groups eliminate the problem of being a twin in a non-twin world. They are becoming more and more common with the incidence of twin birth on the rise. Twin groups provide a forum for education and solidarity to different groups of twins.

Mother of Twins Clubs

Most commonly known are the Mother of Twins Clubs. All over the United States there are local and state groups. A National Mother of Twins Group holds conferences once a year. All of these organizations provide education about twin development and how to parent twins. There is a practical aspect to these parents groups as twins meet other twins and parents meet other parents and form networks and friendships. National Conventions provide the latest research on twin development and parenting twins. Products that parents of twins need are readily accessible at meetings and conferences. Babysitting and playgroups for twins are also an advantage that twin groups provide. Strategies to cope with the stress of raising twins and other multiple birth children is a mission of these organizations.

Twinless Twin Groups

Twin loss groups are relatively new in comparison to the Mother of Twin Clubs. Most well known is Twinless Twins which accepts members who have lost their twin. A bereavement process, education about twin loss, and group therapy support experiences are provided at all meetings whether local, state, or national. Solace, understanding, strategies to cope, and peer support are available to twins who are alone and suffering from this complicated grief experience. Deep understanding and identification with other survivors of twin loss begins the gradual healing process for twins who reach out for solace and solidarity. National, state, and local clubs welcome new members and give referrals for group and individual psychotherapy. Buddies for new members are suggested and easily take on new survivors. Lone twin members can join for a year or two or more as their needs to heal are the primary focus of the group which has long-term members who raise money to keep the group working.

The educational, emotional, and social support provided by these organizations is profound and priceless to lone twins and their families.

Twin Estrangement Groups

My interest in twins is related to my difficult and estranged relationship with my twin sister. After I completed *Alone in the Mirror: Twins in Therapy* in 2012, I received many emails to my website from twins who wanted to understand why they could not get along with one another. I was surprised, flattered, and happy to know that I had written something that made other twins feel more understood and gave them some peace of mind. I started making a list of the emails and phone calls I had received. Eventually I decided to start a twin estrangement group for twins who could not work it out with their sister or brother.

Lonely twins who were suffering emotionally because they missed their twin and felt lost wanted to participate. They also felt frustrated with their twin's anger reaction to them. Some twins I spoke with were ashamed of themselves for not getting along better. Another issue was blame and who was at fault for the fracture in the twinship. I knew that estrangement from my twin was difficult, shameful, and created deep loneliness. I learned that estrangement is painful for countless twins. I could certainly identify with the pain of the twins who reached out to me. With encouragement from twins who were unhappy with one another, I was able to form a twin estrangement group with twins who I only knew for a brief time and with twins I had known for several years. There was an immediate sense of camaraderie.

The purpose of the twin estrangement group was and still is to provide support, insight, and friendship to twins who feel misunderstood by their twin. Onlookers who think twins should get along create deep feelings of shame in twins and this issue is also addressed. The loneliness of being a twin in a non-twin world is discussed at length and strategies to cope with these feelings are suggested. Why twins fight and whose fault is it anyway is a compelling issue for everyone who attends. Practical and sensitive reactions are given and digested by the group. A sense of closeness and attachment that is authentic has developed between the members. It is like we have formed a twin group to replace our twins who can't understand us. When groups must be missed, members always say that they really missed seeing their twin friends. For twins who can attend via Skype on a regular basis the group provides a deep connective understanding that promotes self-esteem and problem-solving. At the present time the group is international, with members from England, Canada, and the United States.

My experience with this group has underlined for me the loneliness that twins can feel in a non-twin world. Longing for closeness can be attained with other twins because of the deep identification that unhappy twins get from one another. While my twin estrangement group cannot be replicated because of its special nature, our group experiences together can inform misunderstood and frustrated twins that their loneliness can be conquered through meaningful relationships that are focused on honesty and real-life issues with other twins.

Certain twin issues have become clearer to me from this group experience. They are as follows:

1 Twin loneliness can be curtailed through friendships with other twins.
2 Twins have certain sensitivities to setting limits and bragging about themselves that is hard for even other twins to understand. Setting boundaries through an action is hard for twins.
3 Twins are relieved to know that other twins don't get along and that for twins anger and even estrangement can be understood as normal given the way they were parented.
4 Relationships are important to twins and this leaves them vulnerable to being abused by non-twins.
5 Twins love to be the center of attention in close relationships, still they can accept too easily that others may not understand without a true and valiant attempt to win their point.
6 The role you play in the twinship is very hard to overcome completely. It is possible with the help of others who know it is a problem for you.

What We Get from Twin Group

I have asked twin group members to share their experiences with you, the reader. Vince, a member since day one, explains what he learned in group:

> Being in a group helped me to find my way to being an individual. To say I instead of we. To think in a singular way instead of constantly thinking for two. Being in a group of people who had the same or similar problems provided a platform of beginning which allowed for deeper understanding to grow. The insights of other twins allowed me to be an individual. In other words, they pointed out my "twin thinking" and when I became aware of the subtleties of unified thinking it then was easier to know when it was happening and whether it was helpful in solving a problem or hurtful.
>
> Sharing ideas in our twin group allowed for safety and so I did not feel that I was betraying my twinship. The loss of Victor, my treasured twin, will be seven years this July 2016. I am now able to fold him unto myself, as the flowers of morning open in the light of day and then close at the end of day. I no longer feel guilty about being an individual or more to the point terrified of giving up my twinship because I may be dishonoring or abandoning him, or more importantly give up on him.

The more I participate in group I am seen as an individual not a twin. They did not know Victor and while I have regaled some of our more amusing and colorful high jinks, they only know them from my point of view, an individual. The more validation I receive as a single entity and my accomplishment since his passing, a linear time line is established.

The trauma of his loss created chaos and confusion where time and events happened seemingly unrelated to one another, remembered one at a time resembling clouds aloft in a blue sky, never touching, just floating freely seemingly unrelated. Now, as my individuality is maturing, I have come to understand I can go on as a single person with the treasure chest of memories I once had of a life which has passed.

I am one instead of two. A short time ago this statement would have brought me to my knees in terror and fear but now it is the trailing wisp. Gossamer strands which are caught in the morning light when the dew is still dripping and stars can still be seen in its wetness.

As the leader of the group I have lived the intensity of the participants and see their investment in the group experience as healing. Vince feels free to pursue his own life. Sarah has developed a more positive and realistic sense of herself. Sarah shares:

> How have I managed to let my guard down? I feel that my twin support group has enabled me to see myself from a different perspective and in a more positive light. My twin support group has helped me to gain more confidence with myself and my interaction with others. When I have a problem or a question, I have slowly learned to trust my twin friends. Although we are all very different, we have all bonded. We have become friends, confidants, and perhaps each other's pseudo twins. When I have a bad week, I immediately know who will make me feel better. It could be as simple anger at a colleague or the tragic death of a dear aunt, I know my twin friends will listen, empathize, and offer suggestions for a better tomorrow. Because I have a safe place to share, I don't feel as burdened when meeting new people. I don't need to twin with anyone right away in order to share my deepest of secrets. Thus, I can be more superficial (aka normal) and be more OK with it. I save some of the other conversations for my twin night. I love my twin group. I consider each one of them family and look forward to seeing them each week. It doesn't feel quite right to me if I miss a session. They have filled a void in my life. I feel complete and fully dressed when I know that they are a part of my life.

Jackie, a member since day one, starts talking about her understanding of the group experience in narrative form:

> I don't recall having a lot of expectations when we started our twin group. I felt a little excited because I felt like I had learned a lot about how being

a twin has affected me from my several years of individual therapy with Barbara, and I trusted Barbara's ability to direct us through the group dynamics. I felt like I had learned a lot and that I could learn more and help others learn as well.

I think I approached twin group much like I do research—listen carefully and make connections. In the beginning I didn't think much about the people who would be in the group with me. I knew I would get to know them, but in the beginning I was more focused on fitting another meeting into my very busy weekly schedule. I think I sensed that there was a potential for things to happen in group therapy that were different from individual therapy, but I was pretty happy with the work of individual therapy and so going into group therapy I didn't feel that strong need for help that I felt going into individual therapy.

It took a couple of months for our group to begin to gel into its own thing. We started out with eight members, I think. A couple dropped out early on. One member of the group, Karen, was not able to engage with the group process and quit. A couple of new members came in, one of whom was dealing with some very traumatic life events and didn't stay long. The other new member left shortly after. It was through all this shifting around of members that the core of our group—me, Vince, Sandy, and Sarah—formed. We have another addition to our group, Stephen, who is not quite as gelled as the others of us, but if he sticks around he could be. Barbara is not adding any new members.

Overall I have gained from group the following:

1 Seeing the same feelings and responses in other twins helps me see them in myself more clearly. Even when I thought I knew something about myself, that knowledge didn't help me make changes in my life as much as it did when I could see the same thing in others and then recognize it in myself.
2 Getting to know my group members has helped me to see how deeply engrained our "twin-habits" are. I've come to be able to recognize my own "twin-habits," but that doesn't free me from them. Simply recognizing that those habits doesn't mean I can develop alternative habits. But, seeing them so clearly in my group members does make it easier to actually change. It's like having an anchor that holds back those knee jerk reactions so that I can see and feel my old habits and shift my thinking in the midst of things happening.
3 I feel really, really understood. Over the course of our group sessions we have gotten to know the particulars of who each of us is: what we do for a living, what our life was like growing up, what our relationship with our twin is like, etc. But those aren't the details that make me feel really, really understood. It's a much deeper understanding that's connected to how I respond to the world, how I live in the world, how I try to connect with people, and how I have struggled with all of that.

4 Seeing how my group members respond to each other—calling out a group member who is being evasive or closed, or recognizing how their own responses are projections from their own twin relationship—gives me a great sense of respect for each of them, for the risks we have taken with each other and for their genuineness. I think that the members who have quit have quit because they weren't ready or able to deal with being open enough to take the risks or respond genuinely.
5 I feel like everyone in group has my back. These guys are for real. They've called me on my stuff—like when I won't give up on insisting that I have to do everything, be responsible for everything or work harder; or when I'm feeling like I don't want to put myself out there and get credit for my work or attention for my achievements. Even in the midst of them doing this, while I am feeling defensive or annoyed, there's another layer of caring that just makes it all OK.

Sandy, who is an original member and a stalwart defender of truthfulness between twins, shares:

> The twin estrangement group has meant everything to me. I have spent most of my adult life shunned by my twin and marginalized by my family. I thought I was used to being left out and misunderstood but I was actually in a chronic state of confusion. I didn't know that the depth of my loneliness and pain had to do with being a twin until Dr. Klein and this open-hearted, incredibly smart, and brave group of people accepted me into their fold.
>
> I recognize so much of myself in the experiences of my fellow twins in the group. I almost feel that in meeting and getting to know them, I have finally met and am getting to know myself (I'm smiling as I write that because—well—it's such a twin thing). They have helped me grow into myself and have taught me that I can trust my own observations. That—more than anything—has given me a sense of safety and, well, peace.
>
> And thanks to the group, I have traded in my evil twin for the twin I always wanted. Keith and I adopted one another. It started as a bit of a joke but I'm surprised by how much comfort I get from it. It's no joke—once a twin, always a twin.

Stephen who lives across the Atlantic Ocean from us joined later on. He was having problems with deep loneliness, alienation, and despair. As our group is conducted on Skype I was apprehensive that we could all fit on the screen. But we did in fact fit, in many different ways. Stephen felt an immediate connection to the group and is a loyal member. He shares his thoughts:

> Now that I understand that my inner experience is different from most people, I realize that being a twin is an odd and isolating thing. When I interact with another person I process it through a kind of prism that bends the moment in two different perceptions—theirs and mine. When I listen I

hear every other word or phrase even though they're silent. I respond with much more than a sentence and most of that is unspoken too.

Don't get me wrong—this isn't about my twin. He's not part of my life and I'm happy to keep it that way. It's simply about … being a twin. That's who I am, it's the culture I was born into and the imperceptible accent I speak with. My differences are invisible, and for much of my life the challenges of human relationships have bewildered me because I'm surrounded by non-twins and have been out-of-sync. And I had no idea.

On the surface, my problems aren't all that different from non-twins. That's what's hard; when I'm told that how I experience problems and challenges is no different from anyone else's, I second-guess myself and discredit my instincts. It's made me vulnerable to people who have their own gift for exploiting vulnerabilities for their own benefit.

The Twin Group has been a godsend. These are people who perceive the world with the same prism, the people who operate on my frequency and who validate me. Through them I have gained clarity, learned to trust myself and I have become a lot more confident. I feel safer, more able to protect myself. My Twin Group understands perfectly what must seem disjointed to a non-twin. I don't feel so alone in my world anymore. As a group member I am more able to feel vulnerable and more able to ask for help. My feelings are validated and protected by my twin friends. They taught me that I can trust my own observations. That—more than anything—has given me a sense of safety and well, peace.

Along the way new members tried out our twin estrangement group experience. Some twins were disinterested. Some were too threatened. Some were just afraid to be really vulnerable. Recently two new members have joined group. Keith and Dave were immediately engaged in our group process based on insight, empathy, and support.

Keith: Being a part of this group is as close as I can be to having my twin back in my life. There is something very special and unique about the connection and communication style that twins have. I felt completely accepted by the group from the very first day, and this feeling of being a part of a group is so important and rare for me. While I spent 35 years in psychotherapy talking with a therapist, I have been terrified to talk about the horrendous abuse I lived through as a child and teenager with other people. I feared people would reject me if they found out the truth. My shame is very deep. But the group has shown me that I am a survivor who was unfairly victimized. I feel accepted. Having connected with Sandy who never talks to her twin brother made me feel more normal or less alone or odd. When Sandy suggested she would be my new twin sister I sent her adoption papers via email immediately. Being accepted by Sandy and the group as a whole has been very healing for me. I have been less afraid to be myself with other people.

Dave: I was introduced to the group to "see what I thought." I had my assumptions, speculations, and even reservations if I'm really being honest. Well, with all that said, I tried to be open-minded walking in and within the first five minutes of group I can confidently say I no longer had to try: These people were just like me. Yes, I may be the youngest; Yes, I may live thousands of miles from some; Yes, I may be pursuing a different career than any of them: But here is the deal—you know how they say "Try to walk in the shoes of your neighbor for even just one day!"—well, we can (and do in group). I don't feel alone. Something is created here that is much more than the sum of the parts. Everyone is learning equally from one another (and that is quite rare as a phenomenon).

***

My experience with my twin groups has validated my belief that twins can help other twins in very important but unexplored ways. The untold stories that twins keep hidden away should be brought to the forefront of their lives and explored. Psychotherapy that takes into consideration the importance of the twin dynamic is critical to exploring the lives of twins.

Conclusions

I am hoping that the words, feelings, and thoughts of twins that have been presented to enlighten the reader whether therapist, sibling, spouse, parent, or friend about the inner life of attachment that twins share is inspirational. Life struggles of twins are very different than singletons. Separations and new friends come first as a developmental task of living in a non-twin world. Next, accepting that you look different from your twin and are in fact different from your twin creates confusion and shame. Your own internal struggles are made worse by the non-twin world who cannot understand what you are going through. Adulthood is about understanding how to develop a new and more mature relationship with your sister or brother. Finding twin replacements that somehow quell your need for intimacy helps adjustment to the non-twin world.

When individuality is developed in each member of the pair, close companionship and caring will be allowed to flourish. Twin harmony in adulthood is an extremely important and cherished gift. Getting to adult closeness is a challenge that can be accomplished with insight into yourself and your attachment to your twin. Letting go of recreating the fantasy of childhood harmony is essential.

7 The Healing Process in Psychotherapy for Twins

Twins take different journeys in psychotherapy than single-born individuals because of their early attachment, shared memories, and lived experiences. Sharing their development is a primary cornerstone to their personality. This reality must be taken into consideration by mental health professionals and twins seeking out psychological understanding and a more peaceful emotional relationship with their inner life and their outer worlds. Unfortunately, how twins react differently in therapy has not been addressed with any clarity or seriousness of purpose. As twinship becomes more commonplace, new ideas about twin relationships and the intimacy that is shared will be explored.

Underlying Issues of Twins in Psychotherapy

Twins seek out psychotherapy for different reasons that are related to their age, the attachment that they share with their twin, and the stressful events that they have had to process as children and as adults. I have worked with twins who suffered from child abuse and neglect, post-traumatic stress disorder, eating disorders, autistic spectrum disorder, anxiety disorders, bipolar disorder, depression, divorce aftermath, disassociative disorder, and complicated grief reactions. In every life story that I am familiar with twinship was a contributing factor to the presenting problem for seeking out psychotherapy. Attachment issues between the twins were predictive of what type of adult relationship they might share. Patterns of twinship contributed to the degree of separateness that was possible between the pair and the amount of independence they had from one another. Their ability to expand upon their individuality was also related to the pattern of twinship that they shared (Klein, 2012).

Interdependent-Identity Twins

The interdependent-identity twins that were discussed earlier in the book all had some valuable experiences with psychotherapy that had a significant positive outcome. The twins with the more abusive and stressful childhoods were more likely to be quite dependent on one another throughout their lifetimes. At all ages, they served as supportive parental figures when necessary. In some instances, where there was some family stability, interdependent-identity twins had a great deal of hostility and resentment toward one another as they grew into adulthood which they expressed openly to one another. Still over-identified twins could not live without each other. Outward fighting was considered taboo by some twin pairs who swallowed their upset to stay tuned into one another. The centrality of enmeshment between the twins in this pattern of twinship made estrangement very unlikely. Living far away from one another was also unlikely as physical closeness was very important to their overall emotional stability and ability to function in the world.

The development of the therapeutic alliance was less intense with interdependent-identity twins because the twin always remained the ultimate authority—the go-to person. Trusting the therapist was difficult and seemed to have unusual challenges because too much trust in the therapist was a sign of disloyalty to their twin. Interdependent-identity twins need to be in control of the connection they share with close people. Even though they see that they are overly attached to one another they are still afraid to make new connections with new people that are sustainable. Gradually, psychotherapy helps overly close twins to make new relationships and to try different interests. Fear of expansiveness prevents a great deal of adventuresome behavior. Feeling trapped and ensuing anger issues can be put on the back burner when necessary because of the important primitive connection theses twins share.

In the case of suicide or other types of loss, lone twins with an interdependent-identity long for a dependent relationship with their therapist which is crucial and healing. Lone twins need very long-term therapy. Still interdependent-identity twins have problems being close with anyone but their deceased twin. Trying to establish a very in-depth relationship takes time and energy and a cleverness—an ability to think outside of the box—on the part of the therapist. Helping the twin-less twin reach out to others is extremely valuable (Arthurs, 2014; Klein, 2012; Morgan, 2014). Twin loss groups are very effective as a support and for advice.

In general, for very closely-tied twins, separation is extremely difficult and confusing. Fears of expansiveness are not usually the focus of therapy as individuality is underdeveloped. How to develop independence and separate lives should be the primary goal of therapy.

Split-Identity Twins

The split-identity twins described earlier in this book all gained a great deal from psychotherapy. Unlike interdependent-identity twins, they had and continue to have conflicted and disappointing relationships with their sister or brother. Twins who are opposites of one another long to find an ally who would understand their unhappiness and struggles. In my experience, split-identity twins work at establishing a deep and meaningful relationship with their therapist who inevitably will become, on some level, a twin replacement. The therapist has to be very careful not to re-enact the twin dynamic with the twin patient. In other words, the "all knowing and over powering" therapist is going to create a therapeutic impasse (Schave, 1993). Power struggles with split-identity twins need to be addressed and diffused. Goals should be based on what the twin wants to gain, not what the therapist sees as important. In other words, with polarized twins it is hard for the therapist not to become over-identified with the twin, which includes making decisions about goals to strive toward.

For split-identity twins fears of expansiveness need to be outlined, accepted, and worked on. As opposite twins become more whole in the sense that they are more than good or bad individuals, internal tension and depression is reduced. Therapy with split-identity twins involves helping them find their path in life. On this psychological journey they will confront and slowly get over their fears of expansiveness. As a sense of 'true self' develops, more toleration and less anger is apparent between the pair. Estrangement later in life is related to the amount of abuse and neglect that was lived through in childhood. The more abusive the childhood, the more likely estrangement will develop. Speculatively, twins see their twin as a part of the abuse they suffered. Being with one another can be very difficult when abuse memories are triggered. Whether the favored twin is enraged at his sister or brother for not taking care of a problem, or the bad twin is enraged over his brother or sister's expectations, there is a regression back to childhood roles and then estrangement.

Individual-Identity Twins

Finding out how hard it is to be alone in the world without your twin can lead twins who are not in a difficult relationship with their twin into psychotherapy. Said in another way, sometimes your twin is not enough and you need the help of another set of eyes. While individual-identity twins like to form close relationships with their therapist, they are less desperate about being totally attuned and in sync all of the time. Their issues of being a twin in a non-twin world are difficult for them to resolve. Fears of expansiveness are always an issue because they feel the need for their twin's approval which is not always forthcoming. Competitive issues for twins with a strong sense of self are also at the forefront of therapy. While serious fighting may be present at different times, estrangement is not common. Family stress is felt when twins try and integrate their husbands and children. Fortunately, conflicts are not as intense or provocative as seen with split-identity twins.

General Reasons for Psychotherapy

In my 2012 book *Alone in the Mirror: Twins in Therapy* I present many case histories of the process of psychotherapy with twins. The quality of attachment contributes to emotional health and the ability to cope with what life brings to you. Briefly, issues of depression and rage, identity confusion, separation anxiety, narcissistic vulnerabilities such as fears of expansiveness or rigidity, complicated grief reaction, and post-traumatic stress disorder can be presenting problems when twins seek out therapy. For more specific cases consult my earlier book.

Developmental Issues

Infancy

Often twins are born prematurely which will create specific issues that pediatricians are able to handle or refer to specialists in the field. Parents need help with infant twins to develop strategies to get by without totally losing their grip on reality because of the workload and the confusion twins bring into the world of the family. Finding a therapist or a group of other parents of twins is very critical and extremely useful in order to learn how to survive and thrive. Just talking about your day-to-day stress is very calming and helps parents think their problems through with good practical solutions. Knowing that you are not the only mother or father who is having troubling juggling your life with twins gives you inspiration and stamina to keep moving ahead (Cooper, 2004; Friedman, 2008; Gromada, 1981; Malmstrom and Poland, 1999).

Toddler/Pre-School Years

As early as possible parents may need help learning to interact differently with each child. Most often twin separation anxiety brings parents of twins to ask for help. Addressing separation issues early in life is very important to long-range psychological well-being throughout the lifespan. Psychotherapy will help the entire family see their twin children as very attached to one another but also in need of their own times alone with their parents, time alone without one another, separate toys, clothes, and friendships. Separation issues can continue on and off throughout their lifespan which is in some way related to unspoken care and concern for one another. Anxiety related to being apart is reflected upon throughout the book.

Elementary School Years

This is a period of calm for twins as they are gradually learning to have separate lives while being in close proximity to one another. School separation is important and is required in most schools. Language development and assertiveness are common problems that are important to address with the teacher and perhaps a speech therapist (Cooper, 2004). If twins are having trouble functioning without each other they will need to see a mental health professional. It is so much easier to solve the different kinds of dependency issues that can develop in childhood, rather than let twins become more entwined. As well twins may have different problems learning and these struggles need to be attended to with care and kindness. For example, one twin can be very socially adept and unable to read. Their twin may be very shy but a non-stop reader. Both children need to broaden their range of strengths and may require tutoring or psychotherapy.

Adolescence

A very turbulent time for twins who want to go their own way and get angry and confused doing so. Twins may need to learn what it means to be a twin and also follow their own path in life. Parents may need the support of mental health professionals to help understand what is going on between their twin children. It is very normal for parents and twins to be on edge and insecure in the teenage years. Twins may need help settling down. I will say it again. It is very important for individuality to be endorsed at this time of life by parents, teachers, and mental health professionals. Strong thoughts, feelings, and words are characteristics of teenage twins who will love one another and then hate one another very very quickly. The roller-coaster of emotion is normal but very hard to contend without help from therapists who work with teenagers.

Early Adulthood

The search for selfhood alone in the world is very important. Twins will need support separating from their twin and learning how to deal with the non-twin world. Making choices that their brother or sister does not support can cause friction between twins and deep feelings of uncertainty about the choices that are being made. Often this is a time that twins seek out the advice of a mental health professional for help adjusting to new relationships, choices that don't include their twin, and singular responsibilities at work and in their personal life.

Adulthood and Midlife

Real-life disappointments—divorce, family loss, career setbacks, children issues—can bring twins together in a realistic way. This is a good time for therapists to help their patients evaluate their twin relationship realistically and to develop a new and mature sense of their relationship as adult twins. Maturity between twins can really happen and will if attention is paid to the real issues that need a solution.

Senior Twins

Older twin still have "baggage" about their relationship but usually they can put their old feelings aside to help one another with later life struggles. When working with older adults it is important to acknowledge the depth of their positive and negative feelings for each other. If you can, at first make simple straightforward suggestions for practical problems (such as "my twin is always on her iPhone when we are together"). As you get to know your senior twin you can develop a deeper relationship. Get your older twin to see that you can help in ways they have not considered. Do not assume that older twins know how to say no to their twin, even though they have had many opportunities to try and become proficient at defining their ego bouondaries.

Being a Twin in a Non-Twin World

Twins need psychological support adjusting to the prejudices of twinship that are projected onto them by their parents, teachers, friends, colleagues, spouses, and question-asking onlookers. Prejudices based on the idealization of twinship in our culture include believing:

1. Twins are idealized images of a perfect relationship, which certainly is not correct.
2. Twins are always similar.
3. Twins are exact opposites of each other.
4. Twins will love one another always and forever.

All of these beliefs take away from understanding of what it is like to be born married and to not be able to get a divorce. Twinship is a complicated attachment with deep love and real rage and ambivalence. Even when twins are given enough opportunity for individual development, being in a minority in the non-twin world is difficult. Also challenging are the attachment issues which I have gone over many times. Many many sessions can be spent on being a twin in a non-twin world.

Longing for Your Early Twin Attachment

Twins will understand this idea immediately. There is something about having someone understand through a look or a gesture that is extremely remarkable and affirming. Longing for this immediate connection is very common even when twins have tried to separate from one another and have had some success in other relationships. Early memories of this type of childhood and teenage comfort can be a sustaining part of self-esteem for twins. Psychotherapy should address this longing directly in order for twins to develop more mature relationships which are not rigidly categorized as all good or all bad.

Strategies to Help Therapists Better Understand the Problems Twins Have Relating to Each Other and Non-Twins

Initially asking about the twin relationship is extremely important as it will make the twin patient feel accepted and will illuminate the pattern of twinship that is shared. You might ask: How would you describe your relationship with your twin? With this information the therapist will be able to develop a sense of the treatment issues. The big question to gather information about is: How over-involved are the patient and their twin? Begin to listen carefully about how much confusion over separate identity exists. Interest in twin development will positively intensify the therapeutic alliance and transference. As well by underlining the centrality of twinship the clinician affirms the deepness of twin attachment. This affirmation in itself is a way of not adhering to stereotypes and prejudices of our culture. Accepting the uniqueness of twin identity is healing for twins who feel like outsiders in a non-twin world.

Get to know your client over many sessions through exploring whatever comes to mind about their twin relationship. Work through the following questions in several sessions. When these issues are addressed you will you get a better sense of what treatment issues should be the focus of treatment. Wonder, as you ask, is there too much closeness? Too much anger? Too much shame? Too much distance?

Question 1: What Is Your Earliest Memory of Being a Twin?

This question in my experience and research is a direct reflection of the type of bond that twins share. For example, interdependent-identity twins remember, "Our closeness was enforced ... we knew that it was always better to be together. We were always being referred to as we and us." Split-identity twins have very different memories that reflect difference and shame or a sense of being weird. One set of split-identity twins reports remembering "Being a walking side show with four legs," "The girl with two heads," "A strange little couple that made Mon and Dad happy." An individual-identity twin pair remembers, "The closeness of being together in the crib," "Playing together in the backyard." Early memories reflect the pattern of twinship, which is predictive of the direction of therapy. Early memories direct and haunt twins throughout the lifespan (Schave and Ciriello, 1983).

Question 2: How Would You Describe Your Parents' Attitude Toward Having Twins?

From my experience there is a range of responses to this question. Common responses include excitement to fear to indifference. Parental attentiveness directs the quality of parental involvement and whether or not your patient was favored or unfavored or had a totally enmeshed relationship with their sister or brother. Parents who see their children as an unexpected burden will intensify and confuse identity issues between their children. Indifferent parents do not take the time to see their children as individuals. They treat their twins as one to save time, energy, and money.

Parents who are excited about their twins show them off but don't work hard enough to see them as unique. They label their children and create a great deal of anger and resentment that leads to estrangement later in life. While interdependent-identity twins can't separate, opposite-identity twins have problems being together as they grow into adulthood.

Parents who are aware of and value differences will encourage independence and individuality. They also respect the profound bond that their children share. Parental attitudes determine how easily twins can separate from one another in order to develop their own individual identity. Even when parents do a "good enough" job of providing individual attention to their twins and do not use their children as a "walking horse and pony show" for attention, inevitably twins will have problems with separations throughout their lifetimes.

Question 3: What Was the Family's Financial and Social Situation When You Were Born?

Environmental influences are very critical in raising twins. Grandparents, nannies, brothers, and sisters can positively or negatively affect the development of identity. Was mother alone with no husband to support and help her? Did dad help out or do most of the work? Did parents fight about how to raise their twins? Were grandparents a part of your patient's life? How bitter were parents about a divorce? Did twins live a calm life in a rural area or were they brought up in an urban jungle?

While money cannot make a good parent, sometimes families with adequate financial and social resources are more able to provide a stable and nurturing home environment which allows for exposure to more individual experiences for both twins. Poor families who have to deal with life in the survival mode are more likely to have difficulty providing enough individual experiences for their children. Wealthy families can lack common sense and pay too much attention to their children's well-being in the wrong ways. Too much emphasis on equality can lead to treating twins as if they should need the same things and be the same. Giving too much is overstimulating and confusing. Twins who are raised by housekeepers and boarding schools will turn to each other for love that they do not really get at home. Sometimes too much is worse than not enough for twins.

Question 4: Did You Have Siblings? How Did They Feel About Having Twin Brothers or Sisters?

These answers will give you insight into the quality of parental care. Were sisters and brothers put in charge of the twins and given too much responsibility? Was there enough love and attention to go around? Understanding if siblings were asked to be surrogate parents will give you a broader understanding of the quality of parenting that was provided. Often brothers or sisters of twins have to function as parents and provide affirmation and attention to twins. Other alliances within the family will be revealed and give insight into the functional or dysfunctional family structure. Understanding the family dynamics will give you insight into what was neglected by the family and what was given freely. Neglect and emotional abuse will create all types of scars that need to be processed.

Question 5: How Did Your Parents See You as Different than Your Twin?

Sometimes twins will say "they saw us as one." Or they might say "mom saw us as different from the beginning and so did the family." Obviously this response sheds light on the quality of parenting and how "real" differences shaped identity for each twin and the pair. The earlier the differentiation between twins the more likely they will be to develop a strong, substantial, and authentic individual identity. Get as much information as you can from this question as it will help you develop a direction for the "true self" in your patient.

Question 6: When Were You First Separated from Your Twin?

I have already written about the importance of separation at the beginning of the book. I will underline this idea again. How parents handle lived separation experiences between twins is extremely critical to the growth of individual identity. If parents are apprehensive about separation, twins will pick up their worry. When twins are not given enough separate experiences in infancy and early childhood, they will have more difficulty dealing with separation and the non-twin world. Social skills need to be experienced and taught early in the lives of twins. Twins need to learn to be alone and find their own interests and explore ideas without their twin. Some parents are eager to develop separate interests and alone time for their twin children. Other parents take advantage of how twins like to share and play together. Parental energy toward all types of differentiation between twins is crucial.

Question 7: What Was It Like for You to Be Separated from Your Twin?

Try and get an emotional response with a great deal of detail. This answer will reflect more directly the warmth of attachment that twins share. Sometimes twins have a cold or indifferent attitude toward one another. Or they are afraid of their anger at one another and do not communicate well in words. Angry outbursts are common when too much anger is held in check. Or one twin will miss the other twin more and feel guilty or betrayed and keep their anger inside. How twins will deal with being alone and coping with new relationships will be suggested in their separation experiences and coming back together exchanges. Twins who are too close or too angry, even if they have an independent sense of self, will be less inclined to seek out other deep relationships because they will fear re-enacting the twin relationship.

Question 8: Did You Attend School Together?

In rare instances twins are not separated at school because they live in a very small community. But usually schools can separate twins and have a policy to do so. It is best when parents are in favor of school separation and do not leave it to the school to make the decision. Parents should advocate for school separation for their children. This answer will give you insight into the development of individuality as well as the quality of their coping strategies. There are both social and academic lessons that twins need to learn when they are apart from each other. While it may be difficult, strategically or emotionally, more school separation is always better!

Question 9: When Do You Think You Started to Want to Be More Distinctive from Your Twin?

Twins are competitive and measure themselves against one another very early in life. It begins when they look for and demand attention from caregivers. Often a sense of being different develops in early childhood over the ability to "be the best or first." The drive for distinctiveness from the co-twin is crucial to the development of their eventual ability to function in the world away from home. The earlier the quest for individuality the more successful the twin will be in adjusting to new friends and colleagues. If individual development is lagging behind for your patient, work on baby steps to help her/him become more independent from their sister or brother and more comfortable in non-twin relationships. Teach your patient that it is good to be different than their sister or brother.

Question 10: Did You Dress Alike Until You Felt the Need to Be Seen as an Individual?

How twins look in comparison to one another is one of the most troublesome of all issues for twins. There is always some intense anxiety about whether or not both twins still look alike. Siblings are never as self-conscious as twins about being different. While boy–girl twins do not have this problem, same-sex twins secretly want to look alike and are confused or panicked when they do not look alike. Young twins through the lifespan to older twins in their seventies and eighties still are concerned that they look different. I am not exaggerating this point, which is definitely an emotion-based problem for twins. Are twins endorsing their individuality or their twinship when they worry about looking different?

The right and best answer is: we never were dressed alike. Obviously, it is optimal for parents to make the decision to dress their twins differently. Oftentimes parents are not psychologically sophisticated enough to make this decision and fall back on the old-fashioned idea that it is cute to dress twins like clones of one another. This question will shed light on how involved your patient is with their twin identity and the narcissistic rewards that are attained from being in public with each other. Over-identification with twin identity will limit the development of the self and the motivation to seek out non-twin relationships.

Question 11: What Was It Like for You to Have Other Children Know You Were a Twin?

This question sheds light on how self-conscious twins feel about being twins. There is clearly a range of answers to this question. Over-identified twins love being seen as twins and do not need to be seen as individuals. Twins with enough individual identity enjoy being a twin and are proud of their twin. Some twins are ashamed that they don't get along with their sister or brother and want to hide from their twinship. The more self-conscious twins are the harder it is for them to attain harmony with each other as adults. Most likely twins who are uncomfortable being in public together as adults have been split into the bad twin and the good twin. A very long-term goal for uncomfortable twins would be to help your patient understand their self-consciousness about being a twin. Twin estrangement groups are very helpful for twins who can't get along with one other. Twins who have strained relationships learn that they are not alone, which helps them deal with their twin issues more effectively.

Question 12: How Would You Describe the Differences Between You and Your Twin?

Leave a lot of space for this response to develop. Get as much detail as possible. Use your validation of differences as a way to support your patient speaking openly about their independent ideas and relationships. Interdependent-identity twins like to ignore the differences between them or make them into discrete and limited traits. Split-identity twins see themselves as total opposites of one another. Individual-identity twins are more realistic about why they are unique. Their answer reflects the quality of attachment twins share and how close they really are to one another as adults. Oftentimes twins are not close to one another because they have been pitted against each other. Twins who have been raised to be individuals will be able to easily describe differences from their co-twin. As much as possible try and encourage the development of pride in individuality.

Question 13: How Did Your Parents Deal with the Issue of Competition?

Twins naturally measure themselves against one another. Competition between twins is an inevitable part of their development as unique people. Each twin pair deals with competition organically in their own way depending on the discipline that parents enforce when they are fighting. Setting up boundaries for twins about fighting and talking about how competition is only part of life is essential. Too much fighting and competition erodes the good powers of the twin attachment that is very useful in later life.

Twins will be able to deal with each other and other people if parents have dealt realistically, practically, and effectively with competition. In most twinships one twin will lag behind the other but dominance in one area is not permanent. This issue of being different and not always being the best is a lesson that has to be learned. If not, twins will have trouble setting limits for one another and other people. When competition between twins is emphasized, polarization and animosity between twins may develop which can lead to anger and estrangement. When competition is ignored ego boundaries between twins become intertwined and competition will truly be confusing. Competition is always a therapeutic issue for twins, which can be resolved through understanding how you are different from your twin. My sister is proud of me and I am proud of her. So I know it can be done.

Question 14: How Did Your Relationship with Your Twin Change Over Time?

When you ask this question try to point out that you believe that change is normal, predictable, and healthy. Your attitude will allow your patient to feel free to express themselves about difficulties they have encountered because they are twins. If your patient is reluctant to share the changes in their relationships, go through all of the stages of development and ask about change directly. Response will give insight into how much interdependence still exists between your patient and their twin, and how much estrangement is likely to develop and last. If you know the intensity of disharmony you will see that estrangement is a valuable coping strategy.

Question 15: Do You Feel that You Still Have a Distinct Twin Identity?

Explain to your patient that twin identity is based on the shared attachment, experiences, and memories of childhoods. While twin identity is immutable, slight differences in individual experiences create differences in personality structure. If your patient relates to or understands this idea continue to explore their thoughts about the difference between individual identity and twin identity. This is a tricky question. Reactions and responses will give you insight into their self-awareness and maturity.

Question 16: Did You Try to Recreate Twinship with Other Very Close Relationships in Your Life? Was It Hard for You to Develop Adult Relationships Outside of the Twinship?

Self-reflection and self-awareness will be illuminated. These answers point out the progress made learning how to function as a twin in a non-twin world. Hopefully some comfort with non-twins has been or will be established. If there is very little comfort outside of the twinship relationship, it is likely that your patient has an interdependent relationship with their twin. Twins in other patterns of twinship will try and find twin replacements both consciously and unconsciously. Twins struggle with non-twins throughout their lifetimes.

Question 17: Did You Ever Feel that Significant Others Could Not Understand What It Was Like for You to Be a Twin?

Interdependent-identity twins will be confused or ignore this question because they are so entwined. The answers of all other twins will reflect their ability to be honest about their struggles of being a twin. As well their answer will reveal to you how emotionally tuned in your patient is to others in their interpersonal world. You will get a sense of how much individual identity they have developed and their comfort level with being separated from their twin.

Question 18: How Did Your Children Deal with You Being a Twin?

There is a range of responses to this question. It is important to know if children feel like outsiders to their parent's twin relationship. Or do they feel valued and special. When children feel second best this a therapeutic issue to deal with very directly. Most twins will not want to slight their children and will work hard to overcome this issue. More complications can unfold. Oftentimes twins give their children too much attention to make up for what they did not get as children. Parenthood recreates the problems and struggles of your childhood which can be projected unwisely onto children of twins.

Question 19: Did You Ever Feel Lonely in Non-Twin Relationships?

In my opinion the honest answer is YES. Some twins will deny their loneliness because they are ashamed of it, which is a problem in and of itself. Responses will suggest whether or not the patient is feeling depressed or isolated. Loneliness for twins is common but should be dealt with therapeutically through increasing non-twin social interactions and skills. Normalizing the state of loneliness for twins is healing. Monitoring new social activities is also critical. Learn what works for your twin patient and what is not effective in reducing their negativity. Twins can hold on to their longings for their early twin bond and not try to make new friendships.

Question 20: What Kinds of Life Experiences Brought You Closer to Your Twin as an Adult?

New families bring twins closer if there is enough acceptance of creating different family lives and structure. Often twins who cannot accept their unique choices are estranged from each other. Estranged twins will be brought together by a tragedy, divorce, or death. This is a good time to work on the positive aspects of twinship with estranged or alienated twins.

Question 21: What Life Experiences Created Differences and Distance Between You and Your Twin?

Most often romantic partners, families, careers, and special interests allow for individual development which is very important at every stage of development throughout the lifespan. This information will give you insight into your patient's motivation and capacity for individuality. Always endorse individuality, no matter how entwined your patient may seem to be. There is always a reluctance on the part of twins to be different from their twin. At the same time twins enjoy being different and have more to share when they are together.

Question 22: How Would You Describe Your Present Relationship with Your Twin?

Sometimes twins are at peace with their sister or brother, and contentment is a source for therapeutic discussion. Sometimes they are estranged and need to share their disappointments in their twin and family structure. The goals in therapy will be related to this answer. If twins want a better relationship with their twin then this can be a goal. If twins want to get more distance from their sister or brother acceptance of relationship limitations is also a goal. Twin relationships really do change normally throughout the lifespan. Help your patient to accept that change in twin attachment is going to happen. Fighting change will just make life harder for everyone.

What Twins Should Ask the Mental Health Professional

It is important that the patient has some understanding of the mental health professional's knowledge and experiences with twins. Below are important questions to get answered when you are deciding to go into psychotherapy.

What Is Your Understanding of Twinship?

Good enough reaction:

- I am a twin myself.
- I have read about twins and understand the importance of their attachment.
- I am an attachment therapist and very interested in the twin experience of attachment.

Inadequate reaction:

- I am not interested in psychodynamic psychotherapy. I believe in cognitive behavioral approaches.
- I do not understand why the twin relationship is any more important than the sibling relationship.

Do You See Other Twins in Therapy?

Good enough reaction:

- Yes, I have worked with several twins separately and together.
- I am very interested in working with twins and have mentors to discuss any problems I might encounter if I need help.

Inadequate reaction:

- This would be my first experience but I am fascinated by how close and similar twins can be.

Are You a Twin?

Good enough reaction:

- Yes, or my children, or my husband, or my best friend are twins.

Inadequate reaction:

- No, but I am fascinated in stories of good and evil that use twins to highlight problems of opposition.
- No, but I always wanted to be a twin.

Do You Have Any Twins in Your Close Family?

Good enough reaction:

- Yes, I have had some friends that are twins, etc.

Inadequate reaction:

- No, but our family is close and we think that we could be twins.

What Are Your Concerns About Working in Therapy with a Twin?

Good enough reaction:

- I want to help twin patients find their own path.
- I hope that I can identify with their struggles with their friends and family.

Inadequate reaction:

- I am sure that working with twins is no different than working with siblings.

While these questions may seem very pointed, they will help the mental health professional understand that you take your twin issues seriously. And of course the answers to these questions will help you decide on the right clinician to work with.

As you listen to their responses and reactions to these questions try to be open-minded and non-judgmental. Trust your sense of the mental health professional's authenticity as well as their stated knowledge and experience. Remember it is not always possible to see a therapist who is a twin. Your goal should be to work with someone who has the enthusiasm and energy to deal with the complications that you will bring to the work of understanding yourself as an individual and as a twin.

Common Misunderstandings that Create Treatment Impasses with Twins

Closeness and the need for understanding and affirmation is a basic issue for twins. Try and be aware of the following treatment impasses that you can easily fall into as you work on understanding what will help your twin patient's self-awareness and well-being.

Impasse 1: Twin Attachment Is a Secondary Issue

You are surely missing a crucial piece of your patient's presenting problem if you believe this to be true. Twin attachment is always a core issue no matter what the presenting reason for looking for support and understanding may be. If your twin patient says that twinship is not important to them any more, than you know that he or she is in denial or dread about their sister or brother. Try to gently uncover their fear or rage that is provoked when they think about being a twin. Remember, in early adulthood, twins with opposite identities are ashamed of each other or afraid of each other and like to pretend that they are not a twin.

Impasse 2: Don't Bad Mouth The Twin Who Is Being Talked About with Negativity by Your Patient

No matter how enraged a twin is with their twin sister or brother, there is a very deep attachment that is shared. When you criticize the twin sister or brother you are criticizing and shaming your patient and causing confusion. Try and make interpretations with this knowledge in your back pocket. For example, "I can see that you are very angry with your twin" is easier to hear and more appropriate than "You sound like you hate your twin for being so domineering/helpless." Avoid a rigid label about the twin sibling. Try to make a positive connection in the present with the twin attachment that promotes self-understanding. For example, you might ask: What about being a twin made you a stronger individual?

Impasse 3: Don't Over-Analyze Individual Development

Often twins can alarm a therapist because they are so close to one another or seem to have no ego boundaries. For example, I am sure that my first analyst thought I did not know how to say no to my sister. He was correct and it took many many years to learn this lesson. My difficulty in saying no was very frustrating for him. But he was smart enough to realize that I had a problem being a twin. Unfortunately, he was too concerned with my individual development and my resumé. Our goal of my professional success was completed. There was a lot of twin work that was left undone.

If the mental health professional becomes over-focused on individual development you can get on the wrong track or scare away your patient. Try to get your patient to see for themselves the importance of their uniqueness in their twinship and to others in their life. For example, therapist's love to talk about ego boundaries as if there really are ego boundaries that outline who we are. You need to be careful not to judge twins as being enmeshed, as this statement puts twins on the defensive. It is better to ask twins to take responsibility for only their part of a problem they are facing with their twin or twin replacement. Your judgment will breed their judgment which will not help anyone. Clearly judgments create therapeutic impasse. Your responsibility is to help develop a better sense of their individuality.

Impasse 4: Don't Be Reluctant to Bring in the Twin

When twins bring their twin to therapy, in almost every situation, they feel understood by their therapist. Divided alliances do not develop from this intervention. My second analyst saw my twin and I together once. He said "You are both very high strung." This was helpful for both of us to hear because it was true and simple. He did not take sides! You could use this intervention with your twin patients.

In other words, sides and alignments are not established if you are careful to avoid these types of interaction. For example, see each twin as an individual not as an opposite of the other or joined at the hip. Seeing the twin of your patient gives you deep insight into who your patient really is without the use of words. Living through the interactions between twins will help you understand how your patient will relate to you. For example, the quiet twin will relate in a contained manner. The less reserved twin will be more comfortable with confrontation.

Impasse 5: Being a Know-It-All

Collaboration on making goals for psychotherapy is crucial. Learn what your patient wants to understand and take action on it. Keep your judgments and opinions to yourself for a while. Otherwise you will become a twin replacement who makes decisions. You want your patient to learn how to make their own decisions. By the way, it is very hard for twins to learn to make their own decisions, so you will have to be patient and understanding.

Impasse 6: Believing that if One Twin Can Do Something the Other Can Do It as Well

Twins are not copies of one another. Naturally twins develop complementary strengths, which means that when one twin is skilled at something the other twin may not be as competent or interested. This is normal. Work with your patient to develop the strengths that are lacking in their behavioral repertoire if they want to develop these strengths. Assuming that twins have the same strengths reinforces the prejudices that plague twins.

Impasse 7: Competition Is Hard for Twins

Twins have a different sense of competitiveness because they were born to compete with each other. For example, after a long day of fighting with one another almost all young twins want to sleep in the same bed together because of the comfort they receive from being next to each other. When they are together they are good winners and good losers. Keep this in mind! Twins get over being the best or worst at something in a different way than non-twins. Usually twins are proud of one another. Sometimes twins share in their brother or sister's accomplishments *not* because they share ego boundaries and are too enmeshed. Rather, and most definitely, twins appreciate one another because they understand how hard the co-twin has worked to attain their goal.

Competition that is not dealt with by parents, psychotherapists, and teachers leads to anger and estrangement in adulthood. When there is estrangement between the pair based on differences and shame, the split-identity pattern of twinship has not been processed or resolved. You can help your twin patients accept their twin as an adult. Help them come to a peaceful understanding of the limitations of their relationship to one another.

Therapeutic Goals that Promote Mature Twin Relationships

Twins strive for individuality as they mature. Mature twin relationships based on adult challenges can be hard to develop because for twins closeness breeds longings for togetherness and rage at differences. In other words, often when twins are together they regress back into their childhood relationship that gave them comfort. Whether consciously or unconsciously, twins are a part of each other's decision-making. For twins, seeing yourself alone in the mirror is a metaphor with many different meanings. Sadness and loss and the need to decide on your own are the most general meanings of being alone in the mirror. Both twins and their therapists should take into consideration the following ideas as they reflect the different positive and healthy states of mind involved when twins feel they can function without their twin.

1. Pride about being able to stand on your own two feet and not need the support of your twin.
2. Relief that you are free to explore the world on your own.
3. Sadness for twins who are missing each other.
4. Confusion if you are ambivalent about not being copies of one another.
5. A judgment about how psychologically healthy you are.
6. Disappointment and rage about how limited other people are in comparison to your twin.
7. Devastation if your twin is no longer alive and traumatic grief.

These mindsets are realistic goals for psychotherapy with twins.

Conclusions

When working with twins keep in mind that, without even expressing their connection to one another, twins feel deeply attached. Twin attachment grows with the passage of time and countless shared experiences. Without talking twins can communicate their thoughts, feelings, and concerns to one another. Inevitably, twins must come to understand on an intellectual level that their attachment is profound and irrevocable. Parents can encourage this self-awareness, knowledge, and truth by speaking to their children about being twins. Teachers, as well, should acknowledge and develop a dialogue about their student's brother or sister. The psychotherapist's long-range goal is to understand with their patient the profound attachment both magical and difficult that is shared. Helping a twin to see how their bond is an irrevocable aspect of their identity is totally essential to their sense of self, mental health, and happiness. Being a twin in a non-twin world takes time and an investment in coping strategies.

Maturity is always more reachable if the above states of mind which have varied meanings are understood and acknowledged. This is hard to accomplish. The key to mental health is working through in dialogue, and understanding, actions and reactions to the twin relationship. Making sure that the individual's sense of self is strong in its foundation and not riddled with insecurities or lack of psychic structure is essential. Both twins should be able to function on their own. Understanding that separation from the twin is a long process which can be at times disruptive to a positive sense of self and evoke deep feelings of loneliness. Separation is also freedom to be what you want to be. Most of all twins need to decide for themselves if they want to have a mature relationship with their brother or sister.

8 Affirming Relationship Changes for Twins Throughout the Lifespan

Similarities and sharing make twin development a unique experience when compared to single-birth children. Twins share their parents. their early life experiences, and a special verbal and non-verbal communication and language. Twins share an identity as twins. Individual identity in infancy and early childhood is developed through verbal and sensory motor interactions with parents and other caregivers that do not include their twin. The importance of separate experiences to overall emotional health and well-being is primary, alongside the necessary issue of tolerating distance from the twin. Crossover developmental processes of sharing and individuality take time and sensitivity to be played out appropriately in the process of identity development in twins. Without attention to the details of unique identity development, enmeshment or narcissistic injuries are sure to haunt the lives of adult twins (Klein, 2012).

Finding real differences between twins is the first step towards developing an organic individual sense of self in each child. For example, one twin likes the song "Rock away baby." His twin sister likes "Old McDonald had a farm." Sing them their own songs. Show some genuine pride in your children for having favorites. While splitting your twins into opposites such as bad/good or strong/weak is a form of "twin abuse" and should be avoided no matter what, it is critical to make a habit of seeing and responding to differences (Schave, 1982; Schave and Ciriello, 1983). Cementing individual identity is an inoculation that provides immunity to estrangement later in life.

So many parents have told me that it was easy for them to see differences between their children if they were paying attention to developing their individuality. Respond to each child as a special person. Differences in their temperament will grow stronger. After your twins fight over what toy belongs to which one of them, different toys will eventually be favorite for one twin or the other. These little special choices create a sense of individuality and need to be valued, encouraged, and respected. Individuality begins with choices in childhood. Conflicts between twins will be minimized in adolescence. Fears of expansiveness will be more manageable later in life when individuality is encouraged.

Treating twins as one is a toxic recipe that is way too easy to follow if you are an overwhelmed or indifferent parent. While twins will eventually turn to one another, share, and provide parental support, if they are ignored by caregivers there are serious social and emotional consequences as they grow into adulthood (Schave and Ciriello, 1983). Help your children when they fight by fairly establishing what is going on. Conflicts are hard for twins to work through on their own. Being apart is very challenging no matter how much anger is expressed at one another. Try and give your children coping strategies for being separate. Interdependence in adulthood limits the life choices of twins and their ultimate happiness and mental health. When there is too much interdependence between twins, fears of expansiveness are navigated together with the help of psychotherapy.

Establishing differences based on parental projections creates anger, resentment, and estrangement between twins who are dependent on one another until they separate. This is a common occurrence when differences are staged, superficial, and inauthentic. Parents see their twins as narcissistic extensions of themselves and need the attention twins bring from outsiders. Privately these parents are not psychologically sophisticated enough to develop authentic relationships with their twins. In contrast, parents who can experience their children as different give them the gift to become who they truly are as they journey through life.

In infancy and childhood, parents are decision-makers whose optimal role is to develop communication, individuality, and respect. As twins separate and grow into adulthood, they make more of their own decisions. New friendships, career choices, and interests create a shift in the twin relationship. These shifts are to be expected and critical to the maturity of the twins—their overall health and prosperity. New relationships create emotional confusion between the pair. Social skills and anxiety about being on your own can be overwhelming and freeing. It is hard to be on your own and relate to the non-twin world. Who takes care of what your twin did for you without asking? Who understands the look in your eyes? What makes you afraid? Separating and forming new friendships is hard to go through but a necessary price for developing a true self.

Recurring Lifespan Issues

Finding Your Own Path

This is a one baby step at a time process that can be side by side with your twin or on very far away paths. As twins grow older it is helpful for them to acknowledge and respect the different paths they have taken.

Exploring New Friendships and Partners

Some new friendships will be superficial. Others will be more profound. Betrayal and disappointment will become experiences that are difficult to live through. Twins will turn to each other or turn away at these pivotal times. If support is forthcoming then maturity will be built into the twin relationship.

Excepting and Affirming Relationship Changes

This is a part of growing up and realizing that your world is larger than your twinship. Some new interests and friends can be shared but some friends and interests are not "community property." Boundaries between twins can create competition and anger. Or boundaries can provide a sense of freedom. Closed boundaries can strangle twins from realizing their potential.

Dealing with Shameful Feelings About Your Twin

When separations occur at any age there is always shame that reflects uncomfortable feelings about making different choices and being different people. Some twins will be open about their negative feelings about their twin and others will cover them up in an attempt to be in harmony with their sister or brother in the public eye. Brothers and sisters do not feel the intense closeness and shame that twins share. It is often hard for non-twins to understand this source of friction between twins. There is a definite agreement among adult twins that shame about their twin affects their sense of self-worth. Because shame is based on over-identification, the anger and confusion it will provoke is hard to overcome.

Longing for Childhood Closeness

The early memories of walking hand-in-hand and sharing closeness and friendship, and companionship, and even identity is hard to forget on an intellectual level and emotionally. When twins are together they have a sense of power as one which makes them feel like they can conquer any problem that they confront together. I remember the 3-year-old twins who climbed on each other's backs to open cupboards and stereo equipment against the house rules. My sister and I had some red furniture polish which was taken away from us in the hospital. The feeling of success using twin power is incredible and addictive for twins. Double trouble is a form of expansiveness that can be useful if channeled correctly. When double trouble is used to sequester twins from making new friends and following different life paths double trouble can be very destructive indeed.

Fighting Is Not a Long-Term Solution

Fighting is normal for twins from an early age. Children verbally abuse or bully each other. They can be physically aggressive if they have seen this behavior at home or school. Girls can pull each other's hair out. While boys can fist-fight and end up in the emergency room. Still, the worst fighting I have heard about is based on cruel words and thoughts that are meant to be hurtful and demeaning. The long-term use of fighting erodes a twin relationship over time. Estrangement can become a normal and comfortable way of relating to avoid anger. Getting help with anger management or other types of psychotherapy for twins is very important as they grow older. Connecting without anger will help twins rely on each other more easily, which will provide important support. Maturity between twins is always based on some sort of forgiveness. Unfortunately, forgiveness is not always possible.

Loneliness

The most painful and hard to fight emotion for me and for many of the twins I have worked with or known in my personal life is loneliness. This intense emotion is hard to explain to non-twins. After-effects of loneliness are detachment from others or a hyper attempt to recreate the twinship with another. Twins need to understand this painful state of mind and make being alone more tolerable. Feelings of loneliness will change throughout the lifespan.

Psychotherapy Is Critical

At different times in life twins may need the support and insight of psychotherapy. While it helps to work with a mental health professional who is a twin, it is also difficult to find a twin in your neighborhood or community. Getting feedback from a psychological perspective about how you interact with others is very useful for twins as it is healing and allows for more self-differentiation.

Being a Twin in a Non-Twin World

Early life is the best time to be a twin. I am very sure of this statement from all of the twins who have shared their life stories with me. Changes in your perception of the value of twinship will change over time. I, like many other twins, spent many years in young adulthood trying not to be a twin. Struggling with twin identity is a long and complicated journey which you cannot do alone. The more real communication twins have with non-twins, the more likely they will feel comfortable without their twin. Accepting that twin closeness is not normal for single-born individuals takes a lot of time to digest as you travel through your life. Twins can help other twins understand this issue.

When You Help Yourself in Psychotherapy You Help Your Twin

This statement may sound incorrect and uninformed but it is true. Even if therapy makes you acknowledge your anger and disappointment in your twin at any stage of life, it also allows you the freedom to be yourself. Your twin will learn from you that being different and disappointed is a part of everyone's life.

Obstacles to Developing an Adult Relationship with Your Twin

It is easy for twins to "beat around the bush" with one another. By this I mean that far too often twins do not share what is on their mind with their sister or brother, in an attempt not to upset them or themselves. Strangely, being honest with your twin can be frightening if they don't want to hear what you have to say. I know this to be true in my own relationship with my sister. I regret not being more honest in my opinions with her. I would let my anger and frustrations build up and then tell her when it was really too big in my mind. I think she did the same thing. This dishonesty caused fighting and intense anger which eroded our relationship. Saying this, I know how hard it can be to be honest with your twin.

***

Obviously there is no one recipe for sharing a genuine relationship in maturity with your twin. Harmony is a very difficult goal to attain later in life for twins. Looking at how the twins in this book found some peace of mind will help you understand how to approach developing a mature relationship. Parents, other relatives, and therapists will experience success as they try and create the pathways that are encouraged in this book.

In closing I share the profound happiness, delight, and sense of closeness that I have felt working with twins to become more self-focused and tuned into who they are as twins and as individuals. Every group session is important to the members. Whether I start with a theme like, "Why is it hard for twins to be true to themselves?", or an issue that is troubling someone in group, we all present new points of view, insight, and support. Here is a fond memory of a group encounter:

> Dr. Klein: We have two new members today. Keith a fraternal twin who has not had contact with his brother for 30 years. Dave who will be the youngest member of group, only 25, is having trouble separating from his brother. Dave wants his freedom and his own space but worries about how his independence will affect his twin. Can you introduce yourself briefly to the new members? Please tell us how you have developed a more mature relationship with your twin.
>
> Jackie: I am an identical twin who has been in this group for over a year. My sister and I can only get along if I act like I am not a successful women in my own right. While I am a professor and I have a black belt in karate, I have to be diminutive when I am with her. The group encouraged me to write her a letter about how I felt about her ignoring my wedding. She said that when I talked about my wedding I was leaving her out. [This is a synopsis of the conversation.] She hates it when I am more important than her. The group is supporting that my anger and frustration with her is more important than her sadness of feeling less than me.
>
> I believe that I have gained the strength to be myself in all relationships. When someone asks me for help, be it a student or the dean, I can say that I am too busy now but I will call you if I have time. Yesterday I postponed a

meeting with the head of my department because I wanted to attend a rally on campus with Michelle Obama. This was hard for me to do. I had to put myself first—a sign of my new sense of self and my maturity as a twin. I am hoping that I can put myself before my twin next time we see each other.

Vince: I am an identical twin whose twin committed suicide almost seven years ago. I have worked hard to overcome this devastating loss. Finally I am at peace with my life but continue to have difficulties being assertive with doctors and nurses at the hospital where I work. Breaking it off with my horrific mother is still an unattainable goal. Getting over being the caretaker has been very hard for me. The group values my struggles which makes it easier for me to move forward with my own life.

I have had to grow as an individual because my brother is gone. At first I was so lost that I could not believe that the doctors and nurses at the hospital were three-dimensional. I would walk around them to make sure they were real. Barbara was concerned about this unbelievable strangeness in my behavior. I now see the world as it is. I have worked hard to get to my own place in this world. Maturity to me means making my own choices. I do this on a daily basis no matter what other people say about me. I am thankful to be in a better space.

Sarah: I am a school librarian and I have two young children. For more than five years I had no contact with my identical twin sister who refused to accept my husband as a part of our extended family. She blamed me for everything that went wrong in her life. I was terrified of her. I worked hard to establish my career and take care of my family. Recently she divorced and turned to me for support. I have given her some of my thoughts about her situation. Now she visits with her children. My children like having cousins. I am still keeping my distance as I tend to get lost in her problems. I work all the time in group learning how to say no to others who want to use me. It is hard but I am getting better because group members make me be accountable to myself.

My relationship with my twin has changed. I am no longer at her beck and call. I can say no to other teachers and my principal. I have new friendships that revolve around my interests in music and art. I am going back to graduate school to get a doctorate in education. I am enjoying my sense of expansiveness as Barbara has encouraged over the years we have worked together. Maturity to me is being myself and as important as my sister.

Sandy: My twin brother and I have not spoken for at least 25 years. He has literally seen me as invisible and I feel totally humiliated by his behavior. No one in the family has openly supported me or taken my side. I have been on my own my entire life. Even in my two marriages I was the caretaker. Asking for and getting what I deserve is hard. I did not really fall in love until I was in my late forties. That break-up caused me to find support for being a twin. Knowing that other twins don't get along has helped me focus on myself and ask for what I need. Still it is hit and miss with my ability to stand up for myself. Barbara thinks I am very talented in protecting the other twins in group.

I am so delighted to understand my reluctance to follow my own heart. I was told as a child to take care of my brother. Getting over this parental demand has been hard. I take care of others as if they were my twin. Giving up on feeling ashamed that I cannot and will not get along with my brother has freed me to get what I want. I can say it. I want my own garden design business. I want my own house and my own garden.

Stephen: I grew up in London with my identical twin brother. He left London to study at Ohio State where he got his PhD. Now he lives in Hawaii. We are both professors of history. We have lived in separate countries for many decades and visit each other once a year. I feel connected to him and can't imagine what I would do if he died. Vince's situation is hard for me to imagine. I am very lonely and I have been unable to find relief through any type of medication or therapy. When I started going to this group I began to understand what was causing my intense loneliness. I am intensely interested in finding a soulmate and being understood by others. It would be amazing if I could recreate the group with my colleagues.

Having a more mature twin relationship means accepting that my brother and I are no longer as close as we were in childhood or as teenagers. We have gone our separate ways but I still miss the connection we had. I am looking to find a close partner to give me the sense of connection I had with my brother growing up.

Keith: I am so amazed at everyone's kindness and sensitivity to me. I am so ashamed of my family and the reality that my brother and I have not spoken for over 30 years. Like Sandy people who know that I am a twin cannot believe that my brother and I cannot be in the same room together. My brother hates me. He has been so cruel to me that I carry around such enormous shame and feel like no one could ever care about me.

Dave: Wow I can't believe what I am hearing. I hope these deep arguments don't happen to me and my brother. We are having a hard time separating. Maybe our separation is more difficult because we were twin performers growing up. Now I want my own career and he does not care about anything but his boyfriends. I am confused. Should I leave him behind? Of course I should. But I can't.

Dr. Klein: Thank you for introducing yourselves. I can see that you are all sensitive to others and how others treat you. It seems like you all long for harmony in relationships even when you know that the childhood closeness you shared is not easily found as an adult.

The Last Story

When I wrote my dissertation on twin development at USC in 1982 my doctoral advisor invited my twin sister, my then husband, and my children to attend my final oral. The date was April 1, 1982. I was very anxious so my committee informed me that I had graduated at the top of my class on the written part of the exams. I walked into the room where my children were sitting: each had their own friend as company. Maybe I believed they needed a twin like I had as a young person. My sister had left her students at Stanford to be an observer. Marjorie sat next to my husband. We were all appropriately dressed in our 1980s finest.

The oral exam started. Halfway through I could not remember an answer to a question that I was asked to answer, I did know as I had practiced with my husband the night before at the Cheesecake Factory in Beverly Hills. He knew the answer. So I said to him: "will you answer that question for me I am too nervous to remember." The chairman of my committee looked at me and said "this is your examination not your husband's." Dr. Smart was a "meanie," taking time to assert her power over me at that moment.

When Dr. Fox asked me what was the most important thing I had learned I told them that my research suggested that the mother identified differently with each of her twin children. From my research, parenting was the basis of differences in twins. To me it looked like nobody understood this answer. Although I do think my psychiatrist husband could have gotten the closest to understanding my findings. I was polite and did not point out that they had not done their homework reading my dissertation. But then more questions were thrown towards me which I could recall. I passed. I knew that even though it was April Fools' Day, I was a doctor.

I started refining my research outside in the lobby of the education building at USC. Dr. Fox asked me: "Barbara who is the dominant twin you or your sister?" I said "my sister Marjorie." Ten minutes later my sister told me that Dr. Fox had asked her the same question and she had said that I was the dominant twin. Amazingly we did not argue about who had right answer. Obviously our relationship was far more complicated. Probably we silently agreed that it was a "ridiculous question." My sister with some concern in her voice said I hope you will rest on "your laurels." Or she could have said give me a chance to catch up with you. I was beyond listening to her advice.

I wondered why my very smart advisor who had helped me throughout the project was thinking in such a narrow-minded way. I learned that the academic sense of twinship was very different than the real psychological lives of twins. I have been fortunate enough to learn more and more about why twins are different from one another and from single-born children.

Bibliography

Ainslie, R. (1997). *Psychology of Twinship*. Northvale, NJ: Jason Aronson.
Ainsworth, M. (1974). "Infant Mother Attachment and Social Development." In M. Richards (ed.), *The Integration of the Child into a Social World*. London: Cambridge University Press, pp. 29–51.
Ainsworth, M., and Biehar, M. (2015). *Patterns of Attachment: A Psychological Study of the Strange Situation*. New York: Routledge Classic Editions.
Allen, M., Greenspan, S., and Pollin, W. (1976). "The Effect of Parental Perception on Early Development in Twins." *Psychiatry* 39: 65–71.
Arthurs, V. (2014). *Naked Angels*. Pittsburgh, PA: Dorrance Publishing Co.
Baby Center Expert Advice (2015). *Your Likelihood of Having Twins or More*. Nov. Online at: www.babycenter.com.
Bailey, J. M., and Pillard, R. C. (1991). "A Genetic Study of Male Sexual Orientation." *Archives of General Psychiatry* 48: 1089–96.
Baker, D. (1962/2012). *Cassandra at the Wedding*. New York Review of Books Classic, New York Review of Books.
Baker, L., and Daniels, D. (1990). "Non-Shared Environmental Influences and Personality Differences in Adult Twins." *Journal of Personality and Social Psychology* 58(1): 103–10.
Basch, M. (1982). "Discussion: The Significance of Infant Developmental Studies for Psychoanalytic Theory." *Psychoanalytic Inquiry* 1(4): 731–7.
Bass, E., and Davis, L. (1998). *The Courage to Heal*. New York: Harper & Row.
Baumrind, D. (1995). *Child Maltreatment and Optimal Caregiving in Social Contexts*. Garland Reference Library of Social Science. New York: Garland Science.
Beebe, B., and Lachmann, F. (1988). "Mother–Infant Mutual Influence and Precursors of Psychic Structure." In A. Goldberg (ed.), *Progress in Self Psychology*, vol. 3. Hillsdale, NJ: Halstad Press, pp. 33–42.
Bell, R. (1977). *Child Effects on Adults*. Hillsdale, NJ: Halstad Press.
Benjamin, J. (2015). *Nine Tricks to Raising Twins (and Staying Sane)*. Momtastic Parenting. Online at: http://www.momtastic.com/parenting/403205-9-tricks-to-raising-twins-and-staying-sane/
Bouchard, T. (1994). "Genes, Environment, and Personality." *Science* 246(5166): 1700–2.
Bowlby, J. (1958). "The Nature of the Child's Tie to His Mother." *International Journal of Psychoanalysis* 39: 350–73.
Bowlby, J. (1973) *Separation Anxiety and Anger*. New York: Basic Books.
Brandt, R. (2001). *Twin Loss: A Book for Survivor Twins*. Leo, IN: Twinsworld Publishing Co.

Briere, J., and Scott, C. (2006) *Principles of Trauma Therapy: A Guide to Symptoms, Evaluations, and Treatment.* Thousand Oaks, CA: Sage.

Brody, E., and Brody, N. (1976). *Intelligence: Nature, Determinants and Consequences.* New York: Academic Press.

Brooker, W. (2004). *Alice's Adventures: Lewis Carroll in Popular Culture.* London: Continuum International Publishing Group.

Brooker, W. (2005). *Alice's Adventures: Lewis Carroll in Popular Culture.* London: Bloomsbury.

Brothers, D. (2008). *Toward a Psychology of Uncertainty: Trauma-Centered Psychoanalysis.* New York: Analytic Press.

Brothers, D. (2012). "Trauma, Gender and the Dark Side of Twinship." *International Journal of Psychoanalytic Self Psychology* 7(3): 391–405.

Brown-Braun, B. (2010). *You're Not the Boss of Me.* New York: HarperCollins Publishers.

Burlingham, D. (1952). *Twins: A Study of Three Pairs of Identical Twins.* New York: International Universities Press.

Burlingham, D. (1963). "A Study of Identical Twins." In R. Eissler (ed.), *The Psychoanalytic Study of the Child,* vol. 18. New Haven, CT: Yale University Press, pp. 367–423.

Case, B. J. (1991). *We Are Twins But Who Am I?* Portland, OR: Tibbit.

Chess, S., and Thomas, A. (1963). *Behavioral Individuality in Early Childhood.* New York: New York University Press.

Claridge, G. S., Hume, W., and Canter, S. (1973). *Personality Differences and Biological Variations: A Study of Twins.* New York: Pergamon Press.

Clarkin, J., Fongasy, P., and Gabbard, G., eds (2010). *Psychodynamic Psychotherapy for Personality Disorders.* Arlington, VA: American Psychiatric Pub. Inst.

Cohen, D., Allen, M., Pollin, M. Werner, M., and Dibble, E. (1972). "Personality Development in Twins." *Journal of the American Academy of Child Psychiatry,* 11: 625–44.

Cohen, D., Dibble, E., and Grave, J. (1977). "Parental Style in Twin Interaction." *Archives of General Psychiatry* 34: 445–51.

Cooper, C. (2004). *Twins and Multiple Births.* London: Random House.

Cooper, D. (January 2016). "Twin Studies Reveal Eating Disorder Connection." Jan. Online at: www.eatingdisorderhope.com.

Cotton, N. (1985). "The Development of Self Esteem and Self Esteem Regulation." In J. Mack and S. Ablon (eds), *The Development and Sustaining of Self Esteem in Childhood.* New York: International Universities Press, pp. 122–50.

Courtois, C. (1988). *Healing the Incest Wound.* New York: W. W. Norton.

Cox, H., and Lathan, E. (1974). *Selected Prose of Robert Frost.* New York: Macmillan.

Cresswell, J. (1996). *Qualitative Inquiry and Research Design: Choosing among Five Traditions.* Thousand Oaks, CA: Sage Publications.

Davis, E. A. (1937). *The Development of Linguistic Skill in Twins, Singletons, and Sibs and Only Children from 5–10.* Minneapolis, MN: Institute of Child Welfare, University of Minnesota.

Day, E. (1932). "The Development of Language in Twins: A Comparison of Twin and Single Children." *Child Development* 3: 298–316.

Demos, V. (1982). "Affect in Early Infancy: Physiology or Psychology?" *Psychoanalytic Inquiry* 1(4): 533–74.

Department of Health (1992). *Vital and Health Statistics: Health and Demographic Characteristics of Twin Births: United States, 1988.* Series 21, no. 50. June. Hyattsville, MD: US Department of Health.

DeVita-Raeburn, E. (2004). *The Empty Room: Understanding Sibling Loss.* New York: Scribner.

Diaz, N. (2013). *What to Do When You're Having Two: The Twins Survival Guide from Pregnancy Through the First Year.* New York: Penguin Group.

Dibble, E., and Cohen, D. (1981). "Personality Development in Identical Twins: The First Decade of Life." *Psychoanalytic Study of the Child* 36: 45–70.

Diskin, S. (2001). *The End of the Twins: A Memoir of Losing a Brother.* Woodstock, NY: Overlook Press.

Dworkin, R. (1979). "Genetic and Environmental Influences on Person Situation Interactions." *Journal of Personality* 13: 279–93.

Ellis, E. (2014). *Relational Maintenance Behavior and Communication Channel Use among Adult Twins.* Ann Arbor, MI: UMT Dissertation Publishing.

Engel, G. L. (1975). "The Death of a Twin: Mourning and Anniversary Reactions: Fragments of 10 Years of Self-Analysis." *International Journal of Psychoanalysis* 45: 23–40.

Erickson, E. (1950). *Childhood and Society.* New York: W. W. Norton.

Erickson, E. (1968). *Identity: Youth and Crisis.* New York: W. W. Norton.

Farber, S. (1981). *Twins Reared Apart: A Reanalysis.* New York: Basic Books.

Flavell, J. (1977). *Cognitive Development.* Englewood Cliffs, NJ: Prentice-Hall.

Floderus-Myrhed, B., Pederson, N., and Rasmuson, I. (1980). "Assessment of Heritability for Personality Based on a Short Form of the Eysenck Personality Inventory, a Study of 12,898 Twin Pairs." *Behavioral Genetics* 10: 153–61.

Foch, T., O'Connor, M., Plomin, R., and Sherry, T. (1980). "A Twin Study of Specific Behavioral Problems of Socialization as Viewed by Parents." *Journal of Abnormal Child Psychology* 81: 189–99.

Fonagy, P., and Target, M. (2003). *Psychoanalytic Theories: Perspectives from Developmental Psychopathology.* New York: Routledge.

Fonagy, P., Gergely, G., Jurist, E. L., and Target, M. (2005). *Affect Regulation, Mentalization, and the Development of Self.* New York: Other Press.

Frederickson, R. (1992). *Repressed Memories: A Journey to Recovery from Sexual Abuse.* New York: Simon & Schuster.

Friedman, J. A. (2008). *Emotionally Healthy Twins: A New Philosophy for Parenting Two Unique Children.* Jackson, TN: Lifelong Book Perseus Book Group (Member of Da Capo Press)

Friedman, J. A. (2014). *The Same But Different: How Twins Can Live, Love, and Learn to Be Individuals.* Los Angeles, CA: Rocky Pines Press.

Freud, S. (1921). "Three Essays on the Theory of Sexuality". In *Standard Edition of the Complete Psychological Works of Sigmund Freud*, vol. 7. London: Hogarth Press.

Gessell, A. (1941). *Comparative Studies of Twin T. and C.* Genetic Psychological Monographs, ed. C. Murchison. Provincetown, MA: Journal Press.

Gifford, S., Murawski, B., Brazelton, B. T., and Young, G. C. (1966). "Differences in Individual Development within a Pair of Identical Twins." *International Journal of Psychoanalysis* 47: 261–8.

Goldsmith, H., and Gottesman, I. (1981). "Origins of Variation in Behavioral Style: A Longitudinal Study of Temperament in Young Twins." *Child Development* 52: 91–103.

Gromada, K. (1981). "Maternal-Infant Attachment: The First Step Toward Individualizing Twins." *Maternal Care Nursing Journal* 6: 129–34.

Ho, H., Foch, T., and Plomin, R. (1980). "Developmental Stability of the Relative Influence of Genes and Environment on Specific Cognitive Abilities during Childhood." *Developmental Psychology* 16: 340–6.

Hock, R. R. (2009). *Forty Studies That Changed Psychology*, 6th edn. Upper Saddle River, NJ: Pearson/Prentice-Hall.

Holden, C. (1980). "Twins Reunited." *Science* 215: 54–60.
Holmes, J. (2014). *John Bowlby and Attachment Theory*, 2nd edn. New York: Routledge.
Hopwood, C., and Donnellen, B. (2011). "Genetic and Environmental Influences on Personality Trait Stability and Growth During the Transition to Adulthood: A Three-Way Longitudinal Study." *Journal of Personality Psychology* 100(3): 545–56.
Hur, Y. M., and Bouchard, T. J., Jr. (1995). "Genetic Influences on Perceptions of Childhood Family Environment: A Reared Apart Twin Study." *Child Development* (Apr.) 66(2): 330–45.
Jensen, A. R. (1969). "Hierarchical Theories of Mental Ability." In B. Dockrell (ed.), *On Intelligence*. London: Mitchum, pp. 55–80.
Joseph, J. (2015). *The Trouble with Twin Studies*. New York: Routledge.
Juel-Nielsen, N. (1980). *Individual and Environment: Monozygotic Twins Reared Apart*. New York: International University Press.
Kendler, K. S. (2001). "Twin Studies of Psychiatric Illness: An Update." *Archives of General Psychiatry* 58(11): 1005–14.
Kendler, K. S., Neale, M. C., Kessler, R. C., Heath, A. C., and Eaves, L. J. (1992). "Familiar Influences on the Clinical Characteristics of Major Depression: A Twin Study." *Acta Psychiatrica Scandinavica* (Nov.) 86(5): 371–8.
Kendler, K. S., Neale, M. C., Kessler, R. C., Heath, A. C., and Eaves, L. J. (1993). "A Longitudinal Twin Study of Personality and Major Depression in Women." *Archives of General Psychiatry* (Nov.) 50(11): 853–62.
Kendler, K. S., Neale, M. C., Kessler, R. C., Heath, A. C., and Eaves, L. J. (1994). "Parental Treatment and the Equal Environment Assumption in Twin Studies of Psychiatric Illness." *Psychological Medicine* (Aug.) 24(3): 579–90.
Kendler, K. S., Walters, E. E., and Kessler, R. C. (1997). "The Prediction of Length of Major Depressive Episodes: Results from an Epidemiological Sample of Female Twins." *Psychological Medicine* (Jan.) 27(1): 107–17.
King, M., and McDonald, E. (1992). "Homosexuals Who Are Twins: A Study of 46 Probands." *British Journal of Psychiatry* 160: 407–9.
Klein, B. (2003). *Not All Twins Are Alike*. Westport, CT: Praeger.
Klein, B. (2012) *Alone in the Mirror*. New York: Routledge.
Klein, B., and Martinez, J. (2016). *How Twin Studies Can Shed Light on Close Relationships*. Phoenix, AZ: International Coalition of North American Phenomenologists ICAP.
Koch, H. (1966). *Twin and Twin Relations*. Chicago, IL: University of Chicago Press.
Kohut, H. (1984). *How Does Analysis Cure?* Chicago, IL: University of Chicago Press.
Kohut, H. (1977). *The Restoration of the Self*. New York: International University Press.
Lamb, W. (1998). *I Know This Much Is True*. New York: Regan Books.
Lanigan, R. (1988). *Phenomenology of Communication: Merleau Ponty's Thematics in Communicology and Seminology*. Pittsburgh, PA: Duquesne University Press.
Lanigan, R. (2016). Prejudices that twins experience in everyday life. Conversation at International Communication National Association of Phenomenology (INAP), Phoenix, AZ, May 27.
Leonard, M. (1961). "Problems in Identification and Ego Development in Twins." In R. Eissler (ed.), *The Psychoanalytic Study of the Child*, vol. 16. London: Hogarth Press, pp. 29–40.
Lewin, V. (2004). *The Twin in the Transference*. London: Whur Publishers Ltd.
Loehlin, J. C. (2001). "Behavior Genetics and Parenting Theory." *American Psychologist* 56: 169–170.
Lykken, David (1978). "The Diagnosis of Zygosity in Twins." *Behavioral Genetics* 8: 437–63.

Lytton, H., Conway, D., and Suave, R. (1977a). "The Impact of Twinship on Parent–Child Interaction." *Journal of Personality and Social Psychology* 35: 97–107.

Lytton, H., Martin, N., and Evaes, L. (1977b). "Environmental and Genetic Causes of Variation in Ethological Aspects of Behavior in 2 Year Old Boys." *Social Biology* 24: 200–11.

Lytton, M. (1980). *Parent Child Interaction.* New York: Plenum Press.

MacDonald, A., ed. (2010). "Merits of Psychodynamic Therapy." *Harvard Mental Health Letter* (Sept.) 27(3): 1–5.

McGuffin, P., Katz R., Rutherford J. (1991). "Nature, Nurture and Depression: A Twin Study." *Psychological Medicine* (May) 21(2): 329–35.

Mahler, M. (1967). *The Psychological Birth of the Human Infant.* New York: Basic Books.

Malmstrom, P., and Poland, J. (1999). *The Art of Parenting Twins: The Unique Joys and Challenges of Raising Twins and Other Multiples.* New York: Ballantine Books.

Marmorstein, N. R., Von Ranson, K. M., Iacono, W. G., and Succop, P. A. (2007). "Longitudinal Associations between Externalizing Behavior and Dysfunctional Eating Attitudes and Behaviors: A Community-Based Study." *Journal of Clinical Child and Adolescent Psychology* 36: 87–94.

Martin, J. A., Hamilton, B. E., and Osterman, M. J. K. (2012). *Three Decades of Twin Births in the United States, 1980–2009.* Hyattsville, MD: NCHS Data Brief 80. Jan.

Martinez, J. (2011). *Communicative Sexualities: A Communicology of Sexual Experience.* Lanham, MD: Lexington Books.

Matheny, A. (1980). "Bayley's Infant Behavior Record: Behavioral Components and Twin Analysis." *Child Development* 51: 157–67.

Matheny, A., and Dolan, A. (1980). "A Twin Study of Personality and Temperament during Middle Childhood." *Journal of Research and Personality* 14: 224–34.

Miller, A. (1981). *Prisoners of Childhood: The Drama of the Gifted Child and the Search for the True Self.* New York: Basic Books.

Mittler, P. (1971). *The Study of Twins.* London: Penguin Books, Inc.

Morgan, Mary R. (2014). *When Grief Calls Forth the Healing: A Memoir of Losing a Twin.* New York: Open Road Integrated Media.

Neimeyer, R. A. (2004). "Fostering Post-Traumatic Growth: A Narrative Contribution." *Psychological Inquiry* 15: 53–9.

Neimeyer, R. A. (2005–6). "Complicated Grief and the Quest for Meaning: A Constructivist Contribution." *Omega* 52(13): 37–52.

Newman, H., Freeman, F. N., and Holzinger, K. J. (1937). *Twins: Study of Heredity and Environment.* Chicago, IL: University of Chicago Press.

Osborne, R., and Suddick, D. (1973). "Stability of I.Q. Differences in Twins between Ages of Twelve and Twenty." *Psychologic Reports* 32: 1096–8.

Paluszny, M., and Beht-Hallahni, B. (1974). "An Assessment: Monozygotic Twin Relationship by the Semantic Differential." *Archives of General Psychiatry* 31: 110–17.

Paluszny, M., and Gibson, R. (1974). "Twin Interactions in a Normal Nursery School." *American Journal of Psychiatry* 13: 293–6.

Parravani, C. (2013). *Her: A Memoir.* New York: Henry Holt & Co.

Pearlman, E., and Ganon, J. (2000). *Raising Twins from Birth to Adolescence: What Parents Want to Know (and What Twins Want to Tell Them).* New York: Harper Collins.

Piaget, J. (1950). *The Psychology of Intelligence.* London: Routledge.

Piaget, J. (1975). "Intellectual Development of the Adolescent." In *Childhood Psychopathology: An Anthology of Basic Readings.* Madison, CT: International University Press, pp. 104–8.

Piaget, J., and Inhelder, B. (1969). *The Psychology of the Child.* New York: Basic Books (original work published 1966).
Pietilä, S., Bülow, P. H., and Björklund, A. (2012). "Images of Sorrow: Experiences of Losing a Co-Twin in Old Age." *Journal of Aging Studies* 26: 119–28.
Piontelli, A. (2008). *Twins of the World: The Legends They Inspire and the Lives They Lead.* New York: Palgrave Macmillan.
Plomin, R., and Rowe, D. (1977). "A Twin Study of Temperament in Young Children." *Journal of Psychology* 97: 107–13.
Plomin, R., and Willerman, K. (1975). "A Cotwin Control Study of Reflection-Impulsivity in Children." *Journal of Educational Psychology* 47: 537–43.
Pogany, E. (2000). *Twin Brothers Separated by Faith After the Holocaust.* New York: Viking.
Pogrebin, A. (2010). *One and the Same: My Life as an Identical Twin and What I've Learned about Everyone's Struggle to Be Singular.* New York: Anchor.
Rowe, D. (1981). "Environmental and Genetic Influences on Dimensions of Perceived Parenting: A Twin Study." *Developmental Psychology* 17: 203–8.
Rowe, D., and Plomin, R. (1979). "Environmental Influences in Infants Social Responsiveness." *Behavioral Genetics* 9: 519–25.
Rowles, D. (2013). "25 Practical Tips About the Horrors of Raising Twins That You Will Never Learn from Movies and TV." Online at: pajiba.com.
Roy, A., Segal, N. L., and Sarchiapone, M. (1995). "Attempted Suicide among Living Co-Twins of Twin Suicide Victims." *American Journal of Psychiatry* (July) 152(7): 1075–6.
Sandbank, Audrey, ed. (1999). *Twin and Triplet Psychology: A Professional Guide to Working with Multiples.* New York: Routledge.
Scalise, D. (2008). *A Sanity-Saving Guide to Raising Twins from Pregnancy Through the First Year.* New York: American Management Association.
Scarr-Salaptick, S., and Carter-Saltzman, I. (1979). "Twin Method: Defense of a Critical Assumption." *Behavioral Genetics* 9: 527–42.
Schave, B. (1982). "Similarities and Differences in 6-Year Old Identical and Fraternal Twins and Their Parents on Measures of Locus of Control and Normal Development." EdD dissertation, University of Southern California.
Schave, B. (1993). *Forgotten Memories: A Journey Out of the Darkness of Sexual Abuse.* New York: Praeger.
Schave, B., and Ciriello, J. (1983). *Identity and Intimacy in Twins.* New York: Praeger.
Schave, D., and Schave, B. (1989). *Early Adolescence and the Search for Self: A Developmental Perspective.* New York: Praeger.
Scheinfield, A. (1967). *Twins and Supertwins.* New York: Lippincott.
Segal, N. (1999). *Entwined Lives: Twins and What They Tell Us about Human Behavior.* New York: E. P. Dutton.
Segal, N. L. (2001). "When Twins Lose Twins: Implications for Theory and Practice." 10th International Congress on Twin Studies. London, July.
Segal, N. (2003). "Spotlights: Reared-Apart Twin Researchers." *Twin Research* 6: 72–81.
Segal, N. (2005). *Indivisible by Two: Lives of Extraordinary Twins.* Cambridge, MA: Harvard University Press.
Segal N. L., and Bouchard, T. J., Jr. (1993). "Grief Intensity Following the Loss of a Twin and Other Relatives: Test of Kinship Genetic Hypotheses." *Human Biology* (Feb.) 65(1): 87–105.
Seimon, M. (1980). "The Separation-Individuation Process in Adult Twins." *American Journal of Psychotherapy* 35: 387–400.

Shawn, A. (2007). *Wish I Could Be There: Notes from a Phobic Life.* New York: Viking.
Shawn, A. (2011). *Twin: A Memoir.* New York: Viking.
Shedler, J. (2010). "The Efficacy of Psychodynamic Psychotherapy." *American Psychologist* (Feb./Mar.) 65(2): 98–109.
Shields, J. (1962). *Monozygotic Twins Brought Up Apart and Together.* London: Oxford University Press.
Shirley, O. (2016). "The Effects of Opposite Sex Twinship on the Adult Twin." *British Journal of Psychotherapy* 32: 109–24.
Siegel, D., and Bryson, T. (2012). *The Whole Brain Child: 12 Revolutionary Strategies to Nurture Your Child's Developing Mind.* New York: Bantam Books.
Smith, N. (1976). "Longitudinal Personality Comparison in One Pair of Identical Twins." *Catalog of Selected Documents in Psychology* 6: 106.
Socarides, D., and Stolorow, R. (1984–85). "Affects and Self Objects." In C. Kligerman (ed.), *The Annual of Psychoanalysis*, vol. 12–13. Madison, CT: International Universities Press, pp. 105–19.
Spudich, C. "A Phenomenology of Twins' Same Careers: Exploring the Influences of Adult Twins' Relationships on Their Same Careers". A Dissertation Presented to the Graduate Faculty of St. Louis University in Partial Fulfillment of the Requirements for the Degree of Doctor of Philosophy, 2014
Stern, D. (1985). *The Interpersonal World of the Infant: A View from Psychoanalysis and Developmental Psychology.* New York: Basic Books.
Sternberg, R., and Grigorenko, E., eds (1997). *Intelligence, Heredity and Environment.* New York: Cambridge University Press.
Stoller, R. (1968). *Sex and Gender: On the Development of Masculinity and Femininity.* New York: Basic Books.
Stolorow, R. (1993). Fears of Expansiveness in Twins. Private conversation, Aug.
Stolorow, R. (2007). *Trauma and Human Existence.* New York: The Analytic Press.
Stolorow, R. (2011). *World, Affectivity, Trauma: Heidegger and Post-Cartesian Psychoanalysis.* New York: Routledge.
Storrs, Carina, and Goldschmidt, Debra (2015). "U.S. Twin Birth Rate Hits Record High." Dec. 23. Online at: cnn.com.
Sullivan, H. (1953). *The Interpersonal Theory of Harry Stack Sullivan.* New York: W. W. Norton.
Tabor, J., and Joseph, E. (1961). "The Simultaneous Analysis of a Pair of Identical Twins and the Twinning Reaction." In R. Eissler (ed.), *The Psychoanalytic Study of the Child*, vol. 16. London: Hogarth Press, pp. 275–299.
Tancredy, C. M., and Fraley, R. C. (2006). "The Nature of Adult Twin Relationships: An Attachment-Theoretical Perspective." *Journal of Personality and Social Psychology* 90(1): 78–93.
Thorndike, E. (1905). *Measurement of Twins.* New York: Science Press.
Togashi, K. (2015). Friendship in young twins. Private conversation.
Togashi, K., and Kottler, A. (2015). *Kohut's Twinship across Cultures: The Psychology of Being Human.* New York: Routledge.
Torgersen, A. M., and Janson, Harold. (2002). "Why Do Identical Twins Differ in Personality? Shared Environment Reconsidered." *Twin Research* 5(1): 44–52.
Vandenberg, S., and Wilson, K. (1979). "Failure of the Twin Situation to Influence Twin Differences in Cognition." *Behavioral Genetics* 9: 58–60.
Vaziri-Flais, S. (2014). *Raising Twins: Parenting Multiples from Pregnancy through the School Years*, 2nd edn. Elk Grove, IL: American Academy of Pediatrics.

Verghese, A. (2009). *Cutting for Stone*. New York: Vintage Books, Random House.
Wagner-Spiro, P., and Spiro, C. S. (2005). *Divided Minds: Twin Sisters and Their Journey Through Schizophrenia*. New York: St Martin's Griffin.
Werner, E. (1973). "From Birth to Latency: Behavioral Differences in a Multi-Racial Group of Twins." *Child Development* 44: 438–44.
Wilson, R., and Harring, E. (1977). "Twins and Siblings: Concordance for School-Age Mental Development." *Child Development* 48: 211–16.
Wilson, R., Brown, A., and Matheny, A. (1971). "Emergence and Persistence of Behavioral Differences in Twins." *Child Development* 42: 1381–98.
Winnicott, D. (1960). "The Theory of the Parent-Infant Relationship." *International Journal of Psychoanalysis* 41: 585–95.
Winnicott, D. (1970). "The Mother-Infant Experience of Mutuality." In E. Anthony and T. Benedek (eds), *Parenthood: Its Psychology and Psychopathology*. Boston, MA: Little, Brown.
Withrow, R., and Schwiebert, V. (2005). "Twin Loss: Implications for Counselors Working with Surviving Twins." *Journal of Counseling and Development* 83: 21–8
Woodward, J. (1998). *The Lone Twin: A Study in Bereavement and Loss*. London: Free Association Books.
Woodward, J. (2002). "Panel Discussion at the Symposium on Twin Loss." *Twin Research* 5: 150–2.
Woodward, J. (2006). "Working Therapeutically with Lone Twins." *Therapy Today* 17(4): 35–7.
Wright, L. (1998). *Twins and What They Tell Us about Who We Are*. New York: John Wiley & Sons.
Zazzo, R. (1960). *Les Jumeaux, le couple et la personne*. Paris: Presses Universitaires de France.

Index

adolescence 68–72
adoption 22–4
Adrienne and Eileen: adult twin relationships 2, 109–12, 125–6, 130, 163–4, 169
adulthood 113–14; discipline 16; early memories 15–17; inadequate parenting 71; interdependent-identity 10; psychotherapy 114–15, 166–7; secret language 16; stress of separation 16–17; twin power 111; advice for parents of twins 33, 38–9, 52–5, 63–7, 96–8, 106
advice for therapists of twins 32–3, 55–6, 99–103, 110, 126–7, 142
advice for twins 31–2, 96–100, 106, 110, 140–3, 160, 164–5
affectional bonds 38–40, 160
alcoholism 20–24
Alice in Wonderland 139–40
Alone in the Mirror 3, 99, 132, 157
anger and resentment between twins 4, 22, 85–9
anorexia 46, 75
anxiety 22, 73–77
autistic spectrum disorder 67

Benna and Rachel: adult separation 118–19; early memories 22–25; favoritism 22; fighting 89; reconciliation 23; separation stress 23; shame 24

Carroll, Lewis 139
comparison 49–53, 165–6
competition 26–7, 31, 41–2, 52, 85–6, 93, 99–100, 161, 165–6
complicated grief 79–80
concrete operational thinking 64

Dave 130–1, 178

death 23
decision making 7–8
depression 32–33, 39, 105
developmental differences between twins and single born children: comparisons 49–51; dominance 51–2; exaggerated sense of belonging to one another 38; identity and self-differentiation, 43–7; language development 47–9; sharing primary attachment 37; sharing parents and early memories 39; social development 49; twin power 40–2
developmental stages: adolescence 74–5, 154; early adulthood 75, 154; infancy 72, 154; middle age 76, 154; preschool to elementary 73, 154; senior 76–7, 154
developmental lags 66–7
developmental uniqueness 7, 38, 65
differences between twins 3–4, 73–5, 161–2
divorce 23
dominance 40, 51–2, 92, 177
double trouble 28, 36, 40–3
dressing alike 14, 160

early twin memories 10–11, 30–2, 177
eating disorders 68
ego boundaries 4–7, 29, 38, 78–9, 109–11, 177
elementary school 63–5, 160
estrangement 4, 18, 22, 28, 86–95, 98–107
evaluating twin relationships 156–64

favoritism 21, 22
fear of expansiveness 9, 20
fighting and dominance 4, 8, 86–107
formal operational thinking 69

friendships 2, 50–1

genetics 2, 36–37
goals in therapy 8, 168–69
good enough parenting 40, 94, 177
grieving 77, 80
guilt feelings 44, 59, 72, 79–83

halves of a whole 2, 26, 46–7, 124
homosexuality 25, 67

idealization of twinship 3, 5, 128, 177
identity issues 1–4, 161–3, 170–71
individual identity 10, 26, 90–1, 122, 153
interdependent-identity 10–11, 84–5, 93–5, 111, 115–16, 151

Jackie 146–8, 174–5
jealousy 49–53, 165–6

Keith and Kirk: early memories 18–19; estrangement 20; fighting 20, 81; group therapy 149, 176; loneliness 102; independence 116–17; new friendships, 131–2; psychotherapy 117; sexual abuse 19–20

language 16, 42, 48
life span issues 171–4
loneliness 4, 50, 58–9, 75–81, 99–104

Madeline and Vicki: adult separation 126; competition 14; discipline 14; early memories 13–15; inadequate parenting 71; shame 136
Marilyn and Janet: double trouble 29; early memories 27; fighting 91; independence 122–3; psychotherapy 29, 123; separation 28; twin power 41–2
mental health and emotional problems 13, 20–4, 32–3, 45, 73, 75, 76–7
Michael and Mark: early memories 29–30; fighting 91; independence 124–5; independent parenting, 29–30; psychotherapy 124; sexuality 30;

Naked Angels 13
narcissistic issues 3, 26–7, 174
non-twin world 27, 29, 33, 36, 83, 109–11, 124, 128, 156, 163
non-verbal communication 48–50

Not All Twins Are Alike 3, 108

onlookers 5, 83
over-identification 48, 89
over-protection 81

parent abuse 17–18, 20
parent–child attachment: abusive 18, 37; financial and social 159; good enough 171; negligence 34–5
parenting in the twentieth century 36–7
Patricia and Pauline: early memories 24–5; fighting 88–9; homosexuality 25; identity 136; independence 119–20; negligent parenting 73; psychotherapy 121; violence 24
patterns of twinship 3, 9–10, 84–5, 111
perfectionism 3, 26–7, 174
personality developmental 18
post-traumatic stress disorder 19, 21–3, 105–8
power conflicts 40, 51–2, 92, 177
primary attachment 7–8, 31–2, 81, 177
projection 171
psychological differences 10, 18, 25, 86–8, 116, 122–3
psychological negligence abuse 71
psychological separation 7, 60–2, 79–81, 164
psychotherapy 2, 29, 151–5

"real" differences between twins 26

Sandy and Scott: early memories 20–1; estrangement 22; favoritism 21–2; fighting 22–88, group therapy 148, 175; independence 117–18; loneliness 75, 100; parental negligence 71; psychotherapy 118; Sarah 101, 137–8, 146, 175
school separation 14, 61–62, 163
separation experiences 6–7, 42–8, 64, 73, 75–8, 83–4, 163
shame 31–2, 105–6, 136
sharing parents *see* primary attachment
siblings of twins 158
singleton reactions to twins 5–6
socialization 137–9
split identity 10, 18, 25, 86–8, 116, 122–3, 152–3
statistics of twin births 35–6
Stephen 100, 148–9

struggles of twins in a non-twin world: identity confusion with non-twins 136–7; invisibility 129–32; misunderstanding about depth of relationships 132–4; separation anxiety in adulthood 134–5; shame about twinship 135–6
suicide 13, 31

therapeutic impasse 166–8
twin: bond 52, 55–6; estrangement groups 145–50; language *see* language; loss 31, 39, 56–9, 79–83, 106–7, 143, 156; minorities *see* idealization; power *see* dominance; compared to siblings 29, 35, 150; replacements 81–2, 112, 162

untold stories 5, 131, 150

Vince and Victor: early memories 11–12; homosexuality 12–13; identity in non-twin world 136–8; independence 111–12; loneliness 102–3; psychotherapy 112; suicide 13; twin groups 145, 175; twin loss 31; twin power 41

young adulthood 73